Learning the Korn Shell

Learning the Korn Shell

Bill Rosenblatt

O'Reilly & Associates, Inc.
Cambridge · Köln · Paris · Sebastopol · Tokyo

Learning the Korn Shell
by Bill Rosenblatt

Copyright © 1993 O'Reilly & Associates, Inc. All rights reserved.
Printed in the United States of America.

Editor: Mike Loukides

Production Editor: Kismet McDonough

Printing History:

June 1993:	First Edition.
July 1993:	Minor corrections.
January 1994:	Minor corrections.
March 1994:	Minor corrections.

This book is printed on acid-free paper with 85% recycled content, 15% post-consumer waste. O'Reilly & Associates is committed to using paper with the highest recycled content available consistent with high quality.

ISBN: 1-56592-054-6   [8/98]

Table of Contents

Preface   *xv*

Korn Shell Versions xv
Summary of Korn Shell Features xvi
Intended Audience xvii
Code Examples xviii
Chapter Summary xviii
Conventions Used in This Handbook xx
Acknowledgments xxi
We'd Like to Hear From You xxii

1: Korn Shell Basics   *1*

What Is a Shell? 2
Scope of This Book 3
History of UNIX Shells 3
   The Korn Shell 4
   Features of the Korn Shell 5
Getting the Korn Shell 5
Interactive Shell Use 6
   Commands, Arguments, and Options 7
Files 7
   Directories 8
   Filenames and Wildcards 11
Input and Output 15
   Standard I/O 15
   I/O Redirection 17
   Pipelines 17
Background Jobs 19
   Background I/O 20
   Background Jobs and Priorities 21
Special Characters and Quoting 22
   Quoting 23
   Backslash-escaping 24
   Quoting Quotation Marks 25

Continuing Lines 26
Control Keys 26

2: *Command-line Editing*   29

Enabling Command-line Editing 30
The History File 31
Emacs Editing Mode 32
Basic Commands 32
Word Commands 34
Line Commands 35
Moving Around in the History File 36
Filename Completion and Expansion 37
Miscellaneous Commands 38
Keyboard Shortcuts with Aliases 42
Vi Editing Mode 42
Simple Control Mode Commands 43
Entering and Changing Text 45
Deletion Commands 46
Moving Around in the History File 48
Character-finding Commands 50
Filename Completion 51
Miscellaneous Commands 52
The fc Command 53
Finger Habits 56

3: *Customizing Your Environment*   59

The .profile File 60
Aliases 61
Tracked Aliases 64
Options 65
Shell Variables 67
Variables and Quoting 68
Built-in Variables 69
Directory Search Path 77
Customization and Subprocesses 79
Environment Variables 80
The Environment File 81
Customization Hints 82

4: Basic Shell Programming 85

Shell Scripts and Functions 85
    Functions 88
Shell Variables 91
    Positional Parameters 91
    More on Variable Syntax 95
String Operators 96
    Syntax of String Operators 96
    Patterns and Regular Expressions 101
    Pattern-matching Operators 105
    Length Operator 108
Command Substitution 109
Advanced Examples: pushd and popd 114

5: Flow Control 119

if/else 120
    Exit Status and Return 121
    Combinations of Exit Statuses 124
    Condition Tests 126
    Integer Conditionals 135
for 136
case 143
select 147
while and until 150

6: Command-line Options and Typed Variables 155

Command-line Options 155
    shift 156
    Options with Arguments 158
    getopts 159
Integer Variables and Arithmetic 165
    Arithmetic Conditionals 167
    Arithmetic Variables and Assignment 168
Arrays 173
    typeset 176
    Local Variables in Functions 177
    String Formatting Options 178
    Type and Attribute Options 182
    Function Options 183

7: Input/Output and Command-line Processing   *185*

I/O Redirectors 185
    Here-documents 187
    File Descriptors 189
String I/O 191
    print 191
    read 193
Command-line Processing 203
    Quoting 207
    eval 210

8: Process Handling   *221*

Process IDs and Job Numbers 222
Job Control 223
    Foreground and Background 223
    Suspending a Job 225
Signals 227
    Control Key Signals 227
    kill 228
    ps 230
trap 234
    Traps and Functions 235
    Process ID Variables and Temporary Files 237
    Ignoring Signals 239
    Resetting Traps 240
Coroutines 241
    wait 242
    Advantages and Disadvantages of Coroutines 243
    Parallelization 243
    Coroutines with Two-way Pipes 245
    Two-way Pipes Versus Standard Pipes 248
Subshells 248
    Subshell Inheritance 249
    Nested Subshells 249

9: Debugging Shell Programs   *253*

Basic Debugging Aids 254
    Set Options 254
    Fake Signals 257
A Korn Shell Debugger 261

Structure of the Debugger 262
The Preamble 264
Debugger Functions 265
Sample kshdb Session 272
Exercises 274

10: Korn Shell Administration 281

Installing the Korn Shell as the Standard Shell 281
Environment Customization 282
    umask 283
    ulimit 283
    Types of Global Customization 285
System Security Features 286
    Restricted Shell 287
    A System Break-in Scenario 287
    Tracked Aliases 289
    Privileged Mode 289

A: Related Shells 291

The Bourne Shell 292
The IEEE 1003.2 POSIX Shell Standard 294
wksh 298
pdksh 299
bash 300
Workalikes on PC Platforms 302
The Future of the Korn Shell 304

B: Reference Lists 309

Invocation Options 309
Built-in Commands and Keywords 309
Built-in Shell Variables 311
Test Operators 312
Options 313
Typeset Options 314
Emacs Mode Commands 315
Vi Control Mode Commands 316

C: Obtaining Sample Programs
    and Problem Set Answers 319

Figures

1: Korn Shell Basics   *1*

1-1   The shell is a layer around the UNIX operating system   2
1-2   A tree of directories and files   8

4: Basic Shell Programming   *85*

4-1   Ways to run a shell script   87
4-2   Functions have their own positional parameters.   94

5: Flow Control   *119*

5-1   Files produced by a C compiler   130

6: Command-line Options and Typed Variables   *155*

6-1   Local variables in functions   178

7: Input/Output and Command-line Processing   *185*

7-1   Steps in Command-line Processing   205

8: Process Handling   *221*

8-1   Background Jobs in Multiple Windows   232
8-2   Coroutine I/O   246

Tables

1: Korn Shell Basics   *1*

1-1	Sample cd Commands	10
1-2	Basic Wildcards	12
1-3	Using the * Wildcard	13
1-4	Using the Set Construct Wildcards	13
1-5	Popular UNIX Data Filtering Utilities	16
1-6	Special Characters	23
1-7	Control Keys	27

2: Command-line Editing   *29*

2-1	Basic emacs-mode Commands	33
2-2	Emacs-mode Word Commands	34
2-3	Emacs-mode Line Commands	35
2-4	Emacs-mode Commands for Moving Through the History File	36
2-5	Emacs-mode Miscellaneous Commands	39
2-6	Editing Commands in vi Input Mode	42
2-7	Basic vi Control Mode Commands	43
2-8	Commands for Entering vi Input Mode	45
2-9	Some vi-mode Deletion Commands	46
2-10	Abbreviations for vi-mode Delete Commands	47
2-11	Vi Control Mode Commands for Searching the History File	48
2-12	Vi-mode Character-Finding Commands	50
2-13	Miscellaneous vi-mode Commands	52

3: Customizing Your Environment   *59*

3-1	Basic Shell Options	66
3-2	Editing Mode Variables	70
3-3	Mail Variables	70

3-4   Status Variables   79

4: Basic Shell Programming   *85*

4-1   Substitution Operators   97
4-2   Regular Expression Operators   102
4-3   Regular Expression Operator Examples   103
4-4   Shell Versus egrep/awk Regular Expression Operators   104
4-5   Pattern-matching Operators   106
4-6   pushd/popd Example   115

5: Flow Control   *119*

5-1   String Comparison Operators   126
5-2   File Attribute Operators   131
5-3   Arithmetic Test Operators   135

6: Command-line Options and Typed Variables   *155*

6-1   Popular C Compiler Options   163
6-2   Arithmetic Operators   166
6-3   Relational Operators   167
6-4   Sample Integer Expression Assignments   168
6-5   Typeset String Formatting Options   178
6-6   Examples of typeset String Formatting Options   178
6-7   Typeset Type and Attribute Options   181
6-8   Typeset Function Options   182

7: Input/Output and Command-line Processing   *185*

7-1   I/O Redirectors   186
7-2   print Escape Sequences   192
7-3   print Options   192
7-4   read Options   201
7-5   Examples of Quoting Rules   208

8: Process Handling   *221*

8-1   Ways to refer to background jobs   225

9: Debugging Shell Programs   253

9-1   Debugging Options   255
9-2   Fake Signals   257
9-3   kshdb Commands   267

10: Korn Shell Administration   281

10-1 ulimit Resource Options   284

A: Related Shells   291

A-1   File Permission Test Operators   303
A-2   MKS Toolkit Names for Shell Files   304

B: Reference Lists   251

Invocation Options   309
Built-In Commands and Keywords   309
Built-In Shell Variables   311
Test Operators   312
Options   313
Typeset Options   314
Emacs-mode Commands   315
Vi Control Mode Commands   316

Preface

The long, tortuous history of the UNIX operating system has resulted in systems with all kinds of permutations and combinations of features. This means that whenever you walk up to an unfamiliar UNIX system, you need to find out certain things about it in order to use it properly. And even on a given system, you may have a number of choices you can make about what features you want to use.

The most important such decision—if you get to make it—is what *shell* to use. "Shell" is UNIX jargon for the program that allows you to communicate with the computer by entering commands and getting responses. The shell is completely separate from the UNIX operating system *per se*; it's just a program that runs on UNIX. With other systems such as MS-DOS, the Macintosh, and VM/CMS, the *command interpreter* or *user interface* is an integral part of the operating system.

Nowadays there are dozens of different shells floating around, ranging from the original standard, the Bourne shell, to menu-based and graphical interfaces. The most important shells have been the Bourne shell, the C shell, and now the Korn shell—the subject of this book.

Korn Shell Versions

Specifically, this book describes the 1988 version of the Korn shell, which is distributed with all UNIX systems based on System V Release 4. There are various other versions, variations, and implementations on other operating systems; these are described in Appendix A, *Related Shells*.

To find out which version you have, type the command **set -o emacs**, then press CTRL-V. You should see a date followed by a version letter (the letter is unimportant). If you do, you have one of the official versions, whether it be the 1988 version or an older one. But if you don't, then you have a nonstandard version such as *pdksh*, the public domain Korn shell discussed in Appendix A.

Summary of Korn Shell Features

The Korn shell is the most advanced of the shells that are "officially" distributed with UNIX systems. It's a backward-compatible evolutionary successor to the Bourne shell that includes most of the C shell's major advantages as well as a few new features of its own.

Features appropriated from the C shell include:

- **Job control**, including the **fg** and **bg** commands and the ability to stop jobs with CTRL-Z.

- **Aliases**, which allow you to define shorthand names for commands or command lines.

- **Functions** (included in some C shell versions), which increase programmability and allow you to store your own shell code in memory instead of files.

- **Command history**, which lets you recall previously entered commands.

The Korn shell's major new features include:

- **Command-line editing**, allowing you to use *vi* or *emacs*-style editing commands on your command lines.

- **Integrated programming features**: the functionality of several external UNIX commands, including *test, expr, getopt,* and *echo,* has been integrated into the shell itself, enabling common programming tasks to be done more cleanly and without creating extra processes.

- **Control structures**, especially the **select** construct, which enables easy menu generation.

- **Debugging primitives** that make it possible to write tools that help programmers debug their shell code.

- **Regular expressions**, well known to users of UNIX utilities like *grep* and *awk,* have been added to the standard set of filename wildcards and to the shell variable facility.

- **Advanced I/O features**, including the ability to do two-way communication with concurrent processes (*coroutines*).

- **New options and variables** that give you more ways to customize your environment.

- **Increased speed** of shell code execution.

- **Security features** that help protect against "Trojan horses" and other types of break-in schemes.

Intended Audience

This book is designed to appeal most closely to casual UNIX users who are just above the "raw beginner" level. You should be familiar with the process of logging in, entering commands, and doing simple things with files. Although Chapter 1, *Korn Shell Basics*, reviews concepts such as the tree-like file and directory scheme, you may find that it moves too quickly if you're a complete neophyte. In that case, we recommend the O'Reilly & Associates Nutshell Handbook, *Learning the UNIX Operating System*, by Grace Todino and John Strang.

If you're an experienced user, you may wish to skip Chapter 1 altogether. But if your experience is with the C shell, you may find that Chapter 1 reveals a few subtle differences between the Korn and C shells.

No matter what your level of experience is, you will undoubtedly learn many things in this book that make you a more productive Korn shell user—from major features down to details at the "nook-and-cranny" level that you weren't aware of.

If you are interested in shell programming (writing shell *scripts* and *functions* that automate everyday tasks or serve as system utilities), you should find this book useful too. However, we have deliberately avoided drawing a strong distinction between interactive shell use (entering commands during a login session) and shell programming. We see shell programming as a natural, inevitable outgrowth of increasing experience as a user.

Accordingly, each chapter depends on those previous to it, and although the first three chapters are oriented toward interactive use only, subsequent chapters describe interactive user-oriented features in addition to programming concepts.

In fact, if this book has an overriding message, it is: "The Korn shell is an incredibly powerful and grossly undervalued UNIX programming environment. You—yes, *you*—can write useful shell programs, even if you just learned how to log on last week and have never programmed before."

Toward that end, we have decided not to spend much time on features of interest exclusively to low-level systems programmers. Concepts like file descriptors, *errno* error numbers, special file types, etc., can only confuse the casual user, and anyway, we figure that those of you who understand such things are smart enough to extrapolate the necessary information from our cursory discussions.

Code Examples

This book is full of examples of shell commands and programs that are designed to be useful in your everyday life as a user, not just to illustrate the feature being explained. In Chapter 4, *Basic Shell Programming*, and onwards, we include various programming problems, which we call *tasks*, that illustrate particular shell programming concepts. Some tasks have solutions that are refined in subsequent chapters. The later chapters also include programming exercises, many of which build on the tasks in the chapter.

You should feel free to use any code you see in this book and to pass it along to friends and colleagues. We especially encourage you to modify and enhance it yourself.

If you want to try examples but you don't use the Korn shell as your login shell, you must put the following line at the top of each shell script:

```
#!/bin/ksh
```

If your Korn shell isn't installed as the file */bin/ksh*, substitute its pathname in the above.

Chapter Summary

If you want to investigate specific topics rather than read the entire book through, here is a chapter-by-chapter summary:

Chapter 1,   *Korn Shell Basics*, introduces the Korn shell and tells you how to install it as your login shell. Then it gives an introduction to the basics of interactive shell use, including overviews of the UNIX file and directory scheme, standard I/O, and background jobs.

Chapter 2,   *Command-line Editing*, discusses the shell's command history mechanism, including the emacs- and vi-editing modes and the **fc** history command.

Chapter 3,   *Customizing Your Environment*, covers ways to customize your shell environment without programming, by using the *.profile* and environment files. Aliases, options, and shell variables are the customization techniques discussed.

Chapter 4,   *Basic Shell Programming*, is an introduction to shell programming. It explains the basics of shell scripts and functions, and discusses several important "nuts-and-bolts" programming features: string manipulation operators, regular expressions, command-line arguments (positional parameters), and command substitution.

Chapter 5,   *Flow Control*, continues the discussion of shell programming by describing command exit status, conditional expressions, and the shell's flow-control structures: **if**, **for**, **case**, **select**, **while**, and **until**.

Chapter 6,   *Command-line Options and Typed Variables*, goes into depth about positional parameters and command-line option processing, then discusses special types and properties of variables, such as integer arithmetic and arrays, and the **typeset** command.

Chapter 7,   *Input/Output and Command-line Processing*, gives a detailed description of Korn shell I/O, filling in the information omitted in Chapter 1, *Korn Shell Basics*. All of the shell's I/O redirectors are covered, as are the line-at-a-time I/O commands **read** and **print**. Then the chapter discusses the shell's command-line processing mechanism and the **eval** command.

Chapter 8,   *Process Handling*, covers process-related issues in detail. It starts with a discussion of job control, then gets into various low-level information about processes, including process IDs, signals, and traps. The chapter then moves out to a higher level of abstraction to discuss coroutines, two-way pipes, and subshells.

Chapter 9,   *Debugging Shell Programs*, discusses various debugging techniques, starting with simple ones like trace and verbose modes and "fake signal" traps. Then it presents *kshdb*, a Korn shell debugging tool that you can use to debug your own code.

Chapter 10,   *Korn Shell Administration*, gives information for system administrators, including techniques for implementing system-wide shell customization and features related to system security.

Appendix A,   *Related Shells*, compares the 1988 UNIX Korn shell to several similar shells, including the standard Bourne shell, the IEEE 1003.2 POSIX shell standard, the Windowing Korn shell (*wksh*), public domain Korn shell (*pdksh*), the Free Software Foundation's *bash*, and the MKS Toolkit shell for MS-DOS and OS/2.

Appendix B,   *Reference Lists*, contains lists of shell invocation options, built-in commands, built-in variables, conditional test operators, options, **typeset** command options, and emacs and vi editing mode commands.

Appendix C,   *Obtaining the Sample Programs*, lists the ways that you can obtain the major scripts in this book for free, using anonymous FTP or electronic mail.

Conventions Used in This Handbook

We leave it as understood that, when you enter a shell command, you press RETURN at the end. RETURN is labeled ENTER on some keyboards.

Characters called CTRL-*X*, where *X* is any letter, are entered by holding down the CTRL (or CTL, or CONTROL) key and pressing that letter. Although we give the letter in uppercase, you can press the letter without the SHIFT key.

Other special characters are LINEFEED (which is the same as CTRL-J), BACK-SPACE (same as CTRL-H), ESC, TAB, and DEL (sometimes labeled DELETE or RUBOUT).

This book uses the following font conventions:

Italic   is used for UNIX filenames, commands not built into the shell, (which are files anyway), and shell functions. *Italic* is also used for dummy parameters that should be replaced with an actual value, to distinguish the *vi* and *emacs* programs from their Korn-shell modes, and to highlight special terms the first time they are defined.

Bold   is used for Korn shell built-in commands, aliases, variables, and options, as well as command lines when they are within regular text. **Bold** is used for all elements typed in by the user.

`Constant Width`   is used in examples to show the contents of files or the output from commands.

`Constant Bold`   is used in examples to show interaction between the user and the shell; any text the user types in is shown in **`Constant Bold`**. For example:

```
$ pwd
/users/billr/ora/kb
$
```

`Constant Italic`   is used in displayed command lines for dummy parameters that should be replaced with an actual value.

Reverse Video   is used in Chapter 2, *Command-line Editing*, to show the position of the cursor on the command line being edited. For example:

```
grep -l Bob < ~pete/wk/names
```

Standard UNIX utility commands are sometimes mentioned with a number in parentheses (usually 1) following the command's name. The number refers to the section of the UNIX User's Manual in which you'll find reference documentation (a.k.a. "man page") on the utility in question. For example, *grep*(1) means you will find the man page for *grep* in Section 1.

Acknowledgments

Many people contributed to this book in many ways. I'd like to thank the following people for technical advice and/or assistance: for system administration help, John van Vlaanderen and Alexis Rosen. For information on alternative shells, John (again), Sean Wilson (of MKS), Ed Ravin, Mel Rappaport, and Chet Ramey. For identifying the need for a shell debugger, expertise in SunOS and system security, and, indeed, a significant portion of my career, Hal Stern. For debugger suggestions, Tan Bronson. For humanitarian aid, Jessica Lustig. And much thanks to David Korn for all kinds of great "horse's mouth" information—and, of course, for the Korn shell itself.

Thanks to our technical reviewers: Jim Baumbach, Jim Falk, David Korn, Ed Miner, Eric Pearce, and Ed Ravin. I especially appreciate the cooperation of Ed and Ed (in that order) during my "Whaddya mean, it doesn't work?!?" phase.

Several people at O'Reilly & Associates contributed to this effort: Gigi Estabrook and Clairemarie Fisher O'Leary proofread multiple drafts of the manuscript, Kismet McDonough and Donna Woonteiler copyedited the manuscript, Len Muellner implemented the book design macro package, Jennifer Niederst designed the cover and the format of the book, and Chris Reilley created the figures. Finally, an ocean of gratitude to Mike Loukides—editor, motivator, facilitator, constructive nit-picker, and constant voice of reason. He and the other folks at O'Reilly & Associates are some of the most innovative, interesting, and motivated people I've ever had the privilege to work with.

We'd Like to Hear From You

We have tested and verified all of the information in this book to the best of our ability, but you may find that features have changed (or even that we have made mistakes!). Please let us know about any errors you find, as well as your suggestions for future editions, by writing:

```
O'Reilly & Associates, Inc.
101 Morris Street
Sebastopol, CA 95472
1-800-998-9938 (in the US or Canada)
1-707-829-0515 (international/local)
1-707-829-0104 (FAX)
```

You can also send us messages electronically. To be put on the mailing list or request a catalog, send email to:

info@oreilly.com

To ask technical questions or comment on the book, send email to:

bookquestions@oreilly.com

In this chapter:
- *What Is a Shell?*
- *Scope of This Book*
- *History of UNIX Shells*
- *Getting the Korn Shell*
- *Interactive Shell Use*
- *Files*
- *Input and Output*
- *Background Jobs*
- *Special Characters and Quoting*

1

Korn Shell Basics

You've used your computer for simple tasks, such as invoking your favorite application programs, reading your electronic mail, and perhaps examining and printing files. You know that your machine runs the UNIX operating system, or maybe you know it under some other name, like SunOS, Ultrix, HP/UX, AIX, A/UX, UTS, or Xenix. But apart from that, you may not have given too much thought to what goes on inside the machine when you type in a command and hit RETURN.

It is true that several layers of events take place whenever you enter a command, but we're going to consider only the top layer, known as the *shell*. Generically speaking, a shell is any user interface to the UNIX operating system, i.e., any program that takes input from the user, translates it into instructions that the operating system can understand, and conveys the operating system's output back to the user.

There are various types of user interfaces. The Korn shell belongs to the most common category, known as character-based user interfaces. These interfaces accept lines of textual commands that the user types in; they usually produce text-based output. Other types of interfaces include the increasingly common *graphical user interfaces* (GUI), which add the ability to display arbitrary graphics (not just typewriter characters) and to accept input from mice and other pointing devices, touch-screen interfaces (such as those you see on some bank teller machines), and so on.

What Is a Shell?

The shell's job, then, is to translate the user's command lines into operating system instructions. For example, consider this command line:

```
sort -n phonelist > phonelist.sorted
```

This means, "Sort lines in the file *phonelist* in numerical order, and put the result in the file *phonelist.sorted*." Here's what the shell does with this command:

1. Breaks up the line into the pieces *sort*, *-n*, *phonelist*, *>*, and *phonelist.sorted*. These pieces are called words.

2. Determines the purpose of the words: *sort* is a command, *-n* and *phonelist* are arguments, and *>* and *phonelist.sorted*, taken together, are I/O instructions.

3. Sets up the I/O according to *> phonelist.sorted* (output to the file *phonelist.sorted*) and some standard, implicit instructions.

4. Finds the command *sort* in a file and runs it with the option *-n* (numerical order) and the argument *phonelist* (input filename).

Of course, each of these steps really involves several substeps, each of which includes a particular instruction to the underlying operating system.

Remember that the shell itself is not UNIX—just the user interface to it. UNIX is one of the first operating systems to make the user interface independent of the operating system.

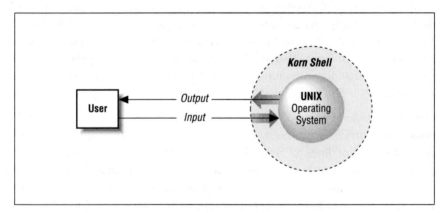

Figure 1-1: The shell is a layer around the UNIX operating system

Scope of This Book

In this book, you will learn about the Korn shell, which is the most recent and powerful of the major UNIX shells. There are two ways to use the Korn shell: as a user interface and as a programming environment.

This chapter and the next cover interactive use. These two chapters should give you enough background to use the shell confidently and productively for most of your everyday tasks.

After you have been using the shell for a while, you will undoubtedly find certain characteristics of your environment (the shell's "look and feel") that you would like to change and tasks that you would like to automate. Chapter 3, *Customizing Your Environment*, shows several ways of doing this.

Chapter 3 also prepares you for shell programming, the bulk of which is covered in Chapters 4 through 6. You need not have any programming experience to understand these chapters and learn shell programming. Chapters 7 and 8 give more complete descriptions of the shell's I/O and process handling capabilities, while Chapter 9 discusses various techniques for debugging shell programs.

You'll learn a lot about the Korn shell in this book; you'll also learn about UNIX utilities and the way the UNIX operating system works in general. It's possible to become a virtuoso shell programmer without any previous programming experience. At the same time, we've carefully avoided going down past a certain level of detail about UNIX internals. We maintain that you shouldn't have to be an internals expert to use and program the shell effectively, and we won't dwell on the few shell features that are intended specifically for low-level systems programmers.

History of UNIX Shells

The independence of the shell from the UNIX operating system *per se* has led to the development of dozens of shells throughout UNIX history—although only a few have achieved widespread use.

The first major shell was the Bourne shell (named after its inventor, Steven Bourne); it was included in the first popular version of UNIX, Version 7, starting in 1979. The Bourne shell is known on the system as *sh*. Although UNIX has gone through many, many changes, the Bourne shell is still popular and essentially unchanged. Several UNIX utilities and administration features depend on it.

The first widely-used alternative shell was the C shell, or *csh*. This was written by Bill Joy at the University of California at Berkeley as part of the Berkeley System Distribution (BSD) version of UNIX that came out a couple of years after Version 7. It's included in most recent UNIX versions.

The C shell gets its name from the resemblance of its commands to statements in the C Programming Language, which makes the shell easier for programmers on UNIX systems to learn. It supports a number of operating system features (e.g., job control; see Chapter 8, *Process Handling*) that were unique to BSD UNIX but by now have migrated to most other modern versions. It also has a few important features (e.g., aliases; see Chapter 3) that make it easier to use in general.

The Korn Shell

The Korn shell, or *ksh*, was invented by David Korn of AT&T Bell Laboratories in the mid-1980s. It is almost entirely upwardly compatible with the Bourne shell,* which means that Bourne shell users can use it right away, and all system utilities that use the Bourne shell can use the Korn shell instead. In fact, some systems have the Korn shell installed as if it were the Bourne shell.

The Korn shell began its public life in 1986 as part of AT&T's "Experimental Toolchest," meaning that its source code was available at very low cost to anyone who was willing to use it without technical support and with the knowledge that it might still have a few bugs. Eventually, AT&T's UNIX System Laboratories (USL) decided to give it full support as a UNIX utility. As of USL's version of UNIX called System V Release 4 (SVR4 for short, 1989), it was distributed with all USL UNIX systems, all third-party versions of UNIX derived from SVR4, and many other versions.

USL's distributed version of the Korn shell, dated November 16, 1988, is what this book describes. Other versions are summarized briefly in Appendix A.

---

*With a few extremely minor exceptions. See Appendix A for the only important one.

Features of the Korn Shell

Although the Bourne shell is still known as the "standard" shell, the Korn shell is becoming increasingly popular and is destined to replace it. In addition to its Bourne shell compatibility, it includes the best features of the C shell as well as several advantages of its own. It also runs more efficiently than any previous shell.

The Korn shell's command-line editing modes are the features that tend to attract people to it at first. With command-line editing, it's much easier to go back and fix mistakes than it is with the C shell's history mechanism—and the Bourne shell doesn't let you do this at all.

The other major Korn shell feature that is intended mostly for interactive users is job control. As Chapter 8, *Process Handling*, explains, job control gives you the ability to stop, start, and pause any number of commands at the same time. This feature was borrowed almost verbatim from the C shell.

The rest of the Korn shell's important advantages are mainly meant for shell customizers and programmers. It has many new options and variables for customization, and its programming features have been significantly expanded to include function definition, more control structures, built-in regular expressions and integer arithmetic, advanced I/O control, and more.

Getting the Korn Shell

You may or may not be using the Korn shell right now. Your system administrator probably set your account up with whatever shell he or she uses as the "standard" on the system. You may not even have been aware that there is more than one shell available.

Yet it's easy for you to determine which shell you are using. Log in to your system and type **echo $SHELL** at the prompt. You will see a response containing **sh**, **csh**, or **ksh**; these denote the Bourne, C, and Korn shells respectively. (There's also a remote chance that you're using a third-party shell such as *bash* or *tcsh*.)

If you aren't using the Korn shell and you want to, then first you need to find out if it exists on your system. Most major UNIX versions released since roughly 1989 come with it—especially those derived from AT&T's System V Release 4. Just type **ksh**. If you get a new dollar-sign prompt ($), then all is well; type **exit** or press **CTRL-D** to go back to your normal shell.

But if you get a "not found" message, your system may not have it. Ask your system administrator or another knowledgeable user; there's a chance that you might have some version of the Korn shell installed on the system in a place (directory) that is not normally accessible to you. But if not, read Appendix A, *Related Shells*, to find out how you can obtain a version of the Korn shell.

Once you know you have the Korn shell on your system, you can invoke it from whatever other shell you use by typing **ksh** as above. However, it's much better to install it as your *login shell*, i.e., the shell that you get automatically whenever you log in. You may be able to do the installation by yourself. Here are instructions that are designed to work on the widest variety of UNIX systems. If something doesn't work (e.g., you type in a command and get a "not found" error message or a blank line as the response), you'll have to abort the process and see your system administrator.

You need to find out where the Korn shell is on your system, i.e., in which directory it's installed. You might be able to find the location by typing **whereis ksh** (especially if you are using the C shell); if that doesn't work, try **whence ksh**, **which ksh**, or this complex command:

```
grep ksh /etc/passwd | awk -F: '{print $7}' | sort -u
```

You should see a response that looks like */bin/ksh* or */usr/local/bin/ksh*.

To install as your login shell, type **chsh** *ksh-name*, where *ksh-name* is the response you got to your **whereis** command (or whatever worked). You'll either get an error message saying that the shell is invalid, or you'll be prompted for your password. Type in your password, then log out and log back in again to start using the Korn shell. If you got an error message, you'll just have to see your system administrator. (For system security reasons, only certain shells are allowed to be installed as login shells.)

Interactive Shell Use

When you use the shell interactively, you engage in a login session that begins when you log in and ends when you **exit** or press CTRL-D.* During a login session, you type *command lines* in to the shell; these are lines of text ending in RETURN that you type in to your terminal or workstation. By

---

*You can set up your shell so that it doesn't accept CTRL-D, i.e., it requires you to type **exit** to end your session. We recommend this, because CTRL-D is too easy to type by accident; see the section on options in Chapter 3, *Customizing Your Environment*.

default, the shell prompts you for each command with a dollar sign, though as you will see in Chapter 3, the prompt can be changed.

Commands, Arguments, and Options

Shell command lines consist of one or more words, which are separated on a command line by blanks or TABs. The first word on the line is the *command*. The rest (if any) are *arguments* (also called *parameters*) to the command, which are names of things on which the command will act.

For example, the command line **lp myfile** consists of the command *lp* (print a file) and the single argument **myfile**. *lp* treats **myfile** as the name of a file to print. Arguments are often names of files, but not necessarily: in the command line **mail billr**, the *mail* program treats **billr** as the name of the user to which a message will be sent.

An *option* is a special type of argument that gives the command specific information on what it is supposed to do. Options usually consist of a dash followed by a letter; we say "usually" because this is a convention rather than a hard-and-fast rule. The command **lp -h myfile** contains the option **-h**, which tells *lp* not to print the "banner page" before it prints the file.

Sometimes options take their own arguments. For example, **lp -d hp3si -h myfile** has two options and one argument. The first option is **-d hp3si**, which means "Send the output to the printer (destination) called **hp3si**". The second option and argument are as above.

Files

Although arguments to commands aren't always files, files are the most important types of "things" on any UNIX system. A file can contain any kind of information, and indeed there are different types of files. Three types are by far the most important:

Regular files Also called text files; these contain readable characters. For example, this book was created from several regular files that contain the text of the book plus human-readable formatting instructions to the *troff* word processor.

Executable files

> Also called programs; these are invoked as commands. Some can't be read by humans; others—the shell scripts that we'll examine in this book—are just special text files. The shell itself is a (non-human-readable) executable file called *ksh*.

Directories   Like folders that contain other files—possibly other directories (called *subdirectories*).

Directories

Let's review the most important concepts about directories. The fact that directories can contain other directories leads to a hierarchical structure, more popularly known as a *tree*, for all files on a UNIX system. Figure 1-2 shows part of a typical directory tree; ovals are regular files and rectangles are directories.

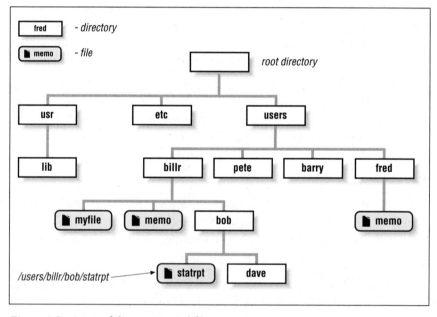

Figure 1-2: A tree of directories and files

The top of the tree is a directory called "root" that has no name on the system.* All files can be named by expressing their location on the system

---

*Most introductory UNIX tutorials say that root has the name /. We stand by this alternative explanation because it is more logically consistent.

relative to root; such names are built by listing all of the directory names (in order from root), separated by slashes (/), followed by the file's name. This way of naming files is called a *full* (or *absolute*) *pathname.*

For example, say there is a file called *memo* that is in the directory *fred*, which is in the directory *users*, which is in the root directory. This file's full pathname is */users/fred/memo.*

The working directory

Of course, it's annoying to have to use full pathnames whenever you need to specify a file. So there is also the concept of the working directory (sometimes called the current directory), which is the directory you are "in" at any given time. If you give a pathname with no leading slash, then the location of the file is worked out relative to the working directory. Such pathnames are called *relative* pathnames; you'll use them much more often than full pathnames.

When you log in to the system, your working directory is initially set to a special directory called your *home* (or *login*) directory. System administrators often set up the system so that everyone's home directory name is the same as their login name, and all home directories are contained in a common directory under root.

For example, */users/billr* is a typical home directory. If this is your working directory and you give the command **lp memo**, then the system looks for the file *memo* in */users/billr*. If you have a directory called *bob* in your home directory, and it contains the file *statreport*, then you can print it with the command **lp bob/statreport**.

Tilde notation

As you can well imagine, home directories occur often in pathnames. Although many systems are organized so that all home directories have a common parent (such as */home* or */users*), you should not have to rely on that being the case, nor should you even have to know what the absolute pathname of someone's home directory is.

Therefore, the Korn shell has a way of abbreviating home directories: just precede the name of the user with a tilde (˜). For example, you could refer to the file *memo* in user fred's home directory as ˜*fred/memo.* This is an absolute pathname, so it doesn't matter what your working directory is when you use it. If fred's home directory has a subdirectory called *bob* and the file is in there instead, you can use ˜*fred/bob/memo* as its name.

Even more convenient, a tilde by itself refers to your own home directory. You can refer to a file called *notes* in your home directory as ˜/*notes* (note the difference between that and ˜*notes*, which the shell would try to interpret as user *notes* home directory). If *notes* is in your *bob* subdirectory, then you can call it ˜/*bob/notes*. This notation is handiest when your working directory is not in your home directory tree, e.g., when it's some "system" directory like */tmp*.

Changing working directories

If you want to change your working directory, use the command **cd**. If you don't remember your working directory, the command **pwd** tells the shell to print it.

cd takes as argument the name of the directory you want to become your working directory. It can be relative to your current directory, it can contain a tilde, or it can be absolute (starting with a slash). If you omit the argument, **cd** changes to your home directory (i.e., it's the same as **cd** ˜).

Table 1-1 gives some sample **cd** commands. Each command assumes that your working directory is */users/billr* just before the command is executed, and that your directory structure looks like Figure 1-2.

Table 1-1: Sample cd Commands

Command	New Working Directory
cd bob	/users/billr/bob
cd bob/dave	/users/billr/bob/dave
cd ˜/bob/dave	/users/billr/bob/dave
cd /usr/lib	/usr/lib
cd ..	/users
cd ../pete	/users/pete
cd ˜pete	/users/pete
cd billr pete	/users/pete
cd illr arry	/users/barry

The first four are straightforward. The next two use a special directory called .. (two dots), which means "parent of this directory." Every directory has one of these; it's a universal way to get to the directory above the current one in the hierarchy—which is called the parent directory.*

The last two examples in the table use a new form of the **cd** command, which is not included in most Bourne shells. The form is **cd** *old new*. It takes the full pathname of the current working directory and tries to find the string **old** in it. If it finds the string, it substitutes **new** and changes to the resulting directory.

In the first of the two examples, the shell substitutes *pete* for *billr* in the current directory name and makes the result the new current directory. The last example shows that the substitution need not be a complete filename: substituting *arry* for *illr* in */users/billr* yields */users/barry*. (If the *old* string can't be found in the current directory name, the shell prints an error message.)

Another new feature of the Korn shell's **cd** command is the form **cd -**, which changes to whatever directory you were in before the current one. For example, if you start out in */usr/lib*, type **cd** without an argument to go to your home directory, and then type **cd -**, you will be back in */usr/lib*.

Filenames and Wildcards

Sometimes you need to run a command on more than one file at a time. The most common example of such a command is *ls*, which lists information about files. In its simplest form, without options or arguments, it lists the names of all files in the working directory except special hidden files, whose names begin with a dot (.).

If you give *ls* filename arguments, it will list those files—which is sort of silly: if your current directory has the files *bob* and *fred* in it and you type **ls bob fred**, the system will simply parrot the filenames back at you.

Actually, *ls* is more often used with options that tell it to list information about the files, like the -l (long) option, which tells *ls* to list the file's owner, size, time of last modification, and other information, or -a (all), which also lists the hidden files described above. But sometimes you want to verify the existence of a certain group of files without having to know all of their names; for example, if you use the *WordPerfect* word processor,

---

*Each directory also has the special directory . (single dot), which just means "this directory." Thus, **cd .** effectively does nothing. Both . and .. are actually special hidden files in each directory that point to the directory itself and to its parent directory, respectively. Root is its own parent.

you might want to see which files in your current directory have names that end in *.wp*.

Filenames are so important in UNIX that the shell provides a built-in way to specify the pattern of a set of filenames without having to know all of the names themselves. You can use special characters, called *wildcards*, in filenames to turn them into patterns. We'll show the three basic types of wildcards that all major UNIX shells support, and we'll save the Korn shell's set of advanced wildcard operators for Chapter 4, *Basic Shell Programming*. Table 1-2 lists the basic wildcards.

Table 1-2: Basic Wildcards

Wildcard	Matches
?	Any single character
*	Any string of characters
[*set*]	Any character in *set*
[!*set*]	Any character *not* in *set*

The ? wildcard matches any single character, so that if your directory contains the files *program.c*, *program.log*, and *program.o*, then the expression **program.?** matches *program.c* and *program.o* but not *program.log*.

The asterisk (*) is more powerful and far more widely-used; it matches any string of characters. The expression **program.*** will match all three files in the previous paragraph; *WordPerfect* users can use the expression *.**wp** to match their input files.*

Table 1-3 should give you a better idea of how the asterisk works. Assume that you have the files *bob*, *darlene*, *dave*, *ed*, *frank*, and *fred* in your working directory.

Notice that * can stand for nothing: both ***ed** and ***e*** match *ed*. Also notice that the last example shows what the shell does if it can't match anything: it just leaves the string with the wildcard untouched.

---

*MS-DOS and VAX/VMS users should note that there is *nothing special* about the dot (.) in UNIX filenames (aside from the leading dot, which "hides" the file); it's just another character. For example, **ls** * lists all files in the current directory; you don't need *.* as you do on other systems.

*Table 1-3: Using the * Wildcard*

Expression	Yields
fr*	frank fred
*ed	ed fred
b*	bob
e	darlene dave ed fred
r	darlene frank fred
*	bob darlene dave ed frank fred
d*e	darlene dave
g*	g*

The remaining wildcard is the *set* construct. A set is a list of characters (e.g., abc), an inclusive range (e.g., a-z), or some combination of the two. If you want the dash character to be part of a list, just list it first or last. Table 1-4 should explain things more clearly.

Table 1-4: Using the Set Construct Wildcards

Expression	Matches
[abc]	a, b, or c
[.,;]	Period, comma, or semicolon
[-_]	Dash and underscore
[a-c]	a, b, or c
[a-z]	All lowercase letters
[!0-9]	All non-digits
[0-9!]	All digits and exclamation point
[a-zA-Z]	All lower- and uppercase letters
[a-zA-Z0-9_-]	All letters, all digits, underscore, and dash

In the original wildcard example, **program.[co]** and **program.[a-z]** both match *program.c* and *program.o*, but not *program.log*.

An exclamation point after the left bracket lets you "negate" a set. For example, [!.;] matches any character except period and semicolon; [!a-zA-Z] matches any character that isn't a letter.

The range notation is handy, but you shouldn't make too many assumptions about what characters are included in a range. It's safe to use a range for uppercase letters, lowercase letters, digits, or any subranges thereof (e.g., **[f-q]**, **[2-6]**). Don't use ranges on punctuation characters or mixed-case letters: e.g., [a-Z] and [A-z] should not be trusted to include all of the letters and nothing more. The problem is that such ranges are not entirely portable between different types of computers.*

The process of matching expressions containing wildcards to filenames is called wildcard expansion. This is just one of several steps the shell takes when reading and processing a command line; another that we have already seen is tilde expansion, where tildes are replaced with home directories where applicable. We'll see others in later chapters, and the full details of the process are enumerated in Chapter 7, *Input/Output and Command-line Processing*.

However, it's important to be aware that the commands that you run only see the results of wildcard expansion. That is, they just see a list of arguments, and they have no knowledge of how those arguments came into being. For example, if you type **ls fr*** and your files are as on the previous page, then the shell expands the command line to **ls fred frank** and invokes the command *ls* with arguments **fred** and **frank**. If you type **ls g***, then (because there is no match) *ls* will be given the literal string **g*** and will complain with the error message, **g* not found**.†

Here is another example that should help you understand why this is important. Suppose you are a C programmer. This just means that you deal with files whose names end in .*c* (programs, a.k.a. source files), .*h* (header files for programs), and .*o* (object code files that aren't human-readable) as well as other files.

Let's say you want to list all source, object, and header files in your working directory. The command **ls *.[cho]** does the trick. The shell expands ***.[cho]** to all files whose names end in a period followed by a **c**, **h**, or **o** and passes the resulting list to *ls* as arguments.

In other words, *ls* will see the filenames just as if they were all typed in individually—but notice that we assumed no knowledge of the actual filenames whatsoever! We let the wildcards do the work.

As you gain experience with the shell, reflect on what life would be like without wildcards. Pretty miserable, we would say.

---

*Specifically, ranges depend on the character encoding scheme your computer uses. The vast majority use ASCII, but IBM mainframes use EBCDIC.

†This is different from the C shell's wildcard mechanism, which prints an error message and doesn't execute the command at all.

Input and Output

The software field—really, any scientific field—tends to advance most quickly and impressively on those few occasions when someone (i.e., not a committee) comes up with an idea that is small in concept yet enormous in its implications. The standard input and output scheme of UNIX has to be on the short list of such ideas, along with such classic innovations as the LISP language, the relational data model, and object-oriented programming.

The UNIX I/O scheme is based on two dazzlingly simple ideas. First, UNIX file I/O takes the form of arbitrarily long sequences of characters (bytes). In contrast, file systems of older vintage have more complicated I/O schemes (e.g., "block," "record," "card image," etc.). Second, everything on the system that produces or accepts data is treated as a file; this includes hardware devices like disk drives and terminals. Older systems treated every device differently. Both of these ideas have made systems programmers' lives much more pleasant.

Standard I/O

By convention, each UNIX program has a single way of accepting input called *standard input*, a single way of producing output called *standard output*, and a single way of producing error messages called *standard error output*, usually shortened to *standard error*. Of course, a program can have other input and output sources as well, as we will see in Chapter 7, *Input/Output and Command-line Processing*.

Standard I/O was the first scheme of its kind that was designed specifically for interactive users at terminals, rather than the older batch style of use that usually involves decks of punch-cards. Since the UNIX shell provides the user interface, it should come as no surprise that standard I/O was designed to fit in very neatly with the shell.

All shells handle standard I/O in basically the same way. Each program that you invoke has all three standard I/O channels set to your terminal or workstation, so that standard input is your keyboard, and standard output and error are your screen or window. For example, the *mail* utility prints messages to you on the standard output, and when you use it to send messages to other users, it accepts your input on the standard input. This means that you view messages on your screen and type new ones in on your keyboard.

When necessary, you can redirect input and output to come from or go to a file instead. If you want to send the contents of a pre-existing file to someone as mail, you redirect *mail*'s standard input so that it reads from that file instead of your keyboard.

You can also hook up programs into a *pipeline*, in which the standard output of one program feeds directly into the standard input of another; for example, you could feed *mail* output directly to the *lp* program so that messages are printed instead of shown on the screen.

This makes it possible to use UNIX utilities as building blocks for bigger programs. Many UNIX utility programs are meant to be used in this way: they each perform a specific type of filtering operation on input text. Although this isn't a textbook on UNIX utilities, they are essential to productive shell use. The more popular filtering utilities are listed in Table 1-5.

Table 1-5: Popular UNIX Data Filtering Utilities

Utility	Purpose
cat	Copy input to output
grep	Search for strings in the input
sort	Sort lines in the input
cut	Extract columns from input
sed	Perform editing operations on input
tr	Translate characters in the input to other characters

You may have used some of these before and noticed that they take names of input files as arguments and produce output on standard output. You may not know, however, that all of them (and most other UNIX utilities) accept input from standard input if you omit the argument.*

For example, the most basic utility is *cat*, which simply copies its input to its output. If you type **cat** with a filename argument, it will print out the contents of that file on your screen. But if you invoke it with no arguments, it will expect standard input and copy it to standard output. Try it: *cat* will wait for you to type a line of text; when you type RETURN, *cat* will parrot the text back at you. To stop the process, hit CTRL-D at the beginning of a

---

*If a particular UNIX utility doesn't accept standard input when you leave out the filename argument, try using – as the argument.

line (see below for what this character means). You will see ˆD when you type CTRL-D. Here's what this should look like:

```
$ cat
Here is a line of text.
Here is a line of text.
This is another line of text.
This is another line of text.
^D
$
```

I/O Redirection

cat is actually short for "catenate," i.e., link together. It accepts multiple filename arguments and copies them to the standard output. But let's pretend, for the moment, that *cat* and other utilities don't accept filename arguments and accept only standard input. As we said above, the shell lets you redirect standard input so that it comes from a file. The notation *command < filename* does this; it sets things up so that *command* takes standard input from a file instead of from a terminal.

For example, if you have a file called *fred* that contains some text, then **cat < fred** will print *fred*'s contents out onto your terminal. **sort < fred** will sort the lines in the *fred* file and print the result on your terminal (remember: we're pretending that utilities don't take filename arguments).

Similarly, *command > filename* causes the *command*'s standard output to be redirected to the named file. The classic "canonical" example of this is **date > now**: the *date* command prints the current date and time on the standard output; the above command saves it in a file called *now*.

Input and output redirectors can be combined. For example: the *cp* command is normally used to copy files; if for some reason it didn't exist or was broken, you could use *cat* in this way:

```
$ cat < file1 > file2
```

This would be similar to **cp file1 file2**.

Pipelines

It is also possible to redirect the output of a command into the standard input of another command instead of a file. The construct that does this is called the pipe, notated as |. A command line that includes two or more commands connected with pipes is called a pipeline.

Pipes are very often used with the *more* command, which works just like *cat* except that it prints its output screen by screen, pausing for the user to type SPACE (next screen), RETURN (next line), or other commands. If you're in a directory with a large number of files and you want to see details about them, **ls -l | more** will give you a detailed listing a screen at a time.

Pipelines can get very complex (see, for example, the **lsd** function in Chapter 4, *Basic Shell Programming*, or the pipeline version of the C compiler driver in Chapter 7, *Input/Output and Command-line Processing*); they can also be combined with other I/O directors. To see a sorted listing of the file *fred* a screen at a time, type **sort < fred | more**. To print it instead of viewing it on your terminal, type **sort < fred | lp**.

Here's a more complicated example. The file */etc/passwd* stores information about users' accounts on a UNIX system. Each line in the file contains a user's login name, user ID number, encrypted password, home directory, login shell, and other info. The first field of each line is the login name; fields are separated by colons (:). A sample line might look like this:

```
billr:5Ae40BGR/tePk:284:93:Bill Rosenblatt:/home/billr:/bin/ksh
```

To get a sorted listing of all users on the system, type:

```
$ cut -d: -f1 < /etc/passwd | sort
```

(Actually, you can omit the <, since *cut* accepts input filename arguments.) The *cut* command extracts the first field (**-f1**), where fields are separated by colons (**-d:**), from the input. The entire pipeline will print a list that looks like this:

```
al
billr
bob
chris
dave
ed
frank
...
```

If you want to send the list directly to the printer (instead of your screen), you can extend the pipeline like this:

```
$ cut -d: -f1 < /etc/passwd | sort | lp
```

Now you should see how I/O directors and pipelines support the UNIX building block philosophy. The notation is extremely terse and powerful. Just as important, the pipe concept eliminates the need for messy temporary files to store output of commands before it is fed into other commands.

For example, to do the same sort of thing as the above command line on other operating systems (assuming that equivalent utilities were available ...), you would need three commands. On DEC's VAX/VMS system, they might look like this:

```
$ cut [etc]passwd /d=":" /f=1 /out=temp1
$ sort temp1 /out=temp2
$ print temp2
```

After sufficient practice, you will find yourself routinely typing in powerful command pipelines that do in one line what it would take several commands (and temporary files) in other operating systems to accomplish.

Background Jobs

Pipes are actually a special case of a more general feature: doing more than one thing at a time. This is a capability that many other commercial operating systems don't have, because of the rigid limits that they tend to impose upon users. UNIX, on the other hand, was developed in a research lab and meant for internal use, so it does relatively little to impose limits on the resources available to users on a computer—as usual, leaning towards uncluttered simplicity rather than overcomplexity.

"Doing more than one thing at a time" means running more than one program at the same time. You do this when you invoke a pipeline; you can also do it by logging on to a UNIX system as many times simultaneously as you wish. (If you try that on an IBM VM/CMS system, for example, you will get an obnoxious "already logged in" message.)

The shell also lets you run more than one command at a time during a single login session. Normally, when you type a command and hit RETURN, the shell will let the command have control of your terminal until it is done; you can't type in further commands until the first one is done. But if you want to run a command that does not require user input and you want to do other things while the command is running, put an ampersand (&) after the command.

This is called running the command in the background, and a command that runs in this way is called a background job; for contrast, a job run the normal way is called a foreground job. When you start a background job, you get your shell prompt back immediately, enabling you to enter other commands.

The most obvious use for background jobs is programs that take a long time to run, such as *sort* or *uncompress* on large files. For example, assume you just got an enormous compressed file loaded into your directory from magnetic tape. Compressed files are created by the *compress* utility, which packs files into smaller amounts of space; they have names of the form *filename.Z*, where *filename* is the name of the original uncompressed file. Let's say the file is *gcc.tar.Z*, which is a compressed archive file that contains well over 10 MB of source code files.

Type **uncompress gcc.tar &** (you can omit the .Z), and the system will start a job in the background that uncompresses the data "in place" and ends up with the file *gcc.tar.* Right after you type the command, you will see a line like this:

```
[1]     4692
```

followed by your shell prompt, meaning that you can enter other commands. Those numbers give you ways of referring to your background job; Chapter 8, *Process Handling*, explains them in detail.

You can check on background jobs with the command **jobs**. For each background job, **jobs** prints a line similar to the above but with an indication of the job's status:

```
[1]  +  Running              uncompress gcc.tar
```

When the job finishes, you will see a message like this right before your shell prompt:

```
[1]  +  Done                 uncompress gcc.tar
```

The message changes if your background job terminated with an error; again, see Chapter 8 for details.

Background I/O

Jobs you put in the background should not do I/O to your terminal. Just think about it for a moment and you'll understand why.

By definition, a background job doesn't have control over your terminal. Among other things, this means that only the foreground process (or, if none, the shell itself) is "listening" for input from your keyboard. If a background job needs keyboard input, it will often just sit there doing nothing until you do something about it (as described in Chapter 8).

If a background job produces screen output, the output will just appear on your screen. If you are running a job in the foreground that produces output too, then the output from the two jobs will be randomly (and often annoyingly) interspersed.

If you want to run a job in the background that expects standard input or produces standard output, the obvious solution is to redirect it so that it comes from or goes to a file. The only exception is that some programs produce small, one-line messages (warnings, "done" messages, etc.); you may not mind if these are interspersed with whatever other output you are seeing at a given time.

For example, the *diff* utility examines two files, whose names are given as arguments, and prints a summary of their differences on the standard output. If the files are exactly the same, *diff* is silent. Usually, you invoke *diff* expecting to see a few lines that are different.

diff, like *sort* and *compress*, can take a long time to run if the input files are very large. Suppose you have two large files that are called *warandpeace.wp* and *warandpeace.wp.old*. The command **diff warandpeace.wp warandpeace.wp.old**** reveals that the author decided to change the name "Ivan" to "Aleksandr" throughout the entire file—i.e., hundreds of differences, resulting in large amounts of output.

If you type **diff warandpeace.wp warandpeace.wp.old &**, then the system will spew lots and lots of output at you, which it will be very difficult to stop—even with the techniques explained in Chapter 7, *Input/Output and Command-line Processing*. However, if you type:

```
$ diff warandpeace.wp warandpeace.wp.old > wpdiff &
```

then the differences will be saved in the file *wpdiff* for you to examine later.

Background Jobs and Priorities

Background jobs can save you a lot of thumb-twiddling time (or can help you diet by eliminating excuses to run to the candy machine). Just remember that such jobs eat up lots of system resources like memory and the processor (CPU). Just because you're running several jobs at once doesn't

---

*You could use **diff warandpeace*** as a shorthand to save typing—as long as there are no other files with names of that form. Remember that *diff* doesn't see the arguments until after the shell has expanded the wildcards. Many people overlook this use of wildcards.

mean that they will run faster than they would if run sequentially—in fact, it's usually worse.

Every job on the system is assigned a *priority*, a number that tells the operating system how much priority to give the job when it doles out resources (the higher the number, the lower the priority). Foreground commands that you enter from the shell usually have the same, standard priority. But background jobs, by default, have lower priority.*

You'll find out in Chapter 3, *Customizing Your Environment*, how you can override this priority assignment so that background jobs run at the same priority as foreground jobs. However, if you're on a multiuser system, then running lots of background jobs may eat up more than your fair share of resources, and you should consider whether having your job run as fast as possible is really more important than being a good citizen.

nice

Speaking of good citizenship, there is also a shell command that lets you lower the priority of any job: the aptly-named *nice*. If you type **nice** *command*, where *command* can be a complex shell command line with pipes, redirectors, etc., then the command will run at a lower priority. You can control just how much lower by giving *nice* a numerical argument; consult the man page for details.†

Special Characters and Quoting

The characters <, >, |, and & are four examples of *special characters* that have particular meanings to the shell. The wildcards we saw earlier in this chapter (*, ?, and [. . .]) are also special characters.

Table 1-6 gives indications of the meanings of all special characters within shell command lines only. Other characters have special meanings in specific situations, such as the regular expressions and string-handling operators we'll see in Chapter 3 and Chapter 4.

---

*This feature was borrowed from the C shell; it is not present in most Bourne shells.

†If you are a system administrator logged in as **root**, then you can also use *nice* to raise a job's priority.

Table 1-6: Special Characters

Character	Meaning	See Chapter
~	Home directory	1
`	Command substitution (archaic)	4
#	Comment	4
$	Variable expression	3
&	Background job	1
*	String wildcard	1
(	Start subshell	8
)	End subshell	8
\	Quote next character	1
|	Pipe	1
[	Start character-set wildcard	1
]	End character-set wildcard	1
{	Start code block	7
}	End code block	7
;	Shell command separator	3
'	Strong quote	1
"	Weak quote	1
<	Input redirect	1
>	Output redirect	1
/	Pathname directory separator	1
?	Single-character wildcard	1

Quoting

Sometimes you will want to use special characters literally, i.e., without their special meanings. This is called *quoting*. If you surround a string of characters with single quotes, you strip all characters within the quotes of any special meaning they might have.

The most obvious situation where you might need to quote a string is with the **print** command, which just takes its arguments and prints them to the standard output. What is the point of this? As you will see in later chapters, the shell does quite a bit of processing on command lines—most of which involves some of the special characters listed in Table 1-6. **print** is a way of making the result of that processing available on the standard output.

But what if we wanted to print the string, 2 * 3 > 5 is a valid inequality? Suppose you typed this:

```
$ print 2 * 3 > 5 is a valid inequality.
```

You would get your shell prompt back, as if nothing happened! But then there would be a new file, with the name *5*, containing "2", the names of all files in your current directory, and then the string 3 **is a valid inequality**. Make sure you understand why.*

However, if you type:

```
$ print '2 * 3 > 5 is a valid inequality.'
```

the result is the string, taken literally. You needn't quote the entire line, just the portion containing special characters (or characters you think *might* be special, if you just want to be sure):

```
$ print '2 * 3 > 5' is a valid inequality.
```

This has exactly the same result.

Notice that Table 1-6 lists double quotes (") as weak quotes. A string in double quotes is subjected to *some* of the steps the shell takes to process command lines, but not all. (In other words, it treats only some special characters as special.) You'll see in later chapters why double quotes are sometimes preferable; Chapter 7, *Input/Output and Command-line Processing*, contains the most comprehensive explanation of the shell's rules for quoting and other aspects of command-line processing. For now, though, you should stick to single quotes.

Backslash-escaping

Another way to change the meaning of a character is to precede it with a backslash (\). This is called backslash-escaping the character. In most cases, when you backslash-escape a character, you quote it. For example:

```
$ print 2 \* 3 \> 5 is a valid inequality.
```

will produce the same results as if you surrounded the string with single quotes. To use a literal backslash, just surround it with quotes ('\') or, even better, backslash-escape it (\\).

---

*This should also teach you something about the flexibility of placing I/O redirectors anywhere on the command line—even in places where they don't seem to make sense.

Here is a more practical example of quoting special characters. A few UNIX commands take arguments that often include wildcard characters, which need to be escaped so the shell doesn't process them first. The most common such command is *find*, which searches for files throughout entire directory trees.

To use *find*, you supply the root of the tree you want to search and arguments that describe the characteristics of the file(s) you want to find. For example, the command **find . -name** *string* searches the directory tree whose root is your current directory for files whose names match the string. (Other arguments allow you to search by the file's size, owner, permissions, date of last access, etc.)

You can use wildcards in the string, but you must quote them, so that the *find* command itself can match them against names of files in each directory it searches. The command **find . -name '*.c'** will match all files whose names end in *.c* anywhere in your current directory, subdirectories, sub-subdirectories, etc.

Quoting Quotation Marks

You can also use a backslash to include double quotes within a quoted string. For example:

```
$ print \"2 \* 3 \> 5\" is a valid inequality.
```

produces the following output:

```
"2 * 3 > 5" is a valid inequality.
```

However, this won't work with single quotes inside quoted expressions. For example, **print 'Bob\'s hair is brown'** will not give you **Bob's hair is brown**. You can get around this limitation in various ways. First, try eliminating the quotes:

```
$ print Bob\'s hair is brown
```

If no other characters are special (as is the case here), this works. Otherwise, you can use the following command:

```
$ print 'Bob'\''s hair is brown'
```

That is, **'\''** (i.e., single quote, backslash, single quote, single quote) acts like a single quote within a quoted string. Why? The first **'** in **'\''** ends the quoted string we started with (**'Bob**), the **\'** inserts a literal single quote, and the next **'** starts another quoted string that ends with the word "brown". If you understand, then you will have no trouble resolving the other bewildering issues that arise from the shell's often cryptic syntax.

Continuing Lines

A related issue is how to continue the text of a command beyond a single line on your terminal or workstation window. The answer is conceptually simple: just quote the RETURN key. After all, RETURN is really just another character.

You can do this in two ways: by ending a line with a backslash, or by not closing a quote mark (i.e., by including RETURN in a quoted string). If you use the backslash, there must be nothing between it and the end of the line—not even spaces or TABs.

Whether you use a backslash or a single quote, you are telling the shell to ignore the special meaning of the RETURN character. After you press RETURN, the shell understands that you haven't finished your command line (i.e., since you haven't typed a "real" RETURN), so it responds with a secondary prompt, which is > by default, and waits for you to finish the line. You can continue a line as many times as you wish.

For example, if you want the shell to print the first sentence of Thomas Hardy's *The Return of the Native*, you can type this:

```
$ print A Saturday afternoon in November was approaching the \
> time of twilight, and the vast tract of unenclosed wild known \
> as Egdon Heath embrowned itself moment by moment.
```

Or you can do it this way:

```
$ print 'A Saturday afternoon in November was approaching the
> time of twilight, and the vast tract of unenclosed wild known
> as Egdon Heath embrowned itself moment by moment.'
```

Control Keys

Control keys—those that you type by holding down the CONTROL (or CTRL) key and hitting another key—are another type of special character. These normally don't print anything on your screen, but the operating system interprets a few of them as special commands. You already know one of them: RETURN is actually the same as CTRL-M (try it and see). You have probably also used the BACKSPACE or DEL key to erase typos on your command line.

Actually, many control keys have functions that don't really concern you—yet you should know about them for future reference and in case you type them by accident.

Perhaps the most difficult thing about control keys is that they can differ from system to system. The usual arrangement is shown in Table 1-7, which lists the control keys that all major modern versions of UNIX support. Note that CTRL-\ and CTRL-| (control-backslash and control-pipe) are the same character notated two different ways; the same is true of DEL and CTRL-?.

You can use the **stty** command to find out what your settings are and change them if you wish; see Chapter 8, *Process Handling*, for details. If the version of UNIX on your system is one of those that derive from BSD (such as SunOS and Ultrix), type **stty all** to see your control-key settings; you will see something like this:

```
erase  kill   werase rprnt  flush  lnext  susp   intr  quit  stop   eof
^?     ^U     ^W     ^R     ^O     ^V     ^Z/^Y  ^C    ^|    ^S/^Q  ^D
```

Table 1-7: Control Keys

Control Key	stty Name	Function Description
CTRL-C	**intr**	Stop current command
CTRL-D	**eof**	End of input
CTRL-\ or CTRL-|	**quit**	Stop current command, if CTRL-C doesn't work
CTRL-S	**stop**	Halt output to screen
CTRL-Q		Restart output to screen
DEL or CTRL-?	**erase**	Erase last character
CTRL-U	**kill**	Erase entire command line
CTRL-Z	**susp**	Suspend current command (see Chapter 8)

The ^*X* notation stands for CTRL-*X*. If your UNIX version derives from System III or System V (this includes AIX, HP/UX, SCO, and Xenix), type **stty –a**; the resulting output will include this information:

```
intr = ^c; quit = ^|; erase = DEL; kill = ^u; eof = ^d; eol = ^`; swtch = ^`
susp = ^z; dsusp <undef>;
```

The control key you will probably use most often is CTRL-C, sometimes called the *interrupt* key. This stops—or tries to stop—the command that is currently running. You will want to use this when you enter a command and find that it's taking too long, you gave it the wrong arguments by mistake, you change your mind about wanting to run it, or whatever.

Sometimes CTRL-C doesn't work; in that case, if you really want to stop a job, try CTRL-\. But don't just type CTRL-\; always try CTRL-C first! Chapter 8, *Process Handling*, explains why in detail. For now, suffice it to say that CTRL-C gives the running job more of a chance to clean up before exiting, so that files and other resources are not left in funny states.

We've already seen an example of CTRL-D. When you are running a command that accepts standard input from your keyboard, CTRL-D tells the process that your input is finished—as if the process were reading a file and it reached the end of the file. *mail* is a utility in which this happens often. When you are typing in a message, you end by typing CTRL-D. This tells *mail* that your message is complete and ready to be sent. Most utilities that accept standard input understand CTRL-D as the end-of-input character, though many such programs accept commands like **q**, **quit**, **exit**, etc. The shell itself understands CTRL-D as the end-of-input character: as we saw earlier in this chapter, you can normally end a login session by typing CTRL-D at the shell prompt. You are just telling the shell that its command input is finished.

CTRL-S and CTRL-Q are called flow-control characters. They represent an antiquated way of stopping and restarting the flow of output from one device to another (e.g., from the computer to your terminal) that was useful when the speed of such output was low. They are rather obsolete in these days of high-speed local networks and dialup lines. In fact, under the latter conditions, CTRL-S and CTRL-Q are basically a nuisance. The only thing you really need to know about them is that if your screen output becomes "stuck," then you may have hit CTRL-S by accident. Type CTRL-Q to restart the output; any keys you may have hit in between will then take effect.

The final group of control characters gives you rudimentary ways to edit your command line. DEL acts as a backspace key (in fact, some systems use the actual BACKSPACE or CTRL-H key as "erase" instead of DEL); CTRL-U erases the entire line and lets you start over. Again, these are outmoded.* Instead of using these, go to the next chapter and read about Korn shell's editing modes, which are among its most exciting features.

---

*Why are so many outmoded control keys still in use? They have nothing to do with the shell *per se*; instead, they are recognized by the *tty driver*, an old and hoary part of the operating system's lower depths that controls input and output to/from your terminal.

In this chapter:
- *The History File*
- *Emacs Editing Mode*
- *Vi Editing Mode*
- *The fc Command*
- *Finger Habits*

2

Command-line Editing

It's always possible to make mistakes when you type at a computer keyboard, but perhaps even more so when you are using a UNIX shell. UNIX shell syntax is powerful, yet terse, full of odd characters, and not particularly mnemonic, making it possible to construct command lines that are as cryptic as they are complex. The Bourne and C shells exacerbate this situation by giving you extremely limited ways of editing your command lines.

In particular, there is no way to recall a previous command line so that you can fix a mistake. For example, in Chapter 7, *Input/Output and Command-line Processing*, we'll see complex command lines like:

```
$ eval cat $srcname | ccom | as | optimize > $objname
```

If you are an experienced Bourne shell user, undoubtedly you know the frustration of having to retype lines like this. You can use the backspace key to edit, but once you hit RETURN, it's gone forever!

The C shell provided a small improvement via its *history* mechanism, which provides a few very awkward ways of editing previous commands. But there are more than a few people who have wondered, "Why can't I edit my UNIX command lines in the same way I can edit text with an editor?"

This is exactly what the Korn shell allows you to do. It has editing modes that allow you to edit command lines with editing commands similar to those of the two most popular UNIX editors, *vi* and *emacs.** It also provides a much-extended analog to the C shell history mechanism called **fc** (for fix command) that, among other things, allows you to use your favorite editor directly for editing your command lines.

---

*For some unknown reason, the documentation on emacs-mode has been removed from *ksh*(1) manual pages on some UNIX systems. This does not mean, however, that the mode doesn't exist or doesn't work properly.

In this chapter, we will discuss features common to all of the Korn shell's command-history facilities; then we will deal with each such facility in detail. If you use *vi* or *emacs*, you may wish to read only the section on the emulation mode for the one you use.* If you use neither *vi* or *emacs*, but are interested in learning one of the editing modes anyway, we suggest emacs-mode, because it is more of a natural extension of the minimal editing capability you get with the bare shell.

We should mention up front that both emacs- and vi-modes introduce the potential for clashes with control keys set up by the UNIX terminal interface. Recall the control keys shown in Chapter 1, *Korn Shell Basics*, in Table 1-7 and the sample *stty* command output. The control keys shown there override their functions in the editing modes.

During the rest of this chapter, we'll warn you when an editing command clashes with the *default setting* of a terminal-interface control key. But if you (or your system administrator) choose to customize your terminal interface, as we'll show in Chapter 8, *Process Handling*, you're on your own as far as the editing modes are concerned.

Enabling Command-line Editing

There are two ways of entering either editing mode. First, you can set your editing mode by using the environment variable VISUAL. The Korn shell checks to see if this variable ends with *vi* or *macs*.† An excellent way to set VISUAL is to put a line like the following in your *.profile* or environment file:

```
VISUAL=$(whence emacs)
```

or

```
VISUAL=$(whence vi)
```

As you will find out in Chapter 3, *Customizing Your Environment*, and Chapter 4, *Basic Shell Programming*, the **whence** built-in command takes the name of another command as its argument and writes the command's full pathname on the standard output; the form $(*command*) returns the standard output generated by *command* as a string value. Thus, the line above finds out the full pathname of your favorite editor and stores it in the

---

*You will get the most out of these sections if you are already familiar with the editor(s) in question. Good sources for more complete information on the editors are the O'Reilly & Associates Nutshell Handbooks *Learning the vi Editor*, by Linda Lamb, and *Learning GNU Emacs*, by Debra Cameron and Bill Rosenblatt.

†GNU Emacs is often installed as *gmacs* or *gnumacs*.

environment variable VISUAL. The advantage of this code is that it is portable to other systems, which may have the executables for editors stored in
different directories.

The second way of selecting an editing mode is to set the option explicitly
with the **set -o** command:

```
$ set -o emacs
```

or

```
$ set -o vi
```

You will find that the vi- and emacs-editing modes are good at emulating
the basic commands of these editors but not their advanced features; their
main purpose is to let you transfer "finger habits" from your favorite editor
to the shell. **fc** is quite a powerful facility; it is mainly meant to supplant C
shell history and as an "escape hatch" for users of editors other than *vi* or
emacs. Therefore the section on **fc** is mainly recommended to C shell users
and those who don't use either standard editor.

The History File

All of the Korn shell's command history facilities depend on a file that contains commands as you type them in. This file is normally *.sh_history* in
your home directory, but you can call it whatever you like by setting the
environment variable HISTFILE (see Chapter 3, *Customizing Your Environment*). When you run one of the Korn shell's editing modes, you are actually running a mini-editor on your history file.

If you run more than one login session at a time (e.g., more than one *xterm*
on an X Windows workstation), you may find it advantageous to maintain a
separate history file for each login session. Put the following line in your
.profile:

```
HISTFILE=~/.hist$$
```

This creates a history file whose name begins with **.hist** and ends with a
number that is essentially guaranteed to be unique; see Chapter 8, *Process
Handling*, for an explanation of why *.hist$$* generates a unique name.
Unfortunately, if you do this, you will end up with lots of stray history files
hanging around. One way to clean up the unneeded history files is to clean
up after yourself at logout time, as explained in Chapter 4, *Basic Shell Pro-
gramming*. Another way is to put an entry in your personal *crontab* file

(see the man page *crontab*(1))* that removes all history files every day at some benign time like 2 A.M. The following line will do it:

```
0 2 * * * rm ~/.hist*
```

Another environment variable, HISTSIZE, can be used to determine the maximum number of commands kept in the history file. The default is 128 (i.e., the 128 most recent commands), which should be more than adequate.

Emacs Editing Mode

If you are an *emacs* user, you will find it most useful to think of emacs editing mode as a simplified, non-customizable† *emacs* with a single, one-line window. All of the basic commands are available for cursor motion, cut and paste, and search.

Basic Commands

Emacs-mode uses control keys for the most basic editing functions. If you aren't familiar with *emacs*, you can think of these as extensions of the rudimentary "erase" character (usually backspace or DEL) that UNIX provides through its interface to users' terminals. In fact, emacs-mode figures out what your erase character is and uses that as its delete-backward key. For the sake of consistency, we'll assume your erase character is DEL from now on; if it is CTRL-H or something else, you will need to make a mental substitution. The most basic control-key commands are shown in Table 2-1. (*Important:* remember that typing CTRL-D when your command line is empty may log you off!) The basic finger habits of emacs-mode are easy to learn, but they do require that you assimilate a couple of concepts that are peculiar to the *emacs* editor.

The first of these is the use of CTRL-B and CTRL-F for backward and forward cursor motion. These keys have the advantage of being obvious mnemonics, but many people would rather use the arrow keys that are on just about every keyboard nowadays.

---

*Some versions of UNIX do not support personal *crontab* files, though all versions derived from AT&T System V should. If yours does not, you have two options: either use *at* with a script that reschedules itself at the end, or ask your system administrator to put an appropriate command in the system's *crontab* file.

†The public domain Korn shell and *bash* have emacs-modes that are customizable. See Appendix A.

Table 2-1: Basic emacs-mode Commands

Command	Description
CTRL-B	Move backward one character (without deleting)
CTRL-F	Move forward one character
DEL	Delete one character backward
CTRL-D	Delete one character forward
CTRL-Y	Retrieve ("yank") last item deleted

Unfortunately, emacs-mode doesn't use the arrow keys, because the codes that they transmit to the computer aren't completely standardized; emacs-mode was designed to work on the widest variety of terminals possible without needing to do the kind of heavy-duty customization that the full *emacs* does. Just about the only hardware requirement of emacs-mode is that the SPACE character overwrite the character on top of which it is typed.

In emacs-mode, the *point* (sometimes also called *dot*) is an imaginary place just to the left of the character the cursor is on. In the command descriptions in Table 2-1, some say "forward" while others say "backward." Think of forward as "to the right of point" and backward as "to the left of point."

For example, let's say you type in a line and, instead of typing **RETURN**, you type CTRL-B and hold it down so that it repeats. The cursor will move to the left until it is over the first character on the line, like this:

```
$ fgrep -l Bob < ~pete/wk/names
```

Now the cursor is on the **f**, and point is at the beginning of the line, just before the **f**. If you type DEL, nothing will happen because there are no characters to the left of point. However, if you press CTRL-D (the "delete character forward" command) you will delete the first letter:

```
$ grep -l Bob < ~pete/wk/names
```

Point is still at the beginning of the line. If this were the desired command, you could hit **RETURN** now and run it; you don't need to move the cursor back to the end of the line. However, if you wanted to, you could type CTRL-F repeatedly to get there:

```
$ grep -l Bob < ~pete/wk/names
```

At this point, typing CTRL-D wouldn't do anything, but hitting DEL would erase the final **s**. If you type DEL and decide you want the **s** back again, just press CTRL-Y to yank it back. If you think this example is silly, you're right in this particular case, but bear in mind that CTRL-Y undoes the last delete command of any kind, including the delete-word and delete-line commands that we will see shortly.*

Word Commands

The basic commands are really all you need to get around a command line, but a set of more advanced commands lets you do it with fewer keystrokes. These commands operate on *words* rather than single characters; emacs-mode defines a word to be a sequence of one or more alphanumeric characters.

The word commands are shown in Table 2-2. Whereas the basic commands are all single characters, these consist of two keystrokes, ESC followed by a letter. You will notice that the command ESC *X*, where *X* is any letter, often does for a word what CTRL-*X* does for a single character. The multiplicity of choices for delete-word-backward arises from the fact that your erase character could be either CTRL-H or DEL.

Table 2-2: Emacs-mode Word Commands

Command	Description
ESC b	Move one word backward
ESC f	Move one word forward
ESC DEL	Delete one word backward
ESC h	Delete one word backward
ESC CTRL-H	Delete one word backward
ESC d	Delete one word forward

To return to our example: if we type ESC b, point will move back a word. Since / is not an alphanumeric character, emacs-mode will stop there:

```
$ grep -1 Bob < ~pete/wk/names
```

The cursor is on the **n** in *names*, and point is between the / and the **n**. Now let's say we want to change the –1 option of this command from *Bob* to

---

* *emacs* users should note that this usage of CTRL-Y is different from the full editor, which doesn't save character deletes.

Dave. We need to move back on the command line, so we type ESC b two more times. This gets us here:

```
$ grep -l Bob < ~pete/wk/names
```

If we type ESC b again, we end up at the beginning of *Bob*:

```
$ grep -l Bob < ~pete/wk/names
```

Why? Remember that a word is defined as a sequence of alphanumeric characters only; therefore < is not a word, and the next word in the backward direction is *Bob*. We are now in the right position to delete *Bob*, so we type ESC d and get:

```
$ grep -l █< ~pete/wk/names
```

Now we can type in the desired argument:

```
$ grep -l Dave█< ~pete/wk/names
```

The CTRL-Y "undelete" command will retrieve an entire word, instead of a character, if the word was the last thing deleted.

Line Commands

There are still more efficient ways of moving around a command line in emacs-mode. A few commands deal with the entire line; they are shown in Table 2-3.

Table 2-3: Emacs-mode Line Commands

Command	Description
CTRL-A	Move to beginning of line
CTRL-E	Move to end of line
CTRL-K	Delete ("kill") forward to end of line
CTRL-C	Capitalize character after point

CTRL-C is often the "interrupt" key that UNIX provides through its interface to your terminal. If this is the case, CTRL-C in emacs-mode will erase the entire line, as if CTRL-A and CTRL-K were pressed. On systems where the interrupt key is set to something else (often DEL), CTRL-C capitalizes the current character.

Using CTRL-A, CTRL-E, and CTRL-K should be straightforward. Remember that CTRL-Y will always undelete the last thing deleted; if you use CTRL-K, that could be quite a few characters.

Moving Around in the History File

Now we know how to get around the command line efficiently and make changes. But that doesn't address the original issue of recalling previous commands by accessing the history file. Emacs-mode has several commands for doing this, summarized in Table 2-4.

Table 2-4: Emacs-mode Commands for Moving Through the History File

Command	Description
CTRL-P	Move to previous line
CTRL-N	Move to next line
CTRL-R	Search backward
ESC <	Move to first line of history file
ESC >	Move to last line of history file

CTRL-P is by far the one you will use most often—it's the "I made a mistake, let me go back and fix it" key. You can use it as many times as you wish to scroll back through the history file. If you want to get back to the last command you entered, you can hold down CTRL-N until the Korn shell beeps at you, or just type ESC >. As an example, you hit **RETURN** to run the command above, but you get an error message telling you that your option letter was incorrect. You want to change it without retyping the whole thing.

First, you would type CTRL-P to recall the bad command. You get it back with point at the end:

```
$ grep -1 Dave < ~pete/wk/names█
```

After CTRL-A, ESC f, two CTRL-Fs, and CTRL-D, you have:

```
$ grep -█Dave < ~pete/wk/names
```

You decide to try –s instead of –l, so you type s and hit RETURN. You get the same error message, so you give up and look it up in the manual. You find out that the command you want is *fgrep*—not *grep*—after all.

You sigh heavily and go back and find the *fgrep* command you typed in an hour ago. To do this, you type CTRL-R; whatever was on the line will disappear and be replaced by ^R. Then type **fgrep**, and you will see this:

```
$ ^Rfgrep
```

Hit RETURN, and the shell will search backwards through the history file for a line containing "fgrep". If it doesn't find one, it will beep. But if it finds one, it will display it, and your "current line" will be that line (i.e., you will be somewhere in the middle of the history file, not at the end as usual):

```
$ fgrep -1 Bob < ~pete/wk/names█
```

Typing CTRL-R without an argument (i.e., just CTRL-R followed by RETURN) causes the shell to repeat your last backward search. If you try the *fgrep* command by hitting RETURN again, two things will happen. First, of course, the command will run. Second, this line will be entered into the history file at the end, and your "current line" will be at the end as well. You will no longer be in the middle of the history file.

CTRL-R may not work properly on some versions of UNIX, because it is also the default setting for the "reprint" function of the terminal interface. (It works correctly on all the versions we've tried.) If you press CTRL-R and see the command line reprinted, you may want to consider changing the terminal interface's "reprint" key. See the section on *stty* in Chapter 8, *Process Handling*.

CTRL-P and CTRL-R are clearly the most important emacs-mode commands that deal with the history file; you might use CTRL-N occasionally. The others are less useful, and we suspect that they were mainly included for compatibility with the full *emacs* editor.

emacs users should also note that the full editor's "deluxe" search capabilities, such as incremental and regular expression search, are not available in the Korn shell's emacs-mode—with one minor exception: if you use CTRL-R and precede your search string with a ˆ (caret character), it will match only commands that have the search string at the beginning of the line.

Filename Completion and Expansion

One of the most powerful (and typically underused) features of emacs-mode is its *filename completion* facility, inspired by similar features in the full *emacs* editor, the C shell, and (originally) the old DEC TOPS-20 operating system.

The premise behind filename completion is that when you need to type a filename, you should not have to type more than is necessary to identify the file unambiguously. This is an excellent feature; there is an analogous one in vi-mode. We recommend that you get it under your fingers, since it will save you quite a bit of typing.

There are three commands in emacs-mode that relate to filename completion. The most important is ESC ESC.* When you type in a word of text followed by ESC ESC, the Korn shell will attempt to complete the name of a file
in the current directory. Then one of four things can happen:

1. If there is no file whose name begins with the word, the shell will beep
    and nothing further will happen.

2. If there is exactly one way to complete the filename and the file is a reg-
    ular file, the shell will type the rest of the filename and follow it with a
    space so you can type in more command arguments.

3. If there is exactly one way to complete the filename and the file is a
    directory, the shell will complete the filename and follow it with a slash.

4. If there is more than one way to complete the filename, the shell will
    complete out to the longest common prefix among the available
    choices.

For example, assume you have a directory with the files *program.c* and
problem.c. You want to compile the first of these by typing **cc program**.c.
You type **cc pr** followed by ESC ESC. This is not an unambiguous prefix,
since the prefix "pro" is common to both filenames, so the shell only completes out to **cc pro**. You need to type more letters to disambiguate, so you
type **g** and hit ESC ESC again. Then the shell completes out to "**cc pro-
gram.c** ", leaving the extra space for you to type in other filenames or
options.

A related command is ESC *, which expands the prefix to all possible
choices. ESC * acts like the standard * shell wildcard character except that
it expands the choices for you to see and does not execute the command.
In the above example, if you type ESC * instead of ESC ESC, the shell will
expand to "**cc problem.c program.c** ". If you type ESC = instead of ESC *,
you will see a numbered list of expansions printed to standard error.

Miscellaneous Commands

Several miscellaneous commands complete emacs editing mode; they are
shown in Table 2-5.

---

* *emacs* users can think of this as analogous to minibuffer completion with the TAB key.

Table 2-5: Emacs-mode Miscellaneous Commands

Command	Description
CTRL-J	Same as RETURN
CTRL-L	Redisplay the line
CTRL-M	Same as RETURN
CTRL-O	Same as RETURN, then display next line in history file
CTRL-T	Transpose two characters to the right of point and move point forward by one*
CTRL-U	Repeat the following command four times
CTRL-V	Print the version of the Korn shell
CTRL-W	Delete ("wipe") all characters between point and "mark". "Mark" is discussed later in this section.
CTRL-X CTRL-X	Exchange point and mark
CTRL-[	Same as ESC (most keyboards)
CTRL-] x	Search forward on current line for x, where x is any character
ESC c	Change word after point to all capital letters
ESC l	Change word after point to all lowercase letters
ESC p	Save all characters between point and mark as if they were deleted
ESC .	Insert last word in previous command line after point
ESC _	Same as above
ESC CTRL-]x	Search backward for x, where x is any character
ESC SPACE	Set mark at point
ESC#	Insert line in history file for future editing

* CTRL-T behaves slightly differently if you put **set -o gmacs** (instead of **emacs**) in your *.profile*. In this case, it will transpose the two characters to the left of point, leaving point unmoved. This is the only difference between emacs and gmacs modes; the latter conforms to the James Gosling version of the *emacs* editor (a.k.a. Unipress *emacs*). Note: neither of these behaves like CTRL-T in GNU *emacs*, which transposes the characters on either side of point.

Several of these commands may clash with terminal interface control keys on your system. CTRL-U is the default key for "kill line" on most versions of UNIX. BSD-derived systems use CTRL-V and CTRL-W as default settings for the "quote next character" and "word erase" terminal interface functions respectively. CTRL-V is particularly confusing, since it is meant to override other terminal interface control keys but has no effect on emacs-mode commands.

A few miscellaneous commands are worth discussing, even though they may not be among the most useful emacs-mode commands.

CTRL-O is useful for repeating a sequence of commands you have already entered. Just go back to the first command in the sequence and press CTRL-O instead of RETURN. This will execute the command and bring up the next command in the history file. Press CTRL-O again to enter this command and bring up the next one. Repeat this until you see the last command in the sequence; then just hit RETURN.

CTRL-U, if it doesn't perform the line-delete function of your system's terminal interface, repeats the next command four times. If you type CTRL-U twice, the repeat factor becomes 16; for 3 CTRL-Us it's 64; and so on. CTRL-U is possibly most useful when navigating through your history file. If you want to recall a command that you entered a while ago, you could type CTRL-U CTRL-P to go back through the history file four lines at a time; you could think of this as a "fast rewind" through your command history.

Another possible use of CTRL-U is when you want to go from one end of a long pathname to the other. Unlike vi-mode, emacs-mode does not have a concept of "word" that is flexible enough to distinguish between pathnames and filename components. The emacs-mode word motion commands (ESC b and ESC f) will move through a pathname only one component at a time, because emacs-mode treats the slash as a word separator. You can use CTRL-U to help get around this limitation. If you have a line that looks like this:

```
$ ls -1 /a/very/long/pathname/filename█
```

and you need to go back and change "very" to "really" you can type CTRL-U ESC b and your cursor will end up here:

```
$ ls -1 /a/▊ery/long/pathname/filename
```

Then you can make the change:

```
$ ls -1 /a/really▊long/pathname/filename
```

Judicious use of CTRL-U can save you a few keystrokes, but considering the small amount of information you manipulate when you edit command lines, it's probably not an incredibly vital feature. Often, holding down a key to repeat it is just as effective as CTRL-U. Because you'll probably have to redefine the terminal driver's line erase key before you can use CTRL-U, it's probably better to do without CTRL-U.

The mark mentioned in the explanation of CTRL-W should be familiar to *emacs* editor users, but its function in emacs-mode is a subset of that in the full editor. Emacs-mode keeps track of the place at which the last delete was performed (whether a delete character, word, line, or whatever); this place is called the *mark*. If nothing has been deleted on the current line, mark defaults to the beginning of the line. You can also set the mark to where your cursor is by typing ESC SPACE. CTRL-X CTRL-X (CTRL-X hit twice) causes the Korn shell to swap point and mark, i.e., to move your cursor to where the mark is and reset mark to where your cursor was before you typed CTRL-X CTRL-X.

The mark concept is not extremely useful because of the small amount of "distance" to travel in command lines. But if you ever have to make a series of changes in the same place in a line, CTRL-X CTRL-X will take you back there. In the previous example, if you wanted to change "really" to "monumentally", one way would be to type CTRL-X CTRL-X to return to the beginning of "really":

```
$ ls -1 /a/really/long/pathname/filename
```

Then you could type ESC d to delete "really" and make the change. Of course, you could do this faster by typing ESC DEL instead of CTRL-X CTRL-X and ESC d.

Of the case-changing commands, ESC l is useful when you hit the CAPS LOCK key by accident and don't notice it immediately. Since all-caps words aren't used too often in the UNIX world, you may not use ESC c very often.

If it seems like there are too many synonyms for RETURN, bear in mind that CTRL-M is actually the same (ASCII) character as RETURN, and that CTRL-J is actually the same as LINEFEED, which UNIX usually accepts in lieu of RETURN anyway.

ESC . and ESC _ are useful if you want to run several commands on a given file. The usual UNIX convention is that a filename is the last argument to a command. Therefore you can save typing by just entering each command followed by SPACE and then typing ESC . or ESC _. For example, say you want to examine a file using *more*, so you type:

```
$ more myfilewithaverylongname
```

Then you decide you want to print it, so you type the print command *lp*. You can avoid typing the very long name by typing **lp** followed by a space and then ESC . or ESC _; the Korn shell will insert *myfilewithaverylong-name* for you.

Keyboard Shortcuts with Aliases

Finally, emacs-mode has an interesting way of defining keyboard shortcuts for commonly used commands by interacting with the Korn shell's alias facility, as described in the next chapter. Here's how it works: if you define an alias called _x, where x is a letter, then emacs-mode will expand the alias when you hit ESC x. The expansion will appear on your screen, but the Korn shell will not run the command, leaving you free to type more or just hit RETURN to run it. We don't find this particularly useful, since you can just define an alias in the normal way instead.

Vi Editing Mode

Like emacs-mode, vi-mode essentially creates a one-line editing window into the history file. Vi-mode is popular because *vi* is the most standard UNIX editor. But the function for which *vi* was designed, writing C programs, has different editing requirements from those of command interpreters. As a result, although it is possible to do complex things in *vi* with relatively few keystrokes, the relatively simple things you need to do in the Korn shell sometimes take too many keystrokes.

Like *vi*, vi-mode has two modes of its own: *input* and *control* mode. The former is for typing commands (as in normal Korn shell use); the latter is for moving around the command line and the history file. When you are in input mode, you can type commands in and hit **RETURN** to run them. In addition, you have minimal editing capabilities via control characters, which are summarized in Table 2-6.

Table 2-6: Editing Commands in vi Input Mode

Command	Description
DEL	Delete previous character
CTRL-W	Erase previous word (i.e., erase until blank)
CTRL-V	"Quote" the next character
ESC	Enter control mode (see below)

Note that at least some of these—depending on which version of UNIX you have—are the same as the editing commands provided by UNIX through its terminal interface.* Vi-mode will use your "erase" character as the "delete previous character" key; usually it is set to DEL or CTRL-H (BACKSPACE). CTRL-V will cause the next character you type to appear in the command line as is; i.e., if it is an editing command (or an otherwise special character like CTRL-D), it will be stripped of its special meaning.

Under normal circumstances, you just stay in input mode. But if you want to go back and make changes to your command line, or if you want to recall previous commands, you need to go into control mode. To do this, hit ESC.

Simple Control Mode Commands

A full range of *vi* editing commands are available to you in control mode. The simplest of these move you around the command line and are summarized in Table 2-7. Vi-mode contains two "word" concepts. The simplest is any sequence of non-blank characters; we'll call this a *non-blank word.* The other is any sequence of only alphanumeric characters (letters and digits) or any sequence of only non-alphanumeric characters; we'll just call this a *word.†*

Table 2-7: Basic vi Control Mode Commands

Command	Description
h	Move left one character
l	Move right one character
w	Move right one word
b	Move left one word
W	Move to beginning of next non-blank word
B	Move to beginning of preceding non-blank word
e	Move to end of current word
E	Move to end of current non-blank word
0	Move to beginning of line
^	Move to first non-blank character in line
$	Move to end of line

---

*In particular, versions of UNIX derived from 4.x BSD have all of these commands built in.

†Neither of these definitions is the same as the definition of a word in emacs-mode.

All of these commands except the last three can be preceded by a number that acts as a repeat count. The last two will be familiar to users of UNIX utilities (such as *grep*) that use regular expressions, as well as to *vi* users.

Time for a few examples. Let's say you type in this line and, before you hit RETURN, decide you want to change it:

```
$ fgrep -l Bob < ~pete/wk/names█
```

As shown, your cursor is beyond the last character of the line. First, type ESC to enter control mode; your cursor will move back one space so that it is on the **s**. Then if you type **h**, your cursor will move back to the **e**. If you type **3h** from the **e**, you will end up at the **n**.

Now we will see the difference between the two "word" concepts. Go back to the end of the line by typing **$**. If you type **b**, the word in question is "names", and the cursor will end up on the **n**:

```
$ fgrep -l Bob < ~pete/wk/names
```

If you type **b** again, the next word is the slash (it's a "sequence" of non-alphanumeric characters), so the cursor ends up over it:

```
$ fgrep -l Bob < ~pete/wk/names
```

However, if you typed **B** instead of **b**, the non-blank word would be the entire pathname, and the cursor would end up at the beginning of it—that is, over the tilde:

```
$ fgrep -l Bob < ~pete/wk/names
```

You would have had to type **b** four times—or just **4b**—to get the same effect, since there are four "words" in the part of the pathname to the left of */names*: *wk*, slash, *pete*, and the leading tilde.

At this point, **w** and **W** do the opposite: typing **w** gets you over the **p**, since the tilde is a "word", while typing **W** brings you to the end of the line. But whereas **w** and **W** take you to the beginning of the next word, **e** and **E** take you to the end of the current word. Thus, if you type **w** with the cursor on the tilde, you get to:

```
$ fgrep -l Bob < ~pete/wk/names
```

Then typing **e** gets you to

```
$ fgrep -l Bob < ~pete/wk/names
```

And typing an additional **w** gets you to:

```
$ fgrep -l Bob < ~pete/wk/names
```

On the other hand, **E** gets you to the end of the current non-blank word—in this case, the end of the line. (If you find these commands non-mnemonic, you're right. The only way to assimilate them is through lots of practice.)

Entering and Changing Text

Now that you know how to enter control mode and move around on the command line, you need to know how to get back into input mode so you can make changes and type in additional commands. A number of commands take you from control mode into input mode; they are listed in Table 2-8. All of them enter input mode a bit differently.

Table 2-8: Commands for Entering vi Input Mode

Command	Description
i	Text inserted before current character (insert)
a	Text inserted after current character (append)
I	Text inserted at beginning of line
A	Text inserted at end of line
R	Text overwrites existing text

Most likely, you will use either **i** or **a** consistently, and you may use **R** occasionally. **I** and **A** are abbreviations for **0i** and **$a** respectively. To illustrate the difference between **i**, **a**, and **R**, say we start out with our example line:

```
$ fgrep -l Bob < ~pete/wk/names
```

If you type **i** followed by **end**, you will get:

```
$ fgrep -l Bob < ~pete/wkend/names
```

That is, the cursor will always appear to be under the / before *names*. But if you type **a** instead of **i**, you will notice the cursor move one space to the right. Then if you type **nick**, you will get:

```
$ fgrep -l Bob < ~pete/wk/nicknames
```

That is, the cursor will always be just after the last character you typed, until you type ESC to end your input. Finally, if you go back to the **n** in *names*, type **R** instead, and then type **task**, you will see:

```
$ fgrep -l Bob < ~pete/wk/tasks
```

In other words, you will be *replacing* (hence *R*) instead of inserting text.

Why capital **R** instead of lowercase **r**? The latter is a slightly different command, which replaces only one character and does not enter input mode. With **r**, the next single character overwrites the character under the cursor. So if we start with the original command line and type **r** followed by a semicolon, we get:

```
$ fgrep -l Bob < ~pete/wk;names
```

If you precede **r** with a number *N*, it will allow you to replace the next *N* existing characters on the line—but still not enter input mode. Lowercase **r** is effective for fixing erroneous option letters, I/O redirection characters, punctuation, etc.

Deletion Commands

Now that you know how to enter commands and move around the line, you need to know how to delete. The basic deletion command in vi-mode is **d** followed by one other letter. This letter determines what the unit and direction of deletion is, and it corresponds to a motion command, as listed previously in Table 2-7. Table 2-9 shows some commonly-used examples.

Table 2-9: Some vi-mode Deletion Commands

Command	Description
dh	Delete one character backwards
dl	Delete one character forwards
db	Delete one word backwards
dw	Delete one word forwards
dB	Delete one non-blank word backwards
dW	Delete one non-blank word forwards
d$	Delete to end of line
d0	Delete to beginning of line

These commands have a few variations and abbreviations. If you use a **c** instead of **d**, you will enter input mode after it does the deletion. You can supply a numeric repeat count either before or after the **d** (or **c**). Table 2-10 lists the available abbreviations.

Most people tend to use **D** to delete to end of line, **dd** to delete an entire line, and **x** (as "backspace") to delete single characters. If you aren't a hard-core *vi* user, you may find it difficult to get some of the more esoteric deletion commands under your fingers.

Table 2-10: Abbreviations for vi-mode Delete Commands

Command	Description
D	Equivalent to *d$* (delete to end of line)
dd	Equivalent to *0d$* (delete entire line)
C	Equivalent to *c$* (delete to end of line, enter input mode)
cc	Equivalent to *0c$* (delete entire line, enter input mode)
X	Equivalent to *db* (delete character backwards)
x	Equivalent to *dl* (delete character forwards)

Every good editor provides "un-delete" commands as well as delete commands, and vi-mode is no exception. Vi-mode maintains a *delete buffer* that stores all of the modifications to text on the current line only (note that this is different from the full *vi* editor). The command **u** undoes the last text modification command only, while **U** undoes all such commands on the current line. So if you make one change but want to undo it, type **u**; but if you make lots of changes and find that the original is closer to what you want, you can undo everything by typing **U**. A related command is **.** (dot), which redoes the last text modification command.

There is also a way to save text in the delete buffer without having deleted it in the first place: just type in a delete command but use **y** ("yank") instead of **d**. This does not modify anything, but it allows you to retrieve the yanked text as many times as you like later on. The command to retrieve yanked text is **p**, which inserts the text on the current line to the left of the cursor. The **y** and **p** commands are powerful but far better suited to "real *vi*" tasks like making global changes to documents or programs than to shell commands, so we doubt you'll use them very often.

Moving Around in the History File

The next group of vi control mode commands we will cover allows you to move around in and search your history file. This is the all-important functionality that lets you go back and fix an erroneous command without retyping the entire line. These commands are summarized in Table 2-11.

Table 2-11: Vi Control Mode Commands for Searching the History File

Command	Description
k or –	Move backward one line
j or +	Move forward one line
G	Move to line given by repeat count
?*string*	Search backward for string
/*string*	Search forward for string
n	Repeat search in same direction as previous
N	Repeat search in opposite direction of previous

The first three can be preceded by repeat counts (e.g., **3k** or 3– moves back three lines in the history file).

If you aren't familiar with *vi* and its cultural history, you may be wondering at the wisdom of choosing such seemingly poor mnemonics as **h**, **j**, **k**, and **l** for backward character, forward line, backward line, and forward character, respectively. Well, there actually is a rationale for the choices—other than that they are all together on the standard keyboard.

Bill Joy originally developed *vi* to run on Lear-Siegler ADM-3a terminals, which were the first popular models with addressable cursors (meaning that a program could send an ADM-3a a command to move the cursor to a specified location on the screen). The ADM-3a's **h**, **j**, **k**, and **l** keys had little arrows on them, so Joy decided to use those keys for appropriate commands in *vi*.

Another (partial) rationale for the command choices is that CTRL-H is the traditional backspace key, and CTRL-J denotes linefeed.

Perhaps + and – are better mnemonics than **j** and **k**, but the latter have the advantage of being more easily accessible to touch typists. In either case, these commands are the most basic ones for moving around the history file. To see how they work, let's take the same examples we used when discussing emacs-mode above.

You enter the example command (RETURN works in both input and control modes, as does LINEFEED or CTRL-J):

```
$ fgrep -1 Bob < ~pete/wk/names
```

but you get an error message saying that your option letter was wrong. You want to change it to **-s** without having to retype the entire command. Assuming you are in control mode (you may have to type ESC to put yourself in control mode), you type **k** or **-** to get the command back. Your cursor will be at the beginning of the line:

```
$ fgrep -1 Bob < ~pete/wk/names
```

Type **w** to get to the **-**, then **l** to get to the **1**. Now you can replace it by typing **rs**; press **RETURN** to run the command.

Now let's say you get another error message, and you finally decide to look at the manual page for the *fgrep* command. You remember having done this a while ago today, so rather than typing in the entire *man*(1) command, you search for the last one you used. To do this, type ESC to enter control mode (if you are already in control mode, this will have no effect), then type **/** followed by **man** or **ma**. To be on the safe side, you can also type **^ma**; the **^** means match only lines that begin with **ma**.*

But typing **/^ma** doesn't give you what you want: instead, the shell gives you:

```
$ make myprogram
```

To search for "man" again, you can type **n**, which does another backward search using the last search string. Typing **/** again without an argument and hitting **RETURN** will accomplish the same thing.

The **G** command retrieves the command whose number is the same as the numeric prefix argument you supply. **G** depends on the command numbering scheme described in Chapter 3, *Customizing Your Environment*, in the section "Prompting Variables." Without a prefix argument, it goes to command number 1. This may be useful to former C shell users who still want to use command numbers.

---

*Fans of *vi* and search utilities like *grep* should note that caret (^) for beginning-of-line is the only context operator vi-mode provides for search strings.

Character-finding Commands

There are some additional motion commands in vi-mode, although they are less useful than the ones we saw earlier in the chapter. These commands allow you to move to the position of a particular character in the line. They are summarized in Table 2-12, in which *x* denotes any character.

All of these commands can be preceded by a repeat count.

Table 2-12: Vi-mode Character-Ænding Commands

Command	Description
f*x*	Move right to next occurrence of *x*
F*x*	Move left to previous occurrence of *x*
t*x*	Move right to next occurrence of *x*, then back one space
T*x*	Move left to previous occurrence of *x*, then forward one space
;	Redo last character-finding command
,	Redo last character-finding command in opposite direction

Starting with the previous example: let's say you want to change *Bob* to *Rob*. Make sure that you're at the end of the line (or, in any case, to the left of the *B* in *Bob*); then, if you type **FB**, your cursor will move to the B:

```
$ fgrep -1 Bob < ~pete/wk/names
```

At this point, you could type **r** to replace the *B* with *R*. But let's say you wanted to change *Bob* to *Blob*. You would need to move one space to the right of the *B*. Of course, you could just type l. But, given that you're somewhere to the right of *Bob*, the fastest way to move to the *o* would be to type **TB** instead of **FB** followed by l.

As an example of how the repeat count can be used with character-finding commands, let's say you want to change the filename from *names* to *namÆle* In this case, assuming your cursor is still on the *B*, you need to get to the third *e* to the right, so you can type **3te**, followed by l to put the cursor back on the **e** in *names*.

The character-finding commands also have associated delete commands. Read the command definitions in the previous table and mentally substitute "delete" for move. You'll get what happens when you precede the given character-finding command with a **d**. The deletion includes the character given as argument. For example, assume that your cursor is under the **n** in *names*:

```
$ fgrep -l Bob < ~pete/wk/names
```

If you want to change *names* to *aides*, one possibility is to type **dfm**. This means "delete right to next occurrence of m," i.e., delete "nam." Then you can type **i** (to enter input mode) and then "aid" to complete the change.

One final command rounds out the vi control mode commands for getting around on the current line: you can use the pipe character (|) for moving to a specific column, whose number is given by a numeric prefix argument. Column counts start at 1; count only your input, not the space taken up by the prompt string. The default repeat count is 1, of course, which means that typing | by itself is equivalent to 0 (see Table 2-7).

Filename Completion

Although the character-finding commands and | are not particularly useful, vi-mode provides one additional feature that we think you will use quite often: filename completion. This feature is not part of the real *vi* editor, and it was undoubtedly inspired by similar features in *emacs* and, originally, in the TOPS-20 operating system for DEC mainframes.

The rationale behind filename completion is simple: you should have to type only as much of a filename as is necessary to distinguish it from other filenames in the same directory. Backslash (\) is the command that tells the Korn shell to do filename completion in vi-mode. If you type in a word, type ESC to enter control mode, and then type \, one of four things will happen; they are the same as for ESC ESC in emacs-mode:

1. If there is no file whose name begins with the word, the shell will beep and nothing further will happen.

2. If there is exactly one way to complete the filename and the file is a regular file, the shell will type the rest of the filename, followed by a space in case you want to type in more command arguments.

3. If there is exactly one way to complete the filename and the file is a directory, the shell will complete the filename, followed by a slash.

4. If there is more than one way to complete the filename, the shell will complete out to the longest common prefix among the available choices.

A related command is *****, which is the same as ESC ***** in emacs-mode as described earlier in this chapter.* It behaves similarly to ESC \, but if there

---

*If you count the ESC needed to get out of input mode, the vi-mode command is identical to emacs-mode.

is more than one completion possibility (number four in the list above), it lists all of them and allows you to type further. Thus, it resembles the * shell wildcard character.

Less useful is the command =, which does the same kind of filename expansion as the * shell wildcard, but in a different way. Instead of expanding the filenames onto the command line, it prints them in a numbered list with one filename on each line. Then it gives you your shell prompt back and retypes whatever was on your command line before you typed =. For example, if the files in your directory include *program.c* and *problem.c*, and you type **pro** followed by ESC and then =, you will see this:

```
·$ cc pro
1) problem.c
2) program.c
```

Miscellaneous Commands

Several miscellaneous commands round out vi-mode; some of them are quite esoteric. They are listed in Table 2-13.

Table 2-13: Miscellaneous vi-mode Commands

Command	Description
~	Invert ("twiddle") case of current character(s).
_	Append last word of previous command, enter input mode.
v	Run the **fc** command on the current line (actually, run the command **fc -e ${VISUAL:-${EDITOR:-vi}}**); usually this means run the full *vi* on the current line.
CTRL-L	Start a new line and redraw the current line on it; good for when your screen becomes garbled.
#	Prepend # (comment character) to the line and send it to the history file;* useful for saving a command to be executed later without having to retype it.
@*x*	Insert expansion of alias _x (see below).

* The line is also "executed" by the shell. However, # is the shell's comment character, so the shell ignores it.

The first of these can be preceded by a repeat count. A repeat count of *n* preceding the ˜ changes the case of the next *n* characters.* The cursor will advance accordingly.

A repeat count preceding _ causes the *n*-th word in the previous command to be inserted in the current line; without the count, the last word is used. Omitting the repeat count is useful because a filename is usually the last thing on a UNIX command line, and because users often run several commands in a row on the same file. With this feature, you can type all of the commands (except the first) followed by ESC _, and the shell will insert the filename.

Finally, the command @ allows you to create keyboard shortcuts by interacting with the shell's alias facility (see Chapter 3, *Customizing Your Environment*). If you create an alias called _x, where **x** is a letter, then the shell will expand the alias on the current line (but not run it) if you type @ followed by **x**. As with the similar facility in emacs-mode, we don't find this particularly useful.

The fc Command

fc is a shell built-in command that provides a superset of the C shell history mechanism. You can use it to examine the most recent commands you entered, to edit one or more commands with your favorite "real" editor, and to run old commands with changes without having to type the entire command in again. We'll look at each of these uses.

The –l option to fc lists previous commands. It takes arguments that refer to commands in the history file. Arguments can be numbers or alphanumeric strings; numbers refer to the commands in the history file, while strings refer to the most recent command beginning with the string. fc treats arguments in a rather complex way:

- If you give two arguments, they serve as the first and last commands to be shown.
- If you specify one number argument, only the command with that number is shown.

---

*This, in our opinion, is a design flaw in the *vi* editor that the Korn shell authors might have corrected. Letting the user append a motion command to ˜ and having it behave analogously to d or y would have been much more useful; that way, a word could be case-twiddled with only two keystrokes.

- With a single string argument, it searches for the most recent command starting with that string and shows you everything from that command to the most recent command.

- If you specify no arguments, you will see the last 16 commands you entered. Thus, **fc –l** by itself is equivalent to the C shell **history** command, and indeed the Korn shell defines a built-in alias **history** as:

```
alias history=fc -l
```

As you will find out in Chapter 3, *Customizing Your Environment*, this means that you can type **history** and the Korn shell will run the command **fc –l**.

A few examples should make these options clearer. Let's say you logged in and entered these commands:

```
ls -l
more myfile
vi myfile
wc -l myfile
pr myfile | lp -h
```

If you type **fc –l** (or **history**) with no arguments, you will see the above list with command numbers, as in:

```
1     ls -l
2     more myfile
3     vi myfile
4     wc -l myfile
5     pr myfile | lp -h
```

The option **–n** suppresses the line numbers. If you want to see only commands 2 through 4, type **fc –l 2 4**. If you want to see only the *vi* command, type **fc –l 3**. To see everything from the *vi* command up to the present, type **fc –l v**. Finally, if you want to see commands between *more* and *wc*, you can type **fc –l m w**, **fc –l m 4**, **fc –l 2 4**, etc.

The **–l** option to **fc** is not particularly useful, except as a quick way of remembering what commands you typed recently. Use the **history** alias if you are an experienced C shell user.

The other important option to **fc** is **–e** for "edit." This is useful as an "escape hatch" from vi- and emacs-modes if you aren't used to either of those editors. You can specify the pathname of your favorite editor and edit commands from your history file; then when you have made the changes, the shell will actually execute the new lines.

Let's say your favorite editor is a little home-brew gem called *zed*. You could edit your commands by typing:

```
$ fc -e /usr/local/bin/zed
```

This seems like a lot of work just to fix a typo in your previous command; fortunately, there is a better way. You can set the environment variable FCEDIT to the pathname of the editor you want **fc** to use. If you put a line in your *.profile* or environment file saying:

```
FCEDIT=/usr/local/bin/zed
```

you will get *zed* when you invoke **fc**. FCEDIT defaults to the old line editor *ed*, so that the overall default is also *ed*.

fc is usually used to fix a recent command. Therefore it handles arguments a bit differently than it does for the **fc –l** variation above:

- With no arguments, **fc** loads the editor with the most recent command.
- With a numeric argument, **fc** loads the editor with the command with that number.
- With a string argument, **fc** loads the most recent command starting with that string.
- With two arguments to **fc**, the arguments specify the beginning and end of a range of commands, as above.

Remember that **fc** actually runs the command(s) after you edit them. Therefore the last-named choice can be dangerous. The Korn shell will attempt to execute all commands in the range you specify when you exit your editor. If you have typed in any multiline constructs (like those we will cover in Chapter 5, *Flow Control*), the results could be even more dangerous. Although these might seem like valid ways of generating "instant shell programs," a far better strategy would be to direct the output of **fc –l** with the same arguments to a file; then edit that file and execute the commands when you're satisfied with them:

```
$ fc -l cp > lastcommands
$ vi lastcommands
$ . lastcommands
```

In this case, the shell will not try to execute the file when you leave the editor!

There is one final use for **fc**. If you specify the editor – (i.e., type **fc -e -**), the Korn shell will skip the editing part and just run the command(s) specified by the argument(s). Why is this useful? For one thing, just typing **fc -e** – causes the previous command to repeat, just like the C shell **!!** command.

The Korn shell provides the built-in alias **r** for this, so that if you type **r** and hit **RETURN**, you will repeat the last command.

This form of **fc** allows yet another type of argument, of the form *old=new*, meaning "change occurrences of *old* in the specified previous command to *new* and then run it." For example, if you wanted to run a complex command like the following on two sets of files:

```
$ tbl ch2.tbl | nroff -mS -Tepson > ch2.out
```

you can enter the command and then type **fc -e - 2=3**. (You could also use the alias, **r 2=3**.) This command would then run:

```
tbl ch3.tbl | nroff -mS -Tepson > ch3.out
```

Finger Habits

To paraphrase the old adage, old finger habits die hard. In fact, that is the primary reason for the choices of *vi* and *emacs* for the Korn shell's editing modes. If you are an experienced user of one of these editors, by all means use the corresponding Korn shell editing mode. If you are a *vi* wizard, you probably know how to navigate between any two points on a line in three keystrokes or less.

But if you're not, you should seriously consider adopting emacs-mode finger habits. Because it is based on control keys, just like the minimal editing support you may have already used with the Bourne or C shell, you will find emacs-mode easier to assimilate. Although the full *emacs* is an extremely powerful editor, its command structure lends itself very well to small subsetting: there are several "mini-emacs" style editors floating around for UNIX, MS-DOS, and other systems.

The same cannot be said for *vi*, because its command structure is really meant for use in a full-screen editor. *vi* is quite powerful too, in its way, but its power becomes evident only when it is used for purposes similar to that for which it was designed: editing source code in C and LISP. A *vi* user has the power to move mountains in few keystrokes—but at the cost of doing anything meaningful in very few keystrokes. Unfortunately, the latter is most desired in a command interpreter, especially nowadays when users are spending more time within applications and less time working with the shell.

Both Korn shell editing modes have quite a few commands; you will undoubtedly develop finger habits that include just a few of them. If you use emacs-mode and you aren't familiar with the full *emacs*, here is a sub-set that is easy to learn yet enables you to do just about anything:

- For cursor motion around a command line, stick to CTRL-A and CTRL-E for beginning and end of line, and CTRL-F and CTRL-B for moving around.

- Delete using DEL (or whatever your "erase" key is) and CTRL-D; as with CTRL-F and CTRL-B, hold down to repeat if necessary. Use CTRL-C to erase the entire line.

- Use CTRL-P to retrieve the last command when you make a mistake.

- Use CTRL-R to search for a command you need to run again.

- Definitely use ESC ESC for filename completion.

After a few hours spent learning these finger habits, you will wonder how you ever got along without command-line editing.

In this chapter:
- *The .profile File*
- *Aliases*
- *Options*
- *Shell Variables*
- *Customization and Subprocesses*
- *Customization Hints*

3

Customizing Your Environment

A common synonym for a UNIX shell, or for the interface any computer program presents, is an environment. An *environment* is typically a collection of concepts that expresses the things a computer does in terms designed to be understandable and coherent, and a look and feel that is comfortable.

For example, your desk at work is an environment. Concepts involved in desk work usually include memos, phone calls, letters, forms, etc. The tools on or in your desk that you use to deal with these things include paper, staples, envelopes, pens, a telephone, a calculator, etc. Every one of these has a set of characteristics that express how you use it; such characteristics range from location on your desk or in a drawer (for simple tools) to more sophisticated things like which numbers the memory buttons on your phone are set to. Taken together, these characteristics make up your desk's look and feel.

You customize the look and feel of your desk environment by putting pens where you can most easily reach them, programming your phone buttons, etc. In general, the more customization you have done, the more tailored to your personal needs—and therefore the more productive—your environment is.

Similarly, UNIX shells present you with such concepts as files, directories, and standard input and output, while UNIX itself gives you tools to work with these, such as file manipulation commands, text editors, and print queues. Your UNIX environment's look and feel is determined by your keyboard and display, of course, but also by how you set up your directories, where you put each kind of file, and what names you give to files, directories, and commands. There are also more sophisticated ways of customizing your shell environment.

The most basic means of customization that the Korn shell provides are these:

Aliases   Synonyms for commands or command strings that you can define for convenience.

Options   Controls for various aspects of your environment, which you can turn on and off.

Variables   Place-holders for information that tell the shell and other programs how to behave under various circumstances.

There are also more complex ways to customize your environment, mainly the ability to program the shell, which we will see in later chapters. In this chapter, we will cover the techniques listed above.

While most of the customizations obtainable with the above techniques are straightforward and apply to everyday UNIX use, others are rather arcane and require in-depth technical knowledge to understand. Most of this chapter will concentrate on the former. Because we want to explain things from the perspective of tasks you may want to perform, rather than that of the specific features of the Korn shell, a few little details may fall through the cracks (such as miscellaneous options to certain commands). We suggest you look in Appendix B for this type of information.

The .profile File

If you want to customize your environment, it is most important to know about a file called *.profile* in your home (login) directory. This is a file of shell commands, also called a shell script, that the Korn shell reads and runs whenever you log in to your system.

If you use a large machine in an office or department, the odds are good that your system administrator has already set up a *.profile* file for you that contains a few standard things. This is one of the "hidden" files mentioned in Chapter 1, *Korn Shell Basics;* other common hidden files include *.X11Startup* (for the X Window System), *.emacs* (for the GNU Emacs editor), and *.mailrc* (for the UNIX mail program).

Your *.profile*, together with the environment file that we will see towards the end of this chapter, will be the source of practically all of the customizations we will discuss here as well as in subsequent chapters. Therefore it is very important for you to become comfortable with a text editor like *vi* or *emacs* so that you can try whatever customization techniques strike your fancy.

Bear in mind, however, that if you add commands to your *.profile*, they will not take effect until you log out and log back in again, or type the command **login**.* Of course, you need not immediately add customization commands to your *.profile*—you can always just test them by typing them in yourself.

If you already have a *.profile*, it's likely to contain lines similar to some of these:

```
PATH=/sbin:/usr/sbin:/usr/bin:/etc:/usr/ucb:/local/bin:
stty stop ^S intr ^C erase ^?
EDITOR=/usr/local/bin/emacs
SHELL=/bin/ksh
export EDITOR
```

These commands set up a basic environment for you, so you probably shouldn't change them until you learn about what they do—which you will by the end of this chapter. When you edit your *.profile*, just put your additional lines in afterwards.

Aliases

Perhaps the easiest and most popular type of customization is the *alias*, which is a synonym for a command or command string. This is one of several Korn shell features that were appropriated from the C shell.† You define an alias by entering (or adding to your *.profile*) a line with the following form:

```
alias new=original
```

(Notice that there are no spaces on either side of the equal sign (=); this is required syntax.) The alias command defines new to be an alias for original, so that whenever you type **new**, the Korn shell substitutes *original* internally.

There are a few basic ways to use an alias. The first, and simplest, is as a more mnemonic name for an existing command. Many commonly-used

---

*This has the same effect as logging out and logging in again, although it actually replaces your login session with a new one without explicitly terminating the old session.

†C shell users should note that the Korn shell's alias feature does not support arguments in alias expansions, as C shell aliases do.

UNIX commands have names that are poor mnemonics and therefore are excellent candidates for aliasing, but the classic example is:

```
alias search=grep
```

grep, the UNIX file-searching utility, was named as an acronym for something like "Generalized Regular Expression Parser."* This acronym may mean something to a computer scientist, but not to the office administrator who has to find **Fred** in a list of phone numbers. If you have to find **Fred** and you have the word *search* defined as an alias for *grep*, you can type:

```
$ search Fred phonelist
```

Another popular alias eschews *exit* in favor of a more widely-used command for ending a login session:

```
alias logout=exit
```

If you are a C shell user, you may be used to having a *.logout* file of commands that the shell executes just before you log out. The Korn shell doesn't have this feature as such, but you can mimic it quite easily using an alias:

```
alias logout='. ~/.ksh_logout; exit'
```

This reads commands in from the file *.ksh_logout* in your home directory and then logs you out. The semicolon acts as a statement separator, allowing you to have more than one command on the same line.

You might want the file *.logout* to "clean up" your history files, as we discussed in the last chapter. Recall that we created history files with the filename *.hist$$*, which guarantees a unique name for every shell. To remove these files when the shells exit, just put this line in your *.logout* file:

```
rm ~/.hist$$
```

Some people who aren't particularly good typists like to use aliases for typographical errors they make often. For example:

```
alias emcas=emacs
alias mali=mail
alias gerp=grep
```

This can be handy, but we feel you're probably better off suffering with the error message and getting the correct spelling under your fingers. Another common way to use an alias is as a shorthand for a longer command string.

---

*Another theory has it that *grep* stands for the command "g/re/p", in the old *ed* text editor, which does essentially the same thing as *grep*.

For example, you may have a directory to which you need to go often. It's buried deeply in your directory hierarchy, so you want to set up an alias that will allow you to **cd** there without typing (or even remembering) the entire pathname:

```
alias cdcm='cd work/projects/devtools/windows/confman'
```

Notice the quotes around the full **cd** command; these are necessary if the string being aliased consists of more than one word.*

As another example, a useful option to the *ls* command is -**F**: it puts a slash (/) after directory files and an asterisk (*) after executable files. Since typing a dash followed by a capital letter is inconvenient, many people like to define an alias like this:

```
alias lf='ls -F'
```

A few things about aliases are important to remember. First, the Korn shell makes a textual substitution of the alias for that which it is aliasing; it may help to imagine *ksh* passing your command through a text editor or word processor and issuing a "change" or "substitute" command before interpreting and executing it.

This, in turn, means that any special characters (such as wildcards like * and ?) that result when the alias is expanded are interpreted properly by the shell.† For example, to make it easier to print all of the files in your directory, you could define the alias:

```
alias printall='pr * | lpr'
```

Second, keep in mind that aliases are recursive, which means that it is possible to alias an alias. A legitimate objection to the previous example is that the alias, while mnemonic, is too long and doesn't save enough typing. If we want to keep this alias but add a shorter abbreviation, we could define:

```
alias pa=printall
```

---

*This contrasts with C shell aliases, in which the quotes aren't required.

†An important corollary: wildcards and other special characters cannot be used in the names of aliases, i.e., on the left side of the equal sign.

Recursive aliasing makes it possible to set up an "infinite loop" of definitions, wherein an alias ends up (perhaps after several lookups) being defined as itself. For example, the command:

```
alias ls='ls -l'
```

sets up a possible infinite loop. Luckily, the shell has a mechanism to guard against such dangers. The above command will work as expected (typing **ls** produces a long list with permissions, sizes, owners, etc.), while in more pathological situations such as:

```
alias listfile=ls
alias ls=listfile
```

the alias **listfile** is ignored.

Aliases can only be used for the beginning of a command string—albeit with certain exceptions. In the **cd** example above, you might want to define an alias for the directory name alone, not for the entire command. But if you define:

```
alias cm=work/projects/devtools/windows/confman
```

and then type **cd cm**, the Korn shell will probably print a message like **ksh: cm: not found**.

An obscure, rather ugly feature of the Korn shell's alias facility—one not present in the analogous C shell feature—provides a way around this problem. If the value of an alias (the right side of the equal sign) ends in a blank, then the Korn shell tries to do alias substitution on the next word on the command line. To make the value of an alias end in a blank, you need to surround it with quotes.

Here is how you would use this capability to allow aliases for directory names, at least for use with the **cd** command. Just define:

```
alias cd='cd '
```

This causes the Korn shell to search for an alias for the directory name argument to **cd**, which in the previous example would enable it to expand the alias **cm** correctly.

Tracked Aliases

Another rather obscure feature of the alias facility is the *tracked* alias, which can shorten the time it takes the shell to invoke commands. If you specify this option (as shown under "Options" below), then for all subsequent alias definitions, the shell will internally substitute the full pathname of each command for which an alias is defined. You can also define individual tracked aliases with the option **-t** to the **alias** command, and you can list all tracked aliases by typing **alias -t** by itself.

As you will see later in this chapter, a tracked alias cuts down the number of steps the shell has to take to find the command when you want to run it. More important, however, are its implications for system security; see Chapter 10, *Korn Shell Administration.*

For example, assume that you have defined the alias **em** for the *emacs* editor, which is kept in the executable file */usr/local/bin/emacs.* If you specify that you want aliases tracked, then the first time you type **em myfile**, the shell will substitute the full pathname, i.e., as if you had defined the alias as:

```
alias em=/usr/local/bin/emacs
```

You'll see how this can save time when you read about the PATH environment variable later on.

Finally, there are a few useful adjuncts to the basic **alias** command. If you type **alias** *name* without an equal sign (=) and value, the shell will print the alias' value or **alias** *name* **not found** if it is undefined. If you type **alias** without any arguments, you get a list of all the aliases you have defined as well as several that are built-in. The command **unalias** *name* removes any alias definition for its argument.

Aliases are very handy for creating a comfortable environment, but they are really just kid stuff compared to more advanced customization techniques like scripts and functions, which we will see in the next chapter. These give you everything aliases do plus much more, so if you become proficient at them, you may find that you don't need aliases anymore. However, aliases are ideal for novices who find UNIX to be a rather forbidding place, full of terseness and devoid of good mnemonics.

Options

While aliases let you create convenient names for commands, they don't really let you change the shell's behavior. *Options* are one way of doing this. A shell option is a setting that is either "on" or "off." While several options relate to arcane shell features that are of interest only to programmers, those that we will cover here are of interest to all users.

The basic commands that relate to options are **set -o** *optionnames* and **set +o** *optionnames*, where *optionnames* is a list of option names separated by blanks. The use of plus (+) and minus (−) signs is counterintuitive: the − turns the named option on, while the + turns it off. The reason for this incongruity is that the dash (−) is the conventional UNIX way of specifying options to a command, while the use of + is an afterthought.

Most options also have one-letter abbreviations that can be used in lieu of the **set -o** command; for example, **set -o noglob** can be abbreviated **set -f**. These abbreviations are carry-overs from the Bourne shell. Like several other "extra" Korn shell features, they exist to ensure upward compatibility; otherwise, their use is not encouraged.

Table 3-1 lists the options that are useful to general UNIX users. All of them are off by default except as noted.

Table 3-1: Basic Shell Options

Option	Description
bgnice	Run background jobs at lower priority (on by default)
emacs	Enter emacs editing mode
ignoreeof	Don't allow use of CTRL-D to log off; require the **exit** command
markdirs	When expanding filename wildcards, append a slash (/) to directories
noclobber	Don't allow output redirection (>) to clobber an existing file
noglob	Don't expand filename wildcards like * and ? (wildcard expansion is sometimes called *globbing*)
nounset	Indicate an error when trying to use a variable that is undefined
trackall	Turn on alias tracking*
vi	Enter vi editing mode

* Future releases will have alias tracking enabled at all times and won't support this option.

There are several other options (22 in all; Appendix B lists them). To check the status of an option, just type **set -o**. The Korn shell will print a list of all options along with their settings. There is no direct way to test a single option, but here is a simple shell function to do it:

```
function testopt {
    if [[ -o $1 ]] ; then
        print Option $1 is on.
    else
        print Option $1 is off.
    fi
}
```

Shell functions will be covered in the next chapter. For now, though, if you want to use the **testopt** function, just type it into your *.profile* or environment file (see the section entitled "The Environment File"), then type either **login** or . *.profile*. Then you can type **testopt** *optionname* to check the status of an option.

Shell Variables

There are several characteristics of your environment that you may want to customize but that cannot be expressed as an on/off choice. Characteristics of this type are specified in shell variables. Shell variables can specify everything from your prompt string to how often the shell checks for new mail.

Like an alias, a shell variable is a name that has a value associated with it. The Korn shell keeps track of several built-in shell variables; shell programmers can add their own. By convention, built-in variables have names in all capital letters. The syntax for defining variables is somewhat similar to the syntax for aliases:

```
varname=value
```

There must be no space on either side of the equal sign, and if the value is more than one word, it must be surrounded by quotes. To use the value of a variable in a command, precede its name by a dollar sign ($).

You can delete a variable with the command **unset** *varname*. Normally this isn't useful, since all variables that don't exist are assumed to be null, i.e., equal to the empty string "". But if you use the option **nounset** (see Table 3-1), which causes the shell to indicate an error when it encounters an undefined variable, then you may be interested in **unset**.

The easiest way to check a variable's value is to use the **print** built-in command.* All **print** does is print its arguments, but not until the shell has evaluated them. This includes—among other things that will be discussed later—taking the values of variables and expanding filename wildcards. So, if the variable **fred** has the value **bob**, typing:

```
$ print "$fred"
```

will cause the shell to simply print **bob**. If the variable is undefined, the shell will print a blank line. A more verbose way to do this is:

```
$ print "The value of \$varname is \"$varname\"."
```

The first dollar sign and the inner double quotes are backslash-escaped (i.e., preceded with \ so the shell doesn't try to interpret them; see Chapter 1, *Korn Shell Basics*) so that they appear literally in the output, which for the above example would be:

```
The value of $fred is "bob".
```

Variables and Quoting

Notice that we used double quotes around variables (and strings containing them) in these **print** examples. In Chapter 1 we said that some special characters inside double quotes are still interpreted (while none are intererpreted inside single quotes). We've seen one of these special characters already: the tilde (~), which is expanded to your (or another user's) home directory.

Another special character that "survives" double quotes is the dollar sign— meaning that variables are evaluated. It's possible to do without the double quotes in some cases; for example, we could have written the above **print** command this way:

```
$ print The value of \$varname is \"$varname\".
```

But double quotes are more generally correct.

---

*The Korn shell supports the old command *echo*, which does much the same thing, for backward compatibility reasons. However, we strongly recommend **print** because its options are the same on all UNIX systems, whereas *echo*'s options differ between BSD-derived and System V-derived UNIX versions.

Here's why. Suppose we did this:

```
$ fred='Four spaces between these    words.'
```

Then if we entered the command **print $fred**, the result would be:

```
Four spaces between these words.
```

What happened to the extra spaces? Without the double quotes, the shell split the string into words after substituting the variable's value, as it normally does when it processes command lines. The double quotes circumvent this part of the process (by making the shell think that the whole quoted string is a single word).

Therefore the command **print "$fred"** prints this:

```
Four spaces between these    words.
```

This becomes particularly important when we start dealing with variables that contain user or file input later on.

Double quotes also allow other special characters to work, as we'll see in Chapters 4, 6, and 7,. But for now, we'll revise the "When in doubt, use single quotes" rule in Chapter 1 by adding, "... unless a string contains a variable, in which case you should use double quotes."

Built-in Variables

As with options, some built-in shell variables are meaningful to general UNIX users, while others are arcana for hackers. We'll look at the more generally useful ones here, and we'll save some of the more obscure ones for later chapters. Again, Appendix B, *Reference Lists*, contains a complete list.

Editing mode variables

Several shell variables relate to the command-line editing modes that we saw in the previous chapter. These are listed in Table 3-2.

The first two of these are sometimes used by text editors and other screen-oriented programs, which rely on the variables being set correctly. Although the Korn shell and most windowing systems should know how to set them correctly, you should look at the values of **COLUMNS** and **LINES** if you are having display trouble with a screen-oriented program.

Table 3-2: Editing Mode Variables

Variable	Meaning
COLUMNS	Width, in character columns, of your terminal. The standard value is 80 (sometimes 132), though if you are using a windowing system like X, you could give a terminal window any size you wish.
LINES	Length of your terminal in text lines. The standard value for terminals is 24, but for IBM PC-compatible monitors it's 25; once again, if you are using a windowing system, you can usually resize to any amount.
HISTFILE	Name of history file, on which the editing modes operate.
EDITOR	Pathname of your favorite text editor; the suffix (*macs* or *vi*) determines which editing mode to use.
VISUAL	Similar to EDITOR; used if EDITOR is not set or vice versa.
FCEDIT	Pathname of editor to use with the **fc** command.

Mail Variables

Since the *mail* program is not running all the time, there is no way for it to inform you when you get new mail; therefore the shell does this instead.* The shell can't actually check for incoming mail, but it can look at your mail file periodically and determine whether the file has been modified since the last check. The variables listed in Table 3-3 let you control how this works.

Table 3-3: Mail Variables

Variable	Meaning
MAIL	Name of file to check for incoming mail (i.e., your mail file)
MAILCHECK	How often, in seconds, to check for new mail (default 600 seconds, or 10 minutes)
MAILPATH	List of filenames, separated by colons (:), to check for incoming mail

---

*BSD UNIX users should note that the *biff* command on those systems does a better job of this; while the Korn shell only prints "you have mail" messages right before it prints command prompts, *biff* can do so at any time.

Under the simplest scenario, you use the standard UNIX mail program, and your mail file is */usr/mail/yourname* or something similar. In this case, you would just set the variable **MAIL** to this filename if you want your mail checked:

```
MAIL=/usr/mail/yourname
```

If your system administrator hasn't already done it for you, put a line like this in your *.profile*.

However, some people use nonstandard mailers that use multiple mail files; **MAILPATH** was designed to accommodate this. The Korn shell will use the value of **MAIL** as the name of the file to check, unless **MAILPATH** is set, in which case the shell will check each file in the **MAILPATH** list for new mail. You can use this mechanism to have the shell print a different message for each mail file: for each mail filename in **MAILPATH**, append a question mark followed by the message you want printed.

For example, let's say you have a mail system that automatically sorts your mail into files according to the username of the sender. You have mail files called */usr/mail/you/fritchie, /usr/mail/you/droberts, /usr/mail/you/jphelps,* etc. You define your **MAILPATH** as follows:

```
MAILPATH=/usr/mail/you/fritchie:/usr/mail/you/droberts:\
/usr/mail/you/jphelps
```

If you get mail from Jennifer Phelps, then the file */usr/mail/you/jphelps* will change. The Korn shell will notice the change within 10 minutes and print the message:

```
you have mail in /usr/mail/you/jphelps.
```

If you are in the middle of running a command, the shell will wait until the command finishes (or is suspended) to print the message. To customize this further, you could define **MAILPATH** to be:

```
MAILPATH=\
/usr/mail/you/fritchie?You have mail from Fiona.:\
/usr/mail/you/droberts?Mail from Dave has arrived.:\
/usr/mail/you/jphelps?There is new mail from Jennifer.
```

The backslashes at the end of each line allow you to continue your command on the next line. But be careful: you can't indent subsequent lines. Now, if you get mail from Jennifer, the shell will print:

```
There is new mail from Jennifer.
```

Prompting Variables

If you have seen enough experienced UNIX users at work, you may already have realized that the shell's prompt is not engraved in stone. It seems as though one of the favorite pastimes of UNIX hackers is thinking of cute or innovative prompt strings. We'll give you some of the information you need to do your own here; the rest will come in the next chapter.

Actually, the Korn shell uses four prompt strings. They are stored in the variables **PS1**, **PS2**, **PS3**, and **PS4**. The first of these is called the primary prompt string; it is your usual shell prompt, and its default value is "$ " (a dollar sign followed by a space). Many people like to set their primary prompt string to something containing their login name. Here is one way to do this:

```
PS1="($LOGNAME)--> "
```

LOGNAME is another built-in shell variable, which is set to your login name when you log in. So, **PS1** becomes a left parenthesis, followed by your login name, followed by ")--> ". If your login name is fred, your prompt string will be **"(fred)--> "**. If you are a C shell user and, like many such people, are used to having a command number in your prompt string, the Korn shell can do this similarly to the C shell: if there is an exclamation point in the prompt string, it will substitute the command number. Thus, if you define your prompt string to be:

```
PS1="($LOGNAME !)-->"
```

then your prompts will be like **(fred 1)—>**, **(fred 2)—>**, and so on.

But perhaps the most useful way to set up your prompt string is so that it always contains your current directory. This way, you needn't type **pwd** to remember where you are. Putting your directory in the prompt is more complicated than the above examples, because your current directory changes during your login session, whereas your login name and the name of your machine don't. But we can accommodate this by taking advantage of some of the shell's arcane quoting rules. Here's how:

```
PS1='($PWD)--> '
```

The difference is the single quotes, instead of double quotes, surrounding the string on the right side of the assignment. Notice that this string is evaluated twice: once when the assignment to **PS1** is done (in your *.profile* or environment file) and then again after every command you enter. Here's what each of these evaluations does:

1. The first evaluation just observes the single quotes and returns what is inside them without further processing. As a result, **PS1** contains the string ($PWD)-> .

2. After every command, the shell evaluates **($PWD)—>. PWD** is a built-in variable that is always equal to the current directory, so the result is a primary prompt that always contains the current directory.

We'll add to this example in Chapter 7, *Input/Output and Command-line Processing.* **PS2** is called the secondary prompt string; its default value is >. It is used when you type an incomplete line and hit RETURN, as an indication that you must finish your command. For example, assume that you start a quoted string but don't close the quote. Then if you hit RETURN, the shell will print > and wait for you to finish the string:

```
$ print "This is a long line,      # PS1 for the command
> which is terminated down here"  # PS2 for the continuation
$                                 # PS1 for the next command
```

PS3 and **PS4** relate to shell programming and debugging, respectively; they will be explained in Chapter 5, *Flow Control,* and Chapter 9, *Debugging Shell Programs.*

Terminal Types

The shell variable **TERM** is vitally important for any program that uses your entire screen or window, like a text editor. Such programs include all screen editors (such as *vi* and *emacs*), *more,* and countless third-party applications.

Because users are spending more and more time within programs, and less and less using the shell itself, it is extremely important that your **TERM** is set correctly. It's really your system administrator's job to help you do this (or to do it for you), but in case you need to do it yourself, here are a few guidelines.

The value of **TERM** must be a short character string with lowercase letters that appears as a filename in the *terminfo* database.* This database is a two-tiered directory of files under the root directory */usr/lib/terminfo.* This directory contains subdirectories with single-character names; these in turn

---

*Versions of UNIX not derived from System V use *termcap,* an older-style database of terminal capabilities that uses the single file */etc/termcap* for all terminal descriptions.

contain files of terminal information for all terminals whose names begin with that character. Each file describes how to tell the terminal in question to do certain common things like position the cursor on the screen, go into reverse video, scroll, insert text, and so on. The descriptions are in binary form (i.e., not readable by humans).

Names of terminal description files are the same as that of the terminal being described; sometimes an abbreviation is used. For example, the DEC VT100 has a description in the file */usr/lib/terminfo/v/vt100*, a monitor for a 386-based PC/AT has a description in the file */usr/lib/terminfo/A/AT-386M*. An *xterm* terminal window under the X Window System has a description in */usr/lib/terminfo/x/xterm*.

Sometimes your UNIX software will set up **TERM** correctly; this usually happens for X terminals and PC-based UNIX systems. Therefore, you should check the value of **TERM** by typing **print $TERM** before going any further. If you find that your UNIX system isn't setting the right value for you (especially likely if your terminal is of a different make than your computer), you need to find the appropriate value of **TERM** yourself.

The best way to find the **TERM** value—if you can't find a local guru to do it for you—is to guess the *terminfo* name and search for a file of that name under */usr/lib/terminfo* by using *ls*. For example, if your terminal is a Blivitz BL-35A, you could try:

```
$ cd /usr/lib/terminfo
$ ls b/bl*
```

If you are successful, you will see something like this:

```
bl35a           blivitz35a
```

In this case, the two names are likely to be synonyms for (links to) the same terminal description, so you could use either one as a value of **TERM**. In other words, you could put *either* of these two lines in your *.profile*:

```
TERM=bl35a
TERM=blivitz35a
```

If you aren't successful, *ls* won't print anything, and you will have to make another guess and try again. If you find that *terminfo* contains nothing that resembles your terminal, all is not lost. Consult your terminal's manual to see if the terminal can emulate a more popular model; nowadays the odds of this are excellent.

Conversely, *terminfo* may have several entries that relate to your terminal, for submodels, special modes, etc. If you have a choice of which entry to use as your value of **TERM**, we suggest you test each one out with your text editor or any other screen-oriented programs you use and see which one works best.

The process is much simpler if you are using a windowing system, in which your "terminals" are logical portions of the screen rather than physical devices. In this case, operating system-dependent software was written to control your terminal window(s), so the odds are very good that if it knows how to handle window resizing and complex cursor motion, then it is capable of dealing with simple things like **TERM**. The X Window System, for example, automatically sets "xterm" as its value for **TERM** in an *xterm* terminal window.

Command Search Path

Another important variable is **PATH**, which helps the shell find the commands you enter.

As you probably know, every command you use is actually a file that contains code for your machine to run.* These files are called executable files or just executables for short. They are stored in various different directories. Some directories, like */bin* or */usr/bin*, are standard on all UNIX systems; some depend on the particular version of UNIX you are using; some are unique to your machine; if you are a programmer, some may even be your own. In any case, there is no reason why you should have to know where a command's executable file is in order to run it.

That is where **PATH** comes in. Its value is a list of directories that the shell searches every time you enter a command;† the directory names are separated by colons (:), just like the files in **MAILPATH**. For example, if you type **print $PATH**, you will see something like this:

```
/sbin:/usr/sbin:/usr/bin:/etc:/usr/ucb:/local/bin
```

Why should you care about your path? There are two main reasons. First, once you have read the later chapters of this book and you try writing your own shell programs, you will want to test them and eventually set aside a

---

*Unless it's a built-in command (one of those shown in **boldface**, like **cd** and **print**), in which case the code is simply part of the executable file for the entire shell.

†Unless the command name contains a slash (/), in which case the search does not take place.

directory for them. Second, your system may be set up so that certain "restricted" commands' executable files are kept in directories that are not listed in **PATH**. For example, there may be a directory */usr/games* in which there are executables that are verboten during regular working hours.

Therefore you may want to add directories to your **PATH**. Let's say you have created a *bin* directory under your login directory, which is */home/you*, for your own shell scripts and programs. To add this directory to your **PATH** so that it is there every time you log in, put this line in your *.profile*:

```
PATH=$PATH":/home/you/bin"
```

This sets **PATH** to whatever it was before, followed immediately by a colon and */home/you/bin*.

This is the "safe" way of doing it. When you enter a command, the shell searches directories in the order they appear in **PATH** until it finds an executable file. Therefore, if you have a shell script or program whose name is the same as an existing command, the shell will use the existing command—unless you type in the command's full pathname to disambiguate. For example, if you have created your own version of the *more* command in the above directory and your **PATH** is set up as in the last example, you will need to type **/home/you/bin/more** (or just **~/bin/more**) to get your version.

The more reckless way of resetting your path is to tell the shell to look in your directory first by putting it before the other directories in your **PATH**:

```
PATH="/home/you/bin:"$PATH
```

This is less safe because you are trusting that your own version of the *more* command works properly. But it is also risky for a more important reason: system security. If your **PATH** is set up in this way, you leave open a "hole" that is well known to computer crackers and mischief makers: they can install "Trojan horses" and do other things to steal files or do damage. (See Chapter 10, *Korn Shell Administration*, for more details.) Therefore, unless you have complete control of (and confidence in) everyone who uses your system, use the first of the two methods of adding your own command directory.

If you need to know which directory a command comes from, you need not look at directories in your **PATH** until you find it. The shell built-in command **whence** prints the full pathname of the command you give it as argument, or just the command's name if it's a built-in command itself (like **cd**), an alias, or a function (as we'll see in Chapter 4, *Basic Shell Programming*).

PATH and Tracked Aliases

It is worth noting that a search through the directories in your **PATH** can take time. You won't exactly die if you hold your breath for the length of time it takes for most computers to search your **PATH**, but the large number of disk I/O operations involved in some **PATH** searches can take longer than the command you invoked takes to run!

The Korn shell provides a way to circumvent PATH searches: the tracked alias mechanism we saw earlier in this chapter. First, notice that if you specify a command by giving its full pathname, the shell won't even use your **PATH**—instead, it will just go directly to the executable file.

Tracked aliases do this for you automatically. If you have alias tracking turned on, then the first time you invoke an alias, the shell looks for the executable in the normal way (through **PATH**). Then it stores the full pathname as if it were the alias, so that the next time you invoke the command, the shell will use the full pathname and not bother with **PATH** at all. If you ever change your **PATH**, the shell marks tracked aliases as "undefined," so that it will search for the full pathnames again when you invoke the corresponding commands.

In fact, you can add tracked aliases for the sole purpose of avoiding **PATH** lookup of commands that you use particularly often. Just put a "trivial alias" of the form **alias –t** *command=command* in your *.profile* or environment file; the shell will substitute the full pathname itself.*

Directory Search Path

CDPATH is a variable whose value, like that of **PATH**, is a list of directories separated by colons. Its purpose is to augment the functionality of the **cd** built-in command.

By default, **CDPATH** isn't set (meaning that it is null), and when you type **cd** *dirname*, the shell will look in the current directory for a subdirectory called *dirname*.† If you set **CDPATH**, you give the shell a list of places to look for *dirname*; the list may or may not include the current directory.

---

*Actually, the shell predefines tracked aliases for most widely-used UNIX utilities.

†As with **PATH**, this search is disabled when *dirname* starts with a slash.

Here is an example. Consider the alias for the long **cd** command from earlier in this chapter:

```
alias cdcm="cd work/projects/devtools/windows/confman"
```

Now suppose there were a few directories under this directory to which you need to go often; they are called *src, bin,* and *doc.* You define your **CDPATH** like this:

```
CDPATH=:~/work/projects/devtools/windows/confman
```

In other words, you define your **CDPATH** to be the empty string (meaning the current directory, wherever you happen to be) followed by *~/work/projects/devtools/windows/confman.*

With this setup, if you type **cd doc**, then the shell will look in the current directory for a (sub)directory called *doc.* Assuming that it doesn't find one, it looks in the directory *~/work/projects/devtools/windows/confman.* The shell finds the *dirname* directory there, so you go *directly* there.

This feature gives you yet another way to save typing when you need to **cd** often to directories that are buried deep in your file hierarchy. You may find yourself going to a specific group of directories often as you work on a particular project, and then changing to another set of directories when you switch to another project. This implies that the **CDPATH** feature is only useful if you update it whenever your work habits change; if you don't, you may occasionally find yourself where you don't want to be.

Miscellaneous Variables

We have covered the shell variables that are important from the standpoint of customization. There are also several that serve as status indicators and for various other miscellaneous purposes. Their meanings are relatively straightforward; the more basic ones are summarized in Table 3-4.

The shell sets the values of these variables (the first three at login time, the last two whenever you change directories). Although you can also set their values, just like any other variables, it is difficult to imagine any situation where you would want to.

Table 3-4: Status Variables

Variable	Meaning
HOME	Name of your home (login) directory
SECONDS	Number of seconds since the shell was invoked
SHELL	Pathname of the shell you are running
PWD	Current directory
OLDPWD	Previous directory before the last **cd** command

Customization and Subprocesses

Some of the variables discussed above are used by commands you may run—as opposed to the shell itself—so that they can determine certain aspects of your environment. The majority, however, are not even known outside the shell.

This dichotomy begs an important question: which shell "things" are known outside the shell, and which are only internal? This question is at the heart of many misunderstandings about the shell and shell programming. Before we answer, we'll ask it again in a more precise way: which shell "things" are known to subprocesses? Remember that whenever you enter a command, you are telling the shell to run that command in a subprocess; furthermore, some complex programs may start their own subprocesses.

Now for the answer, which (like many UNIX concepts) is unfortunately not as simple as you might like. A few things are known to subprocesses, but the reverse is not true: subprocesses can never make these things known to the processes that created them.

Which things are known depends on whether the subprocess in question is a Korn shell program (see Chapter 4, *Basic Shell Programming*) or interactive shell. If the subprocess is a Korn shell program, then it's possible to propagate every type of thing we've seen in this chapter—aliases, options, and variables—plus a few we'll see later.

Environment Variables

By default, only one kind of thing is known to all kinds of subprocesses: a special class of shell variables called *environment variables*. Some of the built-in variables we have seen are actually environment variables: **HIST-FILE**, **HOME**, **LOGNAME**, **MAIL**, **MAILPATH**, **PATH**, **PWD**, **SHELL**, and **TERM**.

It should be clear why these and other variables need to be known by subprocesses. We have already seen the most obvious example: text editors like *vi* and *emacs* need to know what kind of terminal you are using; **TERM** is their way of determining this. As another example, most UNIX mail programs allow you to edit a message with your favorite text editor. How does *mail* know which editor to use? The value of **EDITOR** (or sometimes **VISUAL**).

Any variable can become an environment variable. First it must be defined as usual; then it must be *exported* with the command:

```
export varnames
```

(*varnames* can be a list of variable names separated by blanks.)

You can also define variables to be in the environment of a particular subprocess (command) only, by preceding the command with the variable assignment, like this:

```
varname=value command
```

You can put as many assignments before the command as you want.* For example, assume that you're using the *emacs* editor. You are having problems getting it to work with your terminal, so you're experimenting with different values of **TERM**. You can do this most easily by entering commands that look like:

```
TERM=trythisone emacs filename
```

emacs will have *trythisone* defined as its value of **TERM**, yet the environment variable in your shell will keep whatever value (if any) it had before. This syntax is not very widely used, so we won't see it very often throughout the remainder of this book.

---

*There is an obscure option, **keyword**, that (if turned on) lets you put this type of environment variable definition *anywhere* on the command line, not just at the beginning. Future releases, however, won't support this option.

Nevertheless, environment variables are important. Most *.profile* files include definitions of environment variables; the sample built-in *.profile* earlier in this chapter contained two such definitions:

```
EDITOR=/usr/local/bin/emacs
SHELL=/bin/ksh
export EDITOR
```

For some reason, the Korn shell doesn't make **EDITOR** an environment variable by default. This means, among other things, that *mail* will not know which editor to use when you want to edit a message.* Therefore you would have to export it yourself by using the above **export** command in your *.profile.*

The second line in the above code is meant for systems that do not have the Korn shell installed as the default shell, i.e., as */bin/sh.* Some programs run shells as subprocesses within themselves (e.g., many mail programs and the *emacs* editor's shell mode); by convention they use the **SHELL** variable to determine which shell to use.

You can find out which variables are environment variables and what their values are by typing **export** without arguments.

The Environment File

Although environment variables will always be known to subprocesses, the shell must be explicitly told which other variables, options, aliases, etc., are to be communicated to subprocesses. The way to do this is to put all such definitions in a special file called the *environment file* instead of your *.profile.*

You can call the environment file anything you like, as long as you set the environment variable **ENV** to the file's name. The usual way to do this is as follows:

1. Decide which definitions in your *.profile* you want to propagate to subprocesses. Remove them from *.profile* and put them in a file you will designate as your environment file.

---

* Actually, it will default to the line editor *ed.* You don't want that, now do you?

2. Put a line in your *.profile* that tells the shell where your environment file is:

    ```
    ENV=envfilename
    ```

3. For the changes to take effect, type either . .**profile** or **login**.* In either case, your environment file will be run when the shell encounters the **ENV=** statement.

The idea of the environment file comes from the C shell's *.cshrc* file; thus, many Korn shell users who came from the C shell world call their environment files *.kshrc*. (The *rc* suffix for initialization files is practically universal throughout the UNIX world. According to the folklore, it stands for "run commands" and has origins in old DEC operating systems.)

As a general rule, you should put as few definitions as possible in *.profile* and as many as possible in your environment file. Because definitions add to rather than take away from an environment, there is little chance that they will cause something in a subprocess not to work properly. (An exception might be name clashes if you go overboard with aliases.)

The only things that really need to be in *.profile* are commands that aren't definitions but actually run or produce output when you log in. Option and alias definitions should go into the environment file. In fact, there are many Korn shell users who have tiny *.profile* files, e.g.:

```
stty stop ^S intr ^C erase ^?
date
from
export ENV=~/.kshrc
```

(The *from* command, in some versions of UNIX, checks if you have any mail and prints a list of message headers if you do.) Although this is a small *.profile*, this user's environment file could be huge.

Customization Hints

You should feel free to try any of the techniques presented in this chapter. The best strategy is to test something out by typing it into the shell during your login session; then if you decide you want to make it a permanent part of your environment, add it to your *.profile*.

---

*The latter assumes that the Korn shell is defined as your login shell. If it isn't, you must do the former—or better yet, have your system administrator install it as your login shell!

A nice, painless way to add to your *.profile* without going into a text editor makes use of the **print** command and one of the Korn shell's editing modes. If you type a customization command in and later decide to add it to your *.profile*, you can recall it via CTRL-P or CTRL-R (in emacs-mode) or j, -, or ? (vi-mode). Let's say the line is:

```
PS1="($LOGNAME !)-->"
```

After you recall it, edit it so that it is preceded by a **print** command, surrounded by *single* quotes, and followed by an I/O redirector that (as you will see in Chapter 7) appends the output to ˜*/.profile*:

```
$ print 'PS1="($LOGNAME !)-->"' >> ~/.profile
```

Remember that the single quotes are important because they prevent the shell from trying to interpret things like dollar signs, double quotes, and exclamation points.

You should also feel free to snoop around other peoples' *.profiles* for customization ideas. A quick way to examine everyone's *.profile* is as follows: let's assume that all login directories are under */home*. Then you can type:

```
$ cat /home/*/.profile > ~/other_profiles
```

and examine other people's *.profiles* with a text editor at your leisure (assuming you have read permission on them). If other users have environment files, the file you just created will show what they are, and you can examine them as well.

In this chapter:
- *Shell Scripts and Functions*
- *Shell Variables*
- *String Operators*
- *Command Substitution*
- *Advanced Examples: pushd and popd*

4

Basic Shell Programming

If you have become familiar with the customization techniques we presented in the previous chapter, you have probably run into various modifications to your environment that you want to make but can't—yet. Shell programming makes these possible.

The Korn shell has some of the most advanced programming capabilities of any command interpreter of its type. Although its syntax is nowhere near as elegant or consistent as that of most conventional programming languages, its power and flexibility are comparable. In fact, the Korn shell can be used as a complete environment for writing software prototypes.

Some aspects of Korn shell programming are really extensions of the customization techniques we have already seen, while others resemble traditional programming language features. We have structured this chapter so that if you aren't a programmer, you can read this chapter and do quite a bit more than you could with the information in the previous chapter. Experience with a conventional programming language like Pascal or C is helpful (though not strictly necessary) for subsequent chapters. Throughout the rest of the book, we will encounter occasional programming problems, called *tasks*, whose solutions make use of the concepts we cover.

Shell Scripts and Functions

A *script*, or file that contains shell commands, is a shell program. Your *.profile* and environment files, discussed in Chapter 7, *Input/Output and Command-line Processing*, are shell scripts.

You can create a script using the text editor of your choice. Once you have created one, there are two ways to run it. One, which we have already covered, is to type . *scriptname* (i.e., the command is a dot). This causes the commands in the script to be read and run as if you typed them in.

The second way to run a script is simply to type its name and hit **RETURN**, just as if you were invoking a built-in command. This, of course, is the more convenient way. This method makes the script look just like any other UNIX command, and in fact several "regular" commands are implemented as shell scripts (i.e., not as programs originally written in C or some other language), including *spell, man* on some systems, and various commands for system administrators. The resulting lack of distinction between "user command files" and "built-in commands" is one factor in UNIX's extensibility and, hence, its favored status among programmers.

You can run a script by typing its name only if . (the current directory) is part of your command search path, i.e., is included in your PATH variable (as discussed in Chapter 3, *Customizing Your Environment*). If . isn't on your path, you must type . / *scriptname*, which is really the same thing as typing the script's absolute pathname (see Chapter 1, *Korn Shell Basics*).

Before you can invoke the shell script by name, you must also give it "execute" permission. If you are familiar with the UNIX filesystem, you know that files have three types of permissions (read, write, and execute) and that those permissions apply to three categories of user (the file's owner, a *group* of users, and everyone else). Normally, when you create a file with a text editor, the file is set up with read and write permission for you and read-only permission for everyone else.

Therefore you must give your script execute permission explicitly, by using the *chmod*(1) command. The simplest way to do this is to type:

```
$ chmod +x scriptname
```

Your text editor will preserve this permission if you make subsequent changes to your script. If you don't add execute permission to the script and you try to invoke it, the shell will print the message:

```
scriptname: cannot execute.
```

But there is a more important difference between the two ways of running shell scripts. While the "dot" method causes the commands in the script to be run as if they were part of your login session, the "just the name" method causes the shell to do a series of things. First, it runs another copy of the shell as a subprocess; this is called a *subshell*. The subshell then takes commands from the script, runs them, and terminates, handing control back to the parent shell.

Figure 4-1 shows how the shell executes scripts. Assume you have a simple shell script called *fred* that contains the commands *bob* and *dave*. In Figure 4-1.a, typing .**fred** causes the two commands to run in the same shell, just as if you had typed them in by hand. Figure 4-1.b shows what happens when you type just **fred**: the commands run in the subshell while the parent shell waits for the subshell to finish.

You may find it interesting to compare this with the situation in Figure 4-1.c, which shows what happens when you type **fred &**. As you will recall from Chapter 1, *Korn Shell Basics*, the **&** makes the command run in the *background*, which is really just another term for "subprocess." It turns out that the only significant difference between Figure 4-1.c and Figure 4-1.b is that you have control of your terminal or workstation while the command runs—you need not wait until it finishes before you can enter further commands.

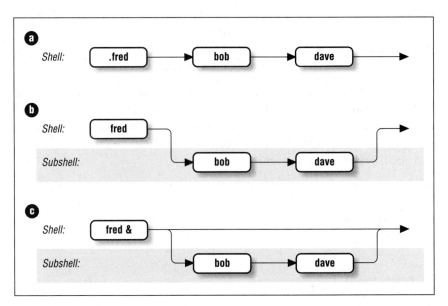

Figure 4-1: Ways to run a shell script

There are many ramifications to using subshells. An important one is that the *export*ed environment variables that we saw in the last chapter (e.g., TERM, LOGNAME, PWD) are known in subshells, whereas other shell variables (such as any that you define in your *.profile* without an *export* statement) are not.

Other issues involving subshells are too complex to go into now; see Chapter 7, *Input/Output and Command-line Processing*, and Chapter 8, *Process Handling*, for more details about subshell I/O and process characteristics, respectively. For now, just bear in mind that a script normally runs in a subshell.

Functions

The Korn shell's *function* feature is an expanded version of a similar facility in the System V Bourne shell and a few other shells. A function is sort of a script-within-a-script; you use it to define some shell code by name and store it in the shell's memory, to be invoked and run later.

Functions improve the shell's programmability significantly, for two main reasons. First, when you invoke a function, it is already in the shell's memory (except for autoloaded functions; see section titled "Autoloaded Functions"); therefore a function runs faster. Modern computers have plenty of memory, so there is no need to worry about the amount of space a typical function takes up. For this reason, most people define as many functions as possible rather than keep lots of scripts around.

The other advantage of functions is that they are ideal for organizing long shell scripts into modular "chunks" of code that are easier to develop and maintain. If you aren't a programmer, ask one what life would be like without functions (also called *procedures* or *subroutines* in other languages) and you'll probably get an earful.

To define a function, you can use either one of two forms:

```
function functname {
    shell commands
}
```

or:

```
functname () {
    shell commands
}
```

There is no difference between the two. Perhaps the first form was created to appeal to Pascal, Modula, and Ada programmers, while the second resembles C; in any case, we will use the first form in this book. You can also delete a function definition with the command **unset -f** *functname*.

When you define a function, you tell the shell to store its name and definition (i.e., the shell commands it contains) in memory. If you want to run the function later, just type in its name followed by any arguments, as if it were a shell script.

You can find out what functions are defined in your login session by typing **functions**.* The shell will print not just the names but the definitions of all functions, in alphabetical order by function name. Since this may result in long output, you might want to pipe the output through *more* or redirect it to a file for examination with a text editor.

Apart from the advantages, there are two important differences betweeen functions and scripts. First, functions do not run in separate processes, as scripts are when you invoke them by name; the "semantics" of running a function are more like those of your *.profile* when you log in or any script when invoked with the "dot" command. Second, if a function has the same name as a script or executable program, the function takes precedence.

This is a good time to show the order of precedence for the various sources of commands. When you type a command to the shell, it looks in the following places until it finds a match:

1. *Keywords* such as **function** and several others, like **if** and **for**, that we will see in Chapter 5, *Flow Control*
2. Aliases†
3. *Built-ins* like **cd** and **whence**
4. Functions
5. Scripts and executable programs, for which the shell searches in the directories listed in the **PATH** environment variable

We'll examine this process in more detail in the section on command-line processing in Chapter 7, *Input/Output and Command-line Processing*.

If you need to know the exact source of a command, there is an option to the **whence** built-in command that we saw in Chapter 3, *Customizing Your Environment*. **whence** by itself will print the pathname of a command if the command is a script or executable program, but it will only parrot the

---

*This is actually an alias for **typeset -f**; see Chapter 6, *Command-line Options and Typed Variables*.

†However, it is possible to define an alias for a keyword, e.g., **alias aslongas=while**. See Chapter 7 for more details.

command's name back if it is anything else. But if you type **whence -v**
commandname, you get more complete information, such as:

```
$ whence -v cd
cd is a shell builtin
$ whence -v function
function is a keyword
$ whence -v man
man is /usr/bin/man
$ whence -v ll
ll is an alias for ls -l
```

We will refer mainly to scripts throughout the remainder of this book, but
unless we note otherwise, you should assume that whatever we say applies
equally to functions.

Autoloaded functions

The simplest place to put your function definitions is in your *.profile* or
environment file. This is fine for a small number of functions, but if you
accumulate lots of them—as many shell programmers eventually do—you
may find that logging in or invoking shell scripts (both of which involve
processing your environment file) takes an unacceptably long time, and
that it's hard to navigate so many function definitions in a single file.

The Korn shell's **autoload** feature addresses these problems. If you put the
command **autoload** *fname** in your *.profile* or environment file, instead of
the function's definition, then the shell won't read in the definition of
fname until it's actually called. **autoload** can take more than one argument.

How does the shell know where to get the definition of an autoloaded
function? It uses the built-in variable **FPATH**, which is a list of directories
like **PATH**. The shell looks for a file called *fname* that contains the definition of function *fname* in each of the directories in **FPATH**.

For example, assume this code is in your environment file:

```
FPATH=~/funcs
autoload dave
```

When you invoke the command *dave*, the shell will look in the directory
~/funcs for a file called *dave* that has the definition of function *dave*. If it

---

autoload is actually an alias for **typeset -fu**; see Chapter 6, *Command-line Options and
Typed Variables*.

doesn't find the file, or if the file exists but doesn't contain the proper function definition, the shell will complain with a "not found" message, just as if the command didn't exist at all.

Function autoloading and **FPATH** are also useful tools for system administrators who need to set up system-wide Korn shell environments. See Chapter 10, *Korn Shell Administration.*

Shell Variables

A major piece of the Korn shell's programming functionality relates to shell variables. We've already seen the basics of variables. To recap briefly: they are named places to store data, usually in the form of character strings, and their values can be obtained by preceding their names with dollar signs ($). Certain variables, called *environment variables*, are conventionally named in all capital letters, and their values are made known (with the **export** statement) to subprocesses.

If you are a programmer, you already know that just about every major programming language uses variables in some way; in fact, an important way of characterizing differences between languages is comparing their facilities for variables.

The chief difference between the Korn shell's variable schema and those of conventional languages is that the Korn shell's places heavy emphasis on character strings. (Thus it has more in common with a special-purpose language like SNOBOL than a general-purpose one like Pascal.) This is also true of the Bourne shell and the C shell, but the Korn shell goes beyond them by having additional mechanisms for handling integers (explicitly) and simple arrays.

Positional Parameters

As we have already seen, you can define values for variables with statements of the form **varname=value**, e.g.:

```
$ fred=bob
$ print "$fred"
bob
```

Some environment variables are predefined by the shell when you log in. There are other built-in variables that are vital to shell programming. We will look at a few of them now and save the others for later.

The most important special, built-in variables are called *positional parameters*. These hold the command-line arguments to scripts when they are invoked. Positional parameters have names **1**, **2**, **3**, etc., meaning that their values are denoted by **$1**, **$2**, **$3**, etc. There is also a positional parameter 0, whose value is the name of the script (i.e., the command typed in to invoke it).

Two special variables contain all of the positional parameters (except positional parameter 0): ***** and **@**. The difference between them is subtle but important, and it's apparent only when they are within double quotes.

"$*" is a single string that consists of all of the positional parameters, separated by the first character in the environment variable **IFS** (internal field separator), which is a space, TAB, and NEWLINE by default. On the other hand, **"$@"** is equal to **"$1"** **"$2"** ... **"$N"**, where *N* is the number of positional parameters. That is, it's equal to *N* separate double-quoted strings, which are separated by spaces. We'll explore the ramifications of this difference in a little while.

The variable **#** holds the number of positional parameters (as a character string). All of these variables are "read-only," meaning that you can't assign new values to them within scripts.

For example, assume that you have the following simple shell script:

```
print "fred: $@"
print "$0: $1 and $2"
print "$# arguments"
```

Assume further that the script is called *fred*. Then if you type **fred bob dave**, you will see the following output:

```
fred: bob dave
fred: bob and dave
2 arguments
```

In this case, $3, $4, etc., are all unset, which means that the shell will substitute the empty (or null) string for them.*

---

*Unless the option **nounset** is turned on.

Positional parameters in functions

Shell functions use positional parameters and special variables like * and # in exactly the same way as shell scripts do. If you wanted to define *fred* as a function, you could put the following in your *.profile* or environment file:

```
function fred {
    print "fred: $*"
    print "$0: $1 and $2"
    print "$# arguments"
}
```

You will get the same result if you type **fred bob dave**.

Typically, several shell functions are defined within a single shell script. Therefore each function will need to handle its own arguments, which in turn means that each function needs to keep track of positional parameters separately. Sure enough, each function has its own copies of these variables (even though functions don't run in their own subshells, as scripts do); we say that such variables are *local* to the function.

However, other variables defined within functions are not local* (they are *global*), meaning that their values are known throughout the entire shell script. For example, assume that you have a shell script called *ascript* that contains this:

```
function afunc {
    print in function $0: $1 $2
    var1="in function"
}

var1="outside of function"
print var1: $var1
print $0: $1 $2
afunc funcarg1 funcarg2
print var1: $var1
print $0: $1 $2
```

If you invoke this script by typing **ascript arg1 arg2**, you will see this output:

```
var1: outside of function
ascript: arg1 arg2
in function afunc: funcarg1 funcarg2
var1: in function
ascript: arg1 arg2
```

---

*However, see the section on **typeset** in Chapter 6, *Command-line Options and Typed Variables*, for a way of making variables local to functions.

In other words, the function *afunc* changes the value of the variable **var1** from "outside of function" to "in function," and that change is known outside the function, while **$0**, **$1**, and **$2** have different values in the function and the main script. Figure 4-2 shows this graphically.

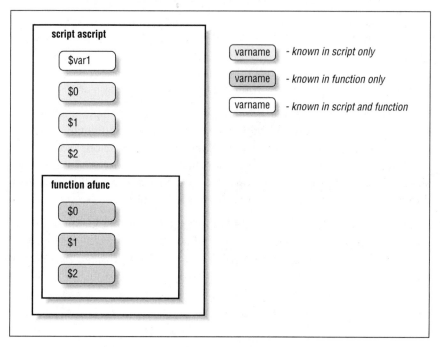

Figure 4-2: Functions have their own positional parameters

It is possible to make other variables local to functions by using the **typeset** command, which we'll see in Chapter 6. Now that we have this background, let's take a closer look at "$@" and "$*". These variables are two of the shell's greatest idiosyncracies, so we'll discuss some of the most common sources of confusion.

- Why are the elements of "$*" separated by the first character of **IFS** instead of just spaces? To give you output flexibility. As a simple example, let's say you want to print a list of positional parameters separated by commas. This script would do it:

```
IFS=,
print $*
```

Changing **IFS** in a script is fairly risky, but it's probably OK as long as nothing else in the script depends on it. If this script were called *arglist*, then the command **arglist bob dave ed** would produce the output **bob,dave,ed.** Chapter 10, *Korn Shell Administration*, contains another example of changing **IFS.**

- Why does "$@" act like *N* separate double-quoted strings? To allow you to use them again as separate values. For example, say you want to call a function within your script with the same list of positional parameters, like this:

```
function countargs {
    print "$# args."
}
```

Assume your script is called with the same arguments as *arglist* above. Then if it contains the command **countargs "$*"**, the function will print **1 args.** But if the command is **countargs "$@"**, the function will print **3 args.**

More on Variable Syntax

Before we show the many things you can do with shell variables, we have to make a confession: the syntax of $*varname* for taking the value of a variable is not quite accurate. Actually, it's the simple form of the more general syntax, which is ${*varname*}.

Why two syntaxes? For one thing, the more general syntax is necessary if your code refers to more than nine positional parameters: you must use ${10} for the tenth instead of $10. Aside from that, consider the example, from Chapter 3, *Customizing Your Environment*, of setting your primary prompt variable (**PS1**) to your login name:

```
PS1="($LOGNAME)--> "
```

This happens to work because the right parenthesis immediately following **LOGNAME** is "special" (in the sense of the special characters introduced in Chapter 1, *Korn Shell Basics*) so that the shell doesn't mistake it for part of the variable name. Now suppose that, for some reason, you want your prompt to be your login name followed by an underscore. If you type:

```
PS1="$LOGNAME_ "
```

then the shell will try to use "LOGNAME_" as the name of the variable, i.e., to take the value of $**LOGNAME_**. Since there is no such variable, the value defaults to *null* (the empty string, ""), and **PS1** is set to just a single space.

For this reason, the full syntax for taking the value of a variable is ${*var-name*}. So if we used

```
PS1="${LOGNAME}_ "
```

we would get the desired $*yourname*_. It is safe to omit the curly brackets ({}) if the variable name is followed by a character that isn't a letter, digit, or underscore.

String Operators

The curly-bracket syntax allows for the shell's *string operators*. String operators allow you to manipulate values of variables in various useful ways without having to write full-blown programs or resort to external UNIX utilities. You can do a lot with string-handling operators even if you haven't yet mastered the programming features we'll see in later chapters.

In particular, string operators let you do the following:

- Ensure that variables exist (i.e., are defined and have non-null values)
- Set default values for variables
- Catch errors that result from variables not being set
- Remove portions of variables' values that match patterns

Syntax of String Operators

The basic idea behind the syntax of string operators is that special characters that denote operations are inserted between the variable's name and the right curly brackets. Any argument that the operator may need is inserted to the operator's right.

The first group of string-handling operators tests for the existence of variables and allows substitutions of default values under certain conditions. These are listed in Table 4-1.*

---

*The colon (:) in each of these operators is actually optional. If the colon is omitted, then change "exists and isn't null" to "exists" in each definition, i.e., the operator tests for existence only.

Table 4-1: Substitution Operators

Operator	Substitution
${*varname*:-*word*}	If *varname* exists and isn't null, return its value; otherwise return *word*.
Purpose:	Returning a default value if the variable is undefined.
Example:	**${count:-0}** evaluates to 0 if **count** is undefined.
${*varname*:=*word*}	If *varname* exists and isn't null, return its value; otherwise set it to *word* and then return its value.*
Purpose:	Setting a variable to a default value if it is undefined.
Example:	**${count:=0}** sets **count** to 0 if it is undefined.
${*varname*:?*message*}	If *varname* exists and isn't null, return its value; otherwise print *varname*: followed by *message*, and abort the current command or script. Omitting *message* produces the default message **parameter null or not set**.
Purpose:	Catching errors that result from variables being undefined.
Example:	**{count:?"undefined!"}** prints "count: undefined!" and exits if **count** is undefined.
${*varname*:+*word*}	If *varname* exists and isn't null, return *word*; otherwise return null.
Purpose:	Testing for the existence of a variable.
Example:	**${count:+1}** returns 1 (which could mean "true") if **count** is defined.

* Pascal, Modula, and Ada programmers may find it helpful to recognize the similarity of this to the assignment operators in those languages.

The first two of these operators are ideal for setting defaults for command-line arguments in case the user omits them. We'll use the first one in our first programming task.

You have a large album collection, and you want to write some software to keep track of it. Assume that you have a file of data on how many albums you have by each artist. Lines in the file look like this:

```
14    Bach, J.S.
1     Balachander, S.
21    Beatles
6     Blakey, Art
```

Write a program that prints the *N* highest lines, i.e., the *N* artists by whom you have the most albums. The default for *N* should be 10. The program should take one argument for the name of the input file and an optional second argument for how many lines to print.

By far the best approach to this type of script is to use built-in UNIX utilities, combining them with I/O redirectors and pipes. This is the classic "building-block" philosophy of UNIX that is another reason for its great popularity with programmers. The building-block technique lets us write a first version of the script that is only one line long:

```
sort -nr $1 | head -${2:-10}
```

Here is how this works: the *sort*(1) program sorts the data in the file whose name is given as the first argument (**$1**). The **-n** option tells *sort* to interpret the first word on each line as a number (instead of as a character string); the **-r** tells it to reverse the comparisons, so as to sort in descending order.

The output of *sort* is piped into the *head*(1) utility, which, when given the argument *-N*, prints the first *N* lines of its input on the standard output. The expression **-${2:-10}** evaluates to a dash (-) followed by the second argument if it is given, or to -10 if it's not; notice that the variable in this expression is **2**, which is the second positional parameter.

Assume the script we want to write is called *highest*. Then if the user types **highest myfile**, the line that actually runs is:

```
sort -nr myfile | head -10
```

Or if the user types **highest myfile 22**, the line that runs is:

```
sort -nr myfile | head -22
```

Make sure you understand how the **:-** string operator provides a default value.

This is a perfectly good, runnable script—but it has a few problems. First, its one line is a bit cryptic. While this isn't much of a problem for such a tiny script, it's not wise to write long, elaborate scripts in this manner. A few minor changes will make the code more readable.

First, we can add comments to the code; anything between # and the end of a line is a comment. At a minimum, the script should start with a few comment lines that indicate what the script does and what arguments it accepts. Second, we can improve the variable names by assigning the values of the positional parameters to regular variables with mnemonic names. Finally, we can add blank lines to space things out; blank lines, like comments, are ignored. Here is a more readable version:

```
#
#       highest filename [howmany]
#
#       Print howmany highest-numbered lines in file filename.
#       The input file is assumed to have lines that start with
#       numbers.  Default for howmany is 10.
#

filename=$1
howmany=${2:-10}

sort -nr $filename | head -$howmany
```

The square brackets around **howmany** in the comments adhere to the convention in UNIX documentation that square brackets denote optional arguments.

The changes we just made improve the code's readability but not how it runs. What if the user were to invoke the script without any arguments? Remember that positional parameters default to null if they aren't defined. If there are no arguments, then **$1** and **$2** are both null. The variable **howmany** (**$2**) is set up to default to 10, but there is no default for **filename** (**$1**). The result would be that this command runs:

```
sort -nr | head -10
```

As it happens, if *sort* is called without a filename argument, it expects input to come from standard input, e.g., a pipe (|) or a user's terminal. Since it doesn't have the pipe, it will expect the terminal. This means that the script will appear to hang! Although you could always type **CTRL-D** or **CTRL-C** to get out of the script, a naive user might not know this.

Therefore we need to make sure that the user supplies at least one argument. There are a few ways of doing this; one of them involves another string operator. We'll replace the line:

```
filename=$1
```

with:

```
filename=${1:?"filename missing."}
```

This will cause two things to happen if a user invokes the script without any arguments: first the shell will print the somewhat unfortunate message:

```
highest: 1: filename missing.
```

to the standard error output. Second, the script will exit without running the remaining code.

With a somewhat "kludgy" modification, we can get a slightly better error message. Consider this code:

```
filename=$1
filename=${filename:?"missing."}
```

This results in the message:

```
highest: filename: missing.
```

(Make sure you understand why.) Of course, there are ways of printing whatever message is desired; we'll find out how in Chapter 5, *Flow Control*.

Before we move on, we'll look more closely at the two remaining operators in Table 4-1 and see how we can incorporate them into our task solution. The := operator does roughly the same thing as :-, except that it has the "side effect" of setting the value of the variable to the given word if the variable doesn't exist.

Therefore we would like to use := in our script in place of :-, but we can't; we'd be trying to set the value of a positional parameter, which is not allowed. But if we replaced:

```
howmany=${2:-10}
```

with just:

```
howmany=$2
```

and moved the substitution down to the actual command line (as we did at the start), then we could use the := operator:

```
sort -nr $filename | head -${howmany:=10}
```

Using := has the added benefit of setting the value of **howmany** to 10 in case we need it afterwards in later versions of the script.

The final substitution operator is :+. Here is how we can use it in our example: Let's say we want to give the user the option of adding a header line to the script's output. If he or she types the option **-h**, then the output will be preceded by the line:

```
ALBUMS  ARTIST
```

Assume further that this option ends up in the variable **header**, i.e., **$header** is **-h** if the option is set or null if not. (Later we will see how to do this without disturbing the other positional parameters.)

The expression:

```
${header:+"ALBUMS  ARTIST\n"}
```

yields null if the variable **header** is null, or **ALBUMS ARTIST\n** if it is non-null. This means that we can put the line:

```
print -n ${header:+"ALBUMS  ARTIST\n"}
```

right before the command line that does the actual work. The **-n** option to **print** causes it *not* to print a LINEFEED after printing its arguments. Therefore this **print** statement will print nothing—not even a blank line—if **header** is null; otherwise it will print the header line and a LINEFEED (\n).

Patterns and Regular Expressions

We'll continue refining our solution to Task 4-1 later in this chapter. The next type of string operator is used to match portions of a variable's string value against *patterns*. Patterns, as we saw in Chapter 1, *Korn Shell Basics*, are strings that can contain wildcard characters (*, ?, and [] for character sets and ranges).

Wildcards have been standard features of all UNIX shells going back (at least) to the Version 6 Bourne shell. But the Korn shell is the first shell to add to their capabilities. It adds a set of operators, called *regular expression* (or *regexp* for short) operators, that give it much of the string-matching power of advanced UNIX utilities like *awk*(1), *egrep*(1) (extended *grep*(1)) and the *emacs* editor, albeit with a different syntax. These capabilities go

beyond those that you may be used to in other UNIX utilities like *grep,*
sed(1) and *vi*(1).

Advanced UNIX users will find the Korn shell's regular expression capabilities occasionally useful for script writing, although they border on overkill.
(Part of the problem is the inevitable syntactic clash with the shell's myriad
other special characters.) Therefore we won't go into great detail about
regular expressions here. For more comprehensive information, the "last
word" on practical regular expressions in UNIX is *sed & awk,* an O'Reilly
Nutshell Handbook by Dale Dougherty. If you are already comfortable
with *awk* or *egrep,* you may want to skip the following introductory section
and go to "Korn Shell Versus awk/egrep Regular Expressions" below,
where we explain the shell's regular expression mechanism by comparing
it with the syntax used in those two utilities. Otherwise, read on.

Regular expression basics

Think of regular expressions as strings that match patterns more powerfully
than the standard shell wildcard schema. Regular expressions began as an
idea in theoretical computer science, but they have found their way into
many nooks and crannies of everyday, practical computing. The syntax
used to represent them may vary, but the concepts are very much the same.

A shell regular expression can contain regular characters, standard wildcard
characters, and additional operators that are more powerful than wildcards.
Each such operator has the form *x(exp),* where *x* is the particular operator
and *exp* is any regular expression (often simply a regular string). The operator determines how many occurrences of *exp* a string that matches the pattern can contain. See Table 4-2 and Table 4-3.

Table 4-2: Regular Expression Operators

Operator	Meaning
*(exp)	0 or more occurrences of *exp*
+(exp)	1 or more occurrences of *exp*
?(exp)	0 or 1 occurrences of *exp*
@(exp1 | exp2 | . . .)	*exp1* or *exp2* or . . .
!(exp)	Anything that doesn't match *exp**

* Actually, !(*exp*) is not a regular expression operator by the standard technical definition,
though it is a handy extension.

Table 4-3: Regular Expression Operator Examples

Expression	Matches
x	*x*
*(*x*)	Null string, *x*, *xx*, *xxx*, ...
+(*x*)	*x*, *xx*, *xxx*, ...
?(*x*)	Null string, *x*
!(*x*)	Any string except *x*
@(*x*)	*x* (see below)

Regular expressions are extremely useful when dealing with arbitrary text, as you already know if you have used *grep* or the regular-expression capabilities of any UNIX editor. They aren't nearly as useful for matching filenames and other simple types of information with which shell users typically work. Furthermore, most things you can do with the shell's regular expression operators can also be done (though possibly with more keystrokes and less efficiency) by piping the output of a shell command through *grep* or *egrep*.

Nevertheless, here are a few examples of how shell regular expressions can solve filename-listing problems. Some of these will come in handy in later chapters as pieces of solutions to larger tasks.

1. The *emacs* editor supports customization files whose names end in *.el* (for Emacs LISP) or *.elc* (for Emacs LISP Compiled). List all *emacs* customization files in the current directory.

2. In a directory of C source code, list all files that are not necessary. Assume that "necessary" files end in *.c* or *.h*, or are named *Makefile* or *README*.

3. Filenames in the VAX/VMS operating system end in a semicolon followed by a version number, e.g., *fred.bob;23*. List all VAX/VMS-style filenames in the current directory.

Here are the solutions:

1. In the first of these, we are looking for files that end in *.el* with an optional *c*. The expression that matches this is ***.el?(c)**.

2. The second example depends on the four standard subexpressions ***.c**, ***.h**, **Makefile**, and **README**. The entire expression is !(*.c|*.h|Makefile|README), which matches anything that does not match any of the four possibilities.

3. The solution to the third example starts with ***\;**: the shell wildcard ***** followed by a backslash-escaped semicolon. Then, we could use the regular expression **+([0-9])**, which matches one or more characters in the range [0-9], i.e., one or more digits. This is almost correct (and probably close enough), but it doesn't take into account that the first digit cannot be 0. Therefore the correct expression is ***\; [1-9]*([0-9])**, which matches anything that ends with a semicolon, a digit from 1 to 9, and *zero* or more digits from 0 to 9.

Regular expression operators are an interesting addition to the Korn shell's features, but you can get along well without them—even if you intend to do a substantial amount of shell programming.

In our opinion, the shell's authors missed an opportunity to build into the wildcard mechanism the ability to match files by *type* (regular, directory, executable, etc., as in some of the conditional tests we will see in Chapter 5, *Flow Control*) as well as by name component. We feel that shell programmers would have found this more useful than arcane regular expression operators.

The following section compares Korn shell regular expressions to analogous features in *awk* and *egrep*. If you aren't familiar with these, skip to the section entitled "Pattern-matching Operators."

Korn shell versus awk/egrep regular expressions

Table 4-4 is an expansion of Table 4-2: the middle column shows the equivalents in *awk/egrep* of the shell's regular expression operators.

Table 4-4: Shell Versus egrep/awk Regular Expression Operators

Korn Shell	egrep/awk	Meaning
* (*exp*)	*exp**	0 or more occurrences of *exp*
+(*exp*)	*exp*+	1 or more occurrences of *exp*
?(*exp*)	*exp*?	0 or 1 occurrences of *exp*
@(*exp1*|*exp2*| ...)	*exp1*|*exp2*| ...	*exp1* or *exp2* or ...
!(*exp*)	(none)	Anything that doesn't match *exp*

These equivalents are close but not quite exact. Actually, an *exp* within any of the Korn shell operators can be a series of *exp1* | *exp2* | . . . alternates. But because the shell would interpret an expression like **dave**|**fred**|**bob** as a pipeline of commands, you must use **@(dave|fred|bob)** for alternates by themselves.

For example:

- **@(dave|fred|bob)** matches **dave**, **fred**, or **bob**.
- ***(dave|fred|bob)** means, "0 or more occurrences of **dave**, **fred**, or **bob**". This expression matches strings like the null string, **dave**, **davedave**, **fred**, **bobfred**, **bobbobdavefredbobfred**, etc.
- **+(dave|fred|bob)** matches any of the above except the null string.
- **?(dave|fred|bob)** matches the null string, **dave**, **fred**, or **bob**.
- **!(dave|fred|bob)** matches anything except **dave**, **fred**, or **bob**.

It is worth re-emphasizing that shell regular expressions can still contain standard shell wildcards. Thus, the shell wildcard **?** (match any single character) is the equivalent to . in *egrep* or *awk*, and the shell's character set operator [. . .] is the same as in those utilities.* For example, the expression **+([0-9])** matches a number, i.e., one or more digits. The shell wildcard character ***** is equivalent to the shell regular expression ***(?)**.

A few *egrep* and *awk* regexp operators do not have equivalents in the Korn shell. These include:

- The beginning- and end-of-line operators ^ and $.
- The beginning- and end-of-word operators \< and \>.
- Repeat factors like \{*N*\} and \{*M,N*\}.

The first two pairs are hardly necessary, since the Korn shell doesn't normally operate on text files and does parse strings into words itself.

Pattern-matching Operators

Table 4-5 lists the Korn shell's pattern-matching operators.

---

*And, for that matter, the same as in *grep*, *sed*, *ed*, *vi*, etc.

Table 4-5: Pattern-matching Operators

Operator	Meaning
${*variable#pattern*}	If the pattern matches the beginning of the variable's value, delete the shortest part that matches and return the rest.
${**variable##***pattern*}	If the pattern matches the beginning of the variable's value, delete the longest part that matches and return the rest.
${**variable%***pattern*}	If the pattern matches the end of the variable's value, delete the shortest part that matches and return the rest.
${*variable%%pattern*}	If the pattern matches the end of the variable's value, delete the longest part that matches and return the rest.

These can be hard to remember, so here's a handy mnemonic device: # matches the front because number signs *precede* numbers; % matches the rear because percent signs *follow* numbers.

The classic use for pattern-matching operators is in stripping off components of pathnames, such as directory prefixes and filename suffixes. With that in mind, here is an example that shows how all of the operators work. Assume that the variable **path** has the value */home /billr/mem/long.file.name*, then:

```
Expression           Result
${path##/*/}                   long.file.name
${path#/*/}              billr/mem/long.file.name
$path            /home/billr/mem/long.file.name
${path%.*}      /home/billr/mem/long.file
${path%%.*}     /home/billr/mem/long
```

The two patterns used here are /*/, which matches anything between two slashes, and .*, which matches a dot followed by anything.

We will incorporate one of these operators into our next programming task.

Task 4-2

> You are writing a C compiler, and you want to use the Korn shell for your front-end.*

Think of a C compiler as a pipeline of data processing components. C source code is input to the beginning of the pipeline, and object code comes out of the end; there are several steps in between. The shell script's task, among many other things, is to control the flow of data through the components and to designate output files.

You need to write the part of the script that takes the name of the input C source file and creates from it the name of the output object code file. That is, you must take a filename ending in *.c* and create a filename that is similar except that it ends in *.o*.

The task at hand is to strip the *.c* off the filename and append *.o*. A single shell statement will do it:

```
objname=${filename%.c}.o
```

This tells the shell to look at the end of **filename** for *.c*. If there is a match, return $filename with the match deleted. So if **filename** had the value **fred.c**, the expression **${filename%.c}** would return **fred**. The *.o* is appended to make the desired **fred.o**, which is stored in the variable **objname**.

If **filename** had an inappropriate value (without *.c*) such as **fred.a**, the above expression would evaluate to **fred.a.o**: since there was no match, nothing is deleted from the value of **filename**, and *.o* is appended anyway. And, if **filename** contained more than one dot—e.g., if it were the *y.tab.c* that is so infamous among compiler writers—the expression would still produce the desired *y.tab.o*. Notice that this would not be true if we used %% in the expression instead of %. The former operator uses the longest match instead of the shortest, so it would match *.tab.o* and evaluate to **y.o** rather than **y.tab.o**. So the single % is correct in this case.

A longest-match deletion would be preferable, however, in the following task.

---

*Don't laugh—many UNIX compilers have shell scripts as front-ends.

> You are implementing a filter that prepares a text file for printer output. You want to put the file's name—without any directory prefix—on the "banner" page. Assume that, in your script, you have the pathname of the file to be printed stored in the variable **pathname**.

Clearly the objective is to remove the directory prefix from the pathname. The following line will do it:

```
bannername=${pathname##*/}
```

This solution is similar to the first line in the examples shown before. If **pathname** were just a filename, the pattern ***/** (anything followed by a slash) would not match and the value of the expression would be **pathname** untouched. If **pathname** were something like *fred/bob*, the prefix *fred/* would match the pattern and be deleted, leaving just **bob** as the expression's value. The same thing would happen if **pathname** were something like */dave/pete/fred/bob*: since the **##** deletes the longest match, it deletes the entire */dave/pete/fred/*.

If we used **#*/** instead of **##*/**, the expression would have the incorrect value *dave/pete/fred/bob*, because the shortest instance of "anything followed by a slash" at the beginning of the string is just a slash (*/*).

The construct **${*variable*##*/}** is actually equivalent to the UNIX utility *basename*(1). *basename* takes a pathname as argument and returns the filename only; it is meant to be used with the shell's command substitution mechanism (see below). *basename* is less efficient than **${*variable*##/*}** because it runs in its own separate process rather than within the shell. Another utility, *dirname*(1), does essentially the opposite of *basename*: it returns the directory prefix only. It is equivalent to the Korn shell expression **${*variable*%/*}** and is less efficient for the same reason.

Length Operator

There are two remaining operators on variables. One is **${#*varname*}**, which returns the length of the value of the variable as a character string. (In Chapter 6, *Command-line Options and Typed Variables*, we will see how to treat this and similar values as actual numbers so they can be used in arithmetic expressions.) For example, if **filename** has the value **fred.c**, then **${#filename}** would have the value **6**. The other operator (**${#*array*[*]}**) has to do with array variables, which are also discussed in Chapter 6.

Command Substitution

From the discussion so far, we've seen two ways of getting values into variables: by assignment statements and by the user supplying them as command-line arguments (positional parameters). There is another way: *command substitution*, which allows you to use the standard output of a command as if it were the value of a variable. You will soon see how powerful this feature is.

The syntax of command substitution is:*

```
$(UNIX command)
```

The command inside the parenthesis is run, and anything the command writes to standard output is returned as the value of the expression. These constructs can be nested, i.e., the UNIX command can contain command substitutions.

Here are some simple examples:

- The value of **$(pwd)** is the current directory (same as the environment variable **$PWD**).

- The value of **$(ls)** is the names of all files in the current directory, separated by NEWLINEs.

- To find out detailed information about a command if you don't know where its file resides, type **ls –l $(whence –p** *command*). The **–p** option forces **whence** to do a pathname lookup and not consider keywords, built-ins, etc.

- To get the contents of a file into a variable, you can use *varname=* **$(<** *filename*). **$(cat** *filename*) will do the same thing, but the shell catches the former as a built-in shorthand and runs it more efficiently.

---

*Bourne and C shell users should note that the command substitution syntax of those shells, `UNIX command` (with backward quotes, a.k.a. grave accents), is also supported by the Korn shell for backward compatibility reasons. However, Korn shell documentation considers this syntax archaic. It is harder to read and less conducive to nesting.

- If you want to edit (with *emacs*) every chapter of your book on the Korn shell that has the phrase "command substitution," assuming that your chapter files all begin with *ch*, you could type:

```
emacs $(grep -l 'command substitution' ch*)
```

The -l option to *grep* prints only the names of files that contain matches.

Command substitution, like variable and tilde expansion, is done within double quotes. Therefore, our rule in Chapter 1, *Korn Shell Basics*, and Chapter 3, *Customizing Your Environment*, about using single quotes for strings unless they contain variables will now be extended: "When in doubt, use single quotes, unless the string contains variables or command substitutions, in which case use double quotes."

You will undoubtedly think of many ways to use command substitution as you gain experience with the Korn shell. One that is a bit more complex than those mentioned previously relates to a customization task that we saw in Chapter 3: personalizing your prompt string.

Recall that you can personalize your prompt string by assigning a value to the variable **PS1**. If you are on a network of computers, and you use different machines from time to time, you may find it handy to have the name of the machine you're on in your prompt string. Most newer versions of UNIX have the command *hostname*(1), which prints the network name of the machine you are on to standard output. (If you do not have this command, you may have a similar one like *gethostname*.) This command enables you to get the machine name into your prompt string by putting a line like this in your *.profile* or environment file:

```
PS1="$(hostname) \$ "
```

(The second dollar sign must be preceded by a backslash so that the shell will take it literally.) For example, if your machine had the name **coltrane**, then this statement would set your prompt string to "**coltrane $** ".

Command substitution helps us with the solution to the next programming task, which relates to the album database in Task 4-1.

Task 4-4

The file used in Task 4-1 is actually a report derived from a bigger table of data about albums. This table consists of several columns, or *fields*, to which a user refers by names like "artist," "title," "year," etc. The columns are separated by vertical bars (|, the same as the UNIX pipe character). To deal with individual columns in the table, field names need to be converted to field numbers.

Suppose there is a shell function called *getfield* that takes the field name as argument and writes the corresponding field number on the standard output. Use this routine to help extract a column from the data table.

The *cut*(1) utility is a natural for this task. *cut* is a data filter: it extracts columns from tabular data.* If you supply the numbers of columns you want to extract from the input, *cut* will print only those columns on the standard output. Columns can be character positions or—relevant in this example—fields that are separated by TAB characters or other delimiters.

Assume that the data table in our task is a file called *albums* and that it looks like this:

```
Coltrane, John|Giant Steps|Atlantic|1960|Ja
Coltrane, John|Coltrane Jazz|Atlantic|1960|Ja
Coltrane, John|My Favorite Things|Atlantic|1961|Ja
Coltrane, John|Coltrane Plays the Blues|Atlantic|1961|Ja
```

Here is how we would use *cut* to extract the fourth (year) column:

```
cut -f4 -d\| albums
```

The **-d** argument is used to specify the character used as field delimiter (TAB is the default). The vertical bar must be backslash-escaped so that the shell doesn't try to interpret it as a pipe.

From this line of code and the *getfield* routine, we can easily derive the solution to the task. Assume that the first argument to *getfield* is the name of the field the user wants to extract. Then the solution is:

```
fieldname=$1
cut -f$(getfield $fieldname) -d\| albums
```

---

*Some older BSD-derived systems don't have *cut*, but you can use *awk* instead. Whenever you see a command of the form:

```
cut -fN -dC filename
```

Use this instead:

```
awk -FC '{print $N}' filename
```

If we called this script with the argument **year**, the output would be:

```
1960
1960
1961
1961
```

Here's another small task that makes use of *cut*.

Task 4-5

Send a mail message to everyone who is currently logged in.

The command *who*(1) tells you who is logged in (as well as which terminal they're on and when they logged in). Its output looks like this:

```
billr      console     May 22 07:57
fred       tty02       May 22 08:31
bob        tty04       May 22 08:12
```

The fields are separated by spaces, not TABs. Since we need the first field, we can get away with using a space as the field separator in the *cut* command. (Otherwise we'd have to use the option to *cut* that uses character columns instead of fields.) To provide a space character as an argument on a command line, you can surround it by quotes:

```
$ who | cut -d' ' -f1
```

With the above *who* output, this command's output would look like this:

```
billr
fred
bob
```

This leads directly to a solution to the task. Just type:

```
$ mail $(who | cut -d' ' -f1)
```

The command **mail billr fred bob** will run and then you can type your message.

Here is another task that shows how useful command pipelines can be in command substitution.

Task 4-6

The *ls* command gives you pattern-matching capability with wildcards, but it doesn't allow you to select files by *modification date*. Devise a mechanism that lets you do this.

This task was inspired by the feature of the VAX/VMS operating system that lets you specify files by date with **BEFORE** and **SINCE** parameters. We'll do this in a limited way now and add features in the next chapter.

Here is a function that allows you to list all files that were last modified on the date you give as argument. Once again, we choose a function for speed reasons. No pun is intended by the function's name:

```
function lsd {
    date=$1
    ls -l | grep -i "^.\{41\}$date" | cut -c55-
}
```

This function depends on the column layout of the **ls ‑l** command. In particular, it depends on dates starting in column 42 and filenames starting in column 55. If this isn't the case in your version of UNIX, you will need to adjust the column numbers.*

We use the *grep* search utility to match the date given as argument (in the form *Mon DD*, e.g., **Jan 15** or **Oct 6**, the latter having two spaces) to the output of **ls ‑l**. This gives us a long listing of only those files whose dates match the argument. The **‑i** option to *grep* allows you to use all lowercase letters in the month name, while the rather fancy argument means, "Match any line that contains 41 characters followed by the function argument." For example, typing **lsd 'jan 15'** causes *grep* to search for lines that match any 41 characters followed by **jan 15** (or **Jan 15**).†

The output of *grep* is piped through our ubiquitous friend *cut* to retrieve the filenames only. The argument to *cut* tells it to extract characters in column 55 through the end of the line.

With command substitution, you can use this function with *any* command that accepts filename arguments. For example, if you want to print all files in your current directory that were last modified today, and today is January 15th, you could type:

```
$ lp $(lsd 'jan 15')
```

---

*For example, **ls ‑l** on SunOS 4.1.x has dates starting in column 33 and filenames starting in column 46.

†Some older BSD-derived versions of UNIX (without System V extensions) do not support the \{*N*\} option. For this example, use 41 periods in a row instead of .\{41\}.

The output of *lsd* is on multiple lines (one for each filename), but LINEFEEDs are legal field separators for the *lp* command, because the environment variable IFS (see earlier in this chapter) contains LINEFEED by default.

Advanced Examples: pushd and popd

We will conclude this chapter with a couple of functions that you may find handy in your everyday UNIX use.

Task 4-7

> The functions *pushd* and *popd* implement a *stack* of directories that enable you to move to another directory temporarily and have the shell remember where you were. The C shell includes these functions, but for some reason the Korn shell omits them. Implement them as shell functions.

We will start by implementing a significant subset of their capabilities and finish the implementation in Chapter 6, *Command-line Options and Typed Variables.*

If you don't know what a stack is, think of a spring-loaded dish receptacle in a cafeteria. When you place dishes on the receptacle, the spring compresses so that the top stays at roughly the same level. The dish most recently placed on the stack is the first to be taken when someone wants food; thus, the stack is known as a "last-in, first-out" or *LIFO* structure.* Putting something onto a stack is known in computer science parlance as *pushing*, and taking something off the top is called *popping*.

A stack is very handy for remembering directories, as we will see; it can "hold your place" up to an arbitrary number of times. The **cd** - form of the **cd** command does this, but only to one level. For example: if you are in *firstdir* and then you change to *seconddir*, you can type **cd** - to go back. But if you start out in *firstdir*, then change to *seconddir*, and then go to *thirddir*, you can use **cd** - only to go back to *seconddir*. If you type **cd** - again, you will be back in *thirddir*, because it is the previous directory.†

---

*Victims of the early-90s recession will also recognize this mechanism in the context of corporate layoff policies.

†Think of **cd** - as a synonym for **cd $OLDPWD**; see the previous chapter.

If you want the "nested" remember-and-change functionality that will take you back to *firstdir*, you need a stack of directories along with the *pushd* and *popd* commands. Here is how these work:*

- The first time **pushd** dir is called, **pushd cd**s to *dir* and pushes the current directory followed by *dir* onto the stack.
- Subsequent calls to **pushd cd** to *dir* and push *dir* only onto the stack.
- **popd** removes the top directory off the stack, revealing a new top. Then it **cd**s to the new top directory.

For example, consider the series of events in Table 4-6. Assume that you have just logged in, and that you are in your home directory (*/home/you*).

We will implement a stack as an environment variable containing a list of directories separated by spaces.

Table 4-6: pushd/popd Example

Command	Stack Contents	Result Directory
pushd fred	/home/you/fred /home/you	/home/you/fred
pushd /etc	/etc /home/you/fred /home/you	/etc
popd	/home/you/fred /home/you	/home/you/fred
popd	/home/you	/home/you
popd	<empty>	(error)

Your directory stack should be initialized to the null string when you log in. To do this, put this in your *.profile*:

```
DIRSTACK=""
export DIRSTACK
```

Do *not* put this in your environment file if you have one. The **export** statement guarantees that DIRSTACK is known to all subprocesses; you want to initialize it only once. If you put this code in an environment file, it will get reinitialized in every subshell, which you probably don't want.

---

*More accurately, this is how the C shell does it, and yes, it *is* somewhat counterintuitive. A more intuitive way would be:

pushd dir: push *dir* (by itself) onto the stack.
popd: **cd** to the top directory, then pop it off.

Next, we need to implement *pushd* and *popd* as functions. Here are our initial versions:

```
function pushd
{
dirname=$1
cd ${dirname:?"missing directory name."}
DIRSTACK="$PWD ${DIRSTACK:-$OLDPWD}"
print "$DIRSTACK"
}

function popd {         # pop directory off stack, cd to new top
    DIRSTACK=${DIRSTACK#* }
    cd ${DIRSTACK%% *}
    print "$PWD"
}
```

Notice that there isn't much code! Let's go through the two functions and see how they work, starting with *pushd*. The first line merely saves the first argument in the variable **dirname** for readability reasons.

The second line's main purpose is to change to the new directory. We use the **:?** operator to handle the error when the argument is missing: if the argument is given, then the expression **${dirname:?"missing directory name."}** evaluates to **$dirname**, but if it is not given, the shell will print the message **pushd: dirname: missing directory name** and exit from the function.

The third line of the function pushes the directory that was current before the change onto the stack. The expression **${DIRSTACK:-$OLDPWD}** evaluates to **$DIRSTACK** if it is non-null or **$OLDPWD** (the current directory before cd) if it is null. The expression within double quotes, then, consists of the argument given, followed by a single space, followed by DIRSTACK or the current directory. The double quotes ensure that all of this is packaged into a single string for assignment back to DIRSTACK. Thus, this line of code handles the special initial case (when the stack is empty) as well as the more usual case (when it's not empty).

The last line merely prints the contents of the stack, with the implication that the leftmost directory is both the current directory and at the top of the stack. (This is why we chose spaces to separate directories, rather than the more customary colons as in PATH and MAILPATH.)

The *popd* function makes yet another use of the shell's pattern-matching operators. Its first line uses the **#** operator, which tries to delete the shortest match of the pattern "* " (anything followed by a space) from the value of DIRSTACK. The result is that the top directory (and the space following it) is deleted from the stack.

The second line of *popd* uses the pattern-matching operator %% to delete the *longest* match to the pattern " *" (a space followed by anything) from DIRSTACK. This extracts the top directory as argument to **cd**, but doesn't affect the value of DIRSTACK because there is no assignment. The final line just prints a confirmation message.

This code is deficient in three ways: first, it has no provision for errors. For example:

- What if the user tries to push a directory that doesn't exist or is invalid?
- What if the user tries *popd* and the stack is empty?

Test your understanding of the code by figuring out how it would respond to these error conditions. The second deficiency is that it implements only some of the functionality of the C shell's *pushd* and *popd* commands—albeit the most useful parts. In the next chapter, we will see how to overcome both of these deficiencies.

The third problem with the code is that it will not work if, for some reason, a directory name contains a space. The code will treat the space as a separator character. We'll accept this deficiency for now. However, when you read about arrays in Chapter 6, *Command-line Options and Typed Variables*, think about how you might use them to rewrite this code and eliminate the problem.

In this chapter:
- *if/else*
- *for*
- *case*
- *select*
- *while and until*

Flow Control

If you are a programmer, you may have read the last chapter—with its claim at the outset that the Korn shell has an advanced set of programming capabilities—and wondered where many features from conventional languages are. Perhaps the most glaringly obvious "hole" in our coverage thus far concerns *flow control* constructs like **if**, **for**, **while**, and so on.

Flow control gives a programmer the power to specify that only certain portions of a program run, or that certain portions run repeatedly, according to conditions such as the values of variables, whether or not commands execute properly, and others. We call this the ability to control the flow of a program's execution.

Almost every shell script or function shown thus far has had no flow control—they have just been lists of commands to be run! Yet the Korn shell, like the C and Bourne shells, has all of the flow control abilities you would expect and more; we will examine them in this chapter. We'll use them to enhance the solutions to some of the programming tasks we saw in the last chapter and to solve tasks that we will introduce here.

Although we have attempted to explain flow control so that non-programmers can understand it, we also sympathize with programmers who dread having to slog through yet another *tabula rasa* explanation. For this reason, some of our discussions relate the Korn shell's flow-control mechanisms to those that programmers should know already. Therefore you will be in a better position to understand this chapter if you already have a basic knowledge of flow control concepts.

The Korn shell supports the following flow control constructs:

if/else	Execute a list of statements if a certain condition is/is not true
for	Execute a list of statements a fixed number of times
while	Execute a list of statements repeatedly *while* a certain condition holds true

until	Execute a list of statements repeatedly *until* a certain condition holds true
case	Execute one of several lists of statements depending on the value of a variable

In addition, the Korn shell provides a new type of flow-control construct:

select	Allow the user to select one of a list of possibilities from a menu

We will cover each of these, but be warned: the syntax is not pretty.

if/else

The simplest type of flow control construct is the *conditional*, embodied in the Korn shell's **if** statement. You use a conditional when you want to choose whether or not to do something, or to choose among a small number of things to do, according to the truth or falsehood of *conditions*. Conditions test values of shell variables, characteristics of files, whether or not commands run successfully, and other factors. The shell has a large set of built-in tests that are relevant to the task of shell programming.

The **if** construct has the following syntax:

```
if condition
then
    statements
[elif condition
    then statements...]
[else
    statements]
fi
```

The simplest form (without the **elif** and **else** parts, a.k.a. *clauses*) executes the *statements* only if the *condition* is true. If you add an **else** clause, you get the ability to execute one set of statements if a condition is true or another set of statements if the condition is false. You can use as many **elif** (a contraction of "else if") clauses as you wish; they introduce more conditions, and thus more choices for which set of statements to execute. If you use one or more **elif**s, you can think of the **else** clause as the "if all *else* fails" part.

Exit Status and Return

Perhaps the only aspect of this syntax that differs from that of conventional languages like C and Pascal is that the "condition" is really a list of statements rather than the more usual Boolean (true or false) expression. How is the truth or falsehood of the condition determined? It has to do with a general UNIX concept that we haven't covered yet: the *exit status* of commands.

Every UNIX command, whether it comes from source code in C, some other language, or a shell script/function, returns an integer code to its calling process—the shell in this case—when it finishes. This is called the exit status. 0 is *usually* the "OK" exit status, while anything else (1 to 255) *usually* denotes an error.*

if checks the exit status of the *last* statement in the list following the if keyword.† (The list is usually just a single statement.) If the status is 0, the condition evaluates to true; if it is anything else, the condition is considered false. The same is true for each condition attached to an **elif** statement (if any).

This enables us to write code of the form:

```
if command ran successfully
then
    normal processing
else
    error processing
fi
```

More specifically, we can now improve on the *pushd* function that we saw in the last chapter:

```
function pushd {        # push current directory onto stack
    dirname=$1
    cd ${dirname:?"missing directory name."}
    DIRSTACK="$dirname ${DIRSTACK:-$PWD}"
    print $DIRSTACK
}
```

This function requires a valid directory as its argument. Let's look at how it handles error conditions: if no argument is given, the second line of code prints an error message and exits. This is fine.

---

*Because this is a "convention" and not a "law," there are exceptions. For example, *diff* (1) (find differences between two files) returns 0 for "no differences," 1 for "differences found," or 2 for an error such as an invalid filename argument.

†LISP programmers will find this idea familiar.

However, the function reacts deceptively when an argument is given that isn't a valid directory. In case you didn't figure it out when reading the last chapter, here is what happens: the **cd** fails, leaving you in the same directory you were in. This is also appropriate. But then the third line of code pushes the bad directory onto the stack anyway, and the last line prints a message that leads you to believe that the push was successful.

We need to prevent the bad directory from being pushed and to print an error message. Here is how we can do this:

```
function pushd {                      # push current directory onto stack
    dirname=$1
    if cd ${dirname:?"missing directory name."}   # if cd was successful
    then
        DIRSTACK="$dirname ${DIRSTACK:-$PWD}"
        print $DIRSTACK
    else
        print still in $PWD.
    fi
}
```

The call to **cd** is now inside an **if** construct. If **cd** is successful, it will return 0; the next two lines of code are run, finishing the *pushd* operation. But if the **cd** fails, it returns with exit status 1, and *pushd* will print a message saying that you haven't gone anywhere.

You can usually rely on built-in commands and standard UNIX utilities to return appropriate exit statuses, but what about your own shell scripts and functions? For example, what if you wrote a **cd** function that overrides the built-in command?

Let's say you have the following code in your *.profile* or environment file:

```
function _cd {
    "cd" $*
    print $OLDPWD --> $PWD
}

alias cd=_cd
```

The function *_cd* simply changes directories and prints a message saying where you were and where you are now. Because functions have lower priority than built-in commands in the shell's order of command lookup, we need to define **cd** itself as an alias so that it overrides the built-in **cd**.

The function calls the built-in **cd** command, but notice that it's surrounded in double quotes: that prevents the shell from looking it up as an alias. (This may seem like a kludge in the aliasing mechanism, but it's really just a ramification of the shell's command-line processing rules, which we list in

Chapter 7, *Input/Output and Command-line Processing.**) If it did find **cd** as an alias, the shell would go into an "infinite recursion" in which the alias is expanded to *_cd*, which runs the function, which calls **cd**, which the shell expands to the alias again, etc.

Anyway, we want this function to return the same exit status that the built-in **cd** returns. The problem is that the exit status is reset by every command, so it "disappears" if you don't save it immediately. In this function, the built-in **cd**'s exit status disappears when the **print** statement runs (and sets its own exit status).

Therefore, we need to save the status that **cd** sets and use it as the entire function's exit status. Two shell features we haven't seen yet provide the way. First is the special shell variable **?**, whose value (**$?**) is the exit status of the last command that ran. For example:

```
cd baddir
print $?
```

causes the shell to print **1**, while:

```
cd gooddir
print $?
```

causes the shell to print **0**.

Return

The second feature we need is the statement **return** *N*, which causes the surrounding script or function to exit with exit status *N*. *N* is actually optional; it defaults to 0. Scripts that finish without a **return** statement (i.e., every one we have seen so far) return whatever the last statement returns. If you use **return** within a function, it will just exit the function. (In contrast, the statement **exit** *N* exits the entire script, no matter how deeply you are nested in functions.)

Getting back to our example: if the call to "real" **cd** were last in our *_cd* function, it would behave properly. Unfortunately, we really need the assignment statement where it is, so that we can avoid lots of ugly error

---

*A related result of command-line processing is that if you surround a command with *single* quotes, the shell won't look it up as an alias or as a function.

processing. Therefore we need to save **cd**'s exit status and return it as the function's exit status. Here is how to do it:

```
function _cd {
    "cd" $*
    es=$?
    print $OLDPWD --> $PWD
    return $es
}
```

The second line saves the exit status of **cd** in the variable **es**; the fourth returns it as the function's exit status. We'll see a more substantial "wrapper" for **cd** in Chapter 7.

Exit statuses aren't very useful for anything other than their intended purpose. In particular, you may be tempted to use them as "return values" of functions, as you would with functions in C or Pascal. That won't work; you should use variables or command substitution instead to simulate this effect.

Combinations of Exit Statuses

One of the more obscure parts of Korn shell syntax allows you to combine exit statuses logically, so that you can test more than one thing at a time.

The syntax *statement1* **&&** *statement2* means, "execute *statement1*, and if its exit status is 0, execute *statement2*." The syntax *statement1* **||** *statement2* is the converse: it means, "execute *statement1*, and if its exit status is *not* 0, execute *statement2*."

At first, these look like "if/then" and "if not/then" constructs, respectively. But they are really intended for use within conditions of **if** constructs—as C programmers will readily understand.

It's much more useful to think of these constructs as "and" and "or," respectively. Consider this:

```
if statement1 && statement2
then
    ...
fi
```

In this case, *statement1* is executed. If it returns a 0 status, then presumably it ran without error. Then *statement2* runs. The **then** clause is executed if *statement2* returns a 0 status. Conversely, if *statement1* fails (returns a non-0 exit status), then *statement2* doesn't even run; the "last statement" in the condition was *statement1*, which failed—so the **then** clause doesn't run. Taken all together, it's fair to conclude that the **then** clause runs if *statement1* and *statement2* both succeeded.

Similarly, consider this:

```
if statement1 || statement2
then
    ...
fi
```

If *statement1* succeeds, then *statement2* does *not* run. This makes *statement1* the last statement, which means that the **then** clause runs. On the other hand, if *statement1* fails, then *statement2* runs, and whether the **then** clause runs or not depends on the success of *statement2*. The upshot is that the **then** clause runs if *statement1 or statement2* succeeds.

As a simple example, assume that we need to write a script that checks a file for the presence of two words and just prints a message saying whether *either* word is in the file or not. We can use *grep* for this: it returns exit status 0 if it found the given string in its input, non-0 if not:

```
filename=$1
word1=$2
word2=$3

if grep $word1 $filename || grep $word2 $filename
then
    print "$word1 or $word2 is in $filename."
fi
```

The **then** clause of this code runs if either *grep* statement succeeds. Now assume that we want the script to say whether or not the input file contains *both* words. Here's how to do it:

```
filename=$1
word1=$2
word2=$3

if grep $word1 $filename && grep $word2 $filename
then
    print "$word1 and $word2 are both in $filename."
fi
```

We'll see more examples of these logical operators later in this chapter and in the code for the *kshdb* debugger in Chapter 9, *Debugging Shell Programs.*

Condition Tests

Exit statuses are the only things an **if** construct can test. But that doesn't mean you can check only whether or not commands ran properly. The shell provides a way of testing a variety of conditions with the [[ ]] construct.*

You can use the construct to check many different attributes of a file (whether it exists, what type of file it is, what its permissions and owner-ship are, etc.), compare two files to see which is newer, do comparisons and pattern matching on strings, and more.

[[*condition*]] is actually a statement just like any other, except that the only thing it does is return an exit status that tells whether *condition* is true or not. Thus it fits within the **if** construct's syntax of **if** *statements*.

String comparisons

The double square brackets ([[]]) surround expressions that include various types of *operators*. We will start with the string comparison operators, which are listed in Table 5-1. (Notice that there are no operators for "greater than or equal" or "less than or equal.") In the table, *str* refers to an expression with a string value, and *pat* refers to a pattern that can contain wildcards (just like the patterns in the string-handling operators we saw in the last chapter).

Table 5-1: String Comparison Operators

Operator	True if . . .
str = *pat**	*str* matches *pat*.
str != *pat*	*str* does not match *pat*.
str1 < *str2*	*str1* is less than *str2*.
str1 > *str2*	*str1* is greater than *str2*.
–n *str*	*str* is not null (has length greater than 0).
–z *str*	*str* is null (has length 0).

* Note that there is only one equal sign (=). This is a common source of errors.

---

*The Korn shell also accepts the external *[]* and *test* commands. The [[ ]] construct has many more options and is better integrated into the Korn shell language: specifically, word splitting and wildcard expansion aren't done within [[and]], making quoting less necessary.

We can use one of these operators to improve our *popd* function, which reacts badly if you try to pop and the stack is empty. Recall that the code for *popd* is:

```
function popd {                  # pop directory off the stack, cd there
    DIRSTACK=${DIRSTACK#* }
    cd ${DIRSTACK%% *}
    print "$PWD"
}
```

If the stack is empty, then **$DIRSTACK** is the null string, as is the expression **${DIRSTACK%% *}**. This means that you will change to your home directory; instead, we want *popd* to print an error message and do nothing.

To accomplish this, we need to test for an empty stack, i.e., whether **$DIR-STACK** is null or not. Here is one way to do it:

```
function popd {                  # pop directory off the stack, cd there
    if [[ -n $DIRSTACK ]]; then
        DIRSTACK=${DIRSTACK#* }
        cd ${DIRSTACK%% *}
        print "$PWD"
    else
        print "stack empty, still in $PWD."
    fi
}
```

Notice that instead of putting **then** on a separate line, we put it on the same line as the **if** after a semicolon, which is the shell's standard statement separator character.

We could have used operators other than **–n**. For example, we could have used **–z** and switched the code in the **then** and **else** clauses. We also could have used:*

```
    if [[ $DIRSTACK = "" ]]; then
        ...
```

While we're cleaning up code we wrote in the last chapter, let's fix up the error handling in the *highest* script (Task 4-1). The code for that script is:

```
    filename=${1:?"filename missing."}
    howmany=${2:-10}
    sort -nr $filename | head -$howmany
```

---

*Note that this code does *not* work under the older *[ ]* or *test* syntax, which will complain about a missing argument if the variable is null. This means that it is no longer necessary to surround both sides with double quotes (or to use hacks like **[x$DIRSTACK = x]**) as you had to with the Bourne shell; the Korn shell's **[[/]]** syntax handles null values correctly.

Recall that if you omit the first argument (the filename), the shell prints the message **highest: 1: filename missing**. We can make this better by substituting a more standard "usage" message:

```
if [[ -z $1 ]]; then
    print 'usage: howmany filename [-N]'
else
    filename=$1
    howmany=${2:-10}
    sort -nr $filename | head -$howmany
fi
```

It is considered better programming style to enclose all of the code in the **if-then-else**, but such code can get confusing if you are writing a long script in which you need to check for errors and bail out at several points along the way. Therefore, a more usual style for shell programming is this:

```
if [[ -z $1 ]]; then
    print 'usage: howmany filename [-N]'
    return 1
fi

filename=$1
howmany=${2:-10}
sort -nr $filename | head -$howmany
```

The **return** statement informs any calling program that needs to know whether it ran successfully or not.

As an example of the = and != operators, we can add the shell script front end to a C compiler to our solution for Task 4-2. Recall that we are given a filename ending in *.c* (the source code file), and we need to construct a filename that is the same but ends in *.o* (the object code file). The modifications we will make have to do with other types of files that can be passed to a C compiler.

About C Compilers

Before we get to the shell code, it is necessary to understand a few things about C compilers. We already know that they translate C source code into object code. Actually, they are part of *compilation systems* that also perform several other tasks. The term "compiler" is often used instead of "compilation system," so we'll use it in both senses.

We're interested here in two tasks that compilers perform other than compiling C code: they can translate *assembly language* code into object code, and they can *link* object code files together to form an *executable* program.

Assembly language works at a level that is close to the bare computer; each assembly statement is directly translatable into a statement of object code—as opposed to C or other higher-level languages, in which a single source statement could translate to dozens of object code instructions. Translating a file of assembly language code into object code is called, not surprisingly, *assembling* the code.

Although many people consider assembly language to be quaintly old-fashioned—like a typewriter in this age of WYSIWYG word processing and desktop publishing—some programmers still need to use it when dealing with precise details of computer hardware. It's not uncommon for a program to consist of several files' worth of code in a higher-level language (such as C) and a few low-level routines in assembly language.

The other task we'll worry about is called *linking*. Most real-world programs, unlike those assigned for a first-year programming class, consist of several files of source code, possibly written by several different programmers. These files are compiled into object code; then the object code must be combined to form the final, runnable program, known as an *executable*. The task of combining is often called "linking": each object code component usually contains references to other components, and these references must be resolved or "linked" together.

C compilation systems are capable of assembling files of assembly language into object code and linking object code files into executables. In particular, a compiler calls a separate *assembler* to deal with assembly code and a *linker* (also known as a "loader," "linking loader," or "link editor") to deal with object code files. These separate tools are known in the UNIX world as *as* and *ld*, respectively. The C compiler itself is invoked with the command *cc*.

We can express all of these steps in terms of the suffixes of files passed as arguments to the C compiler. Basically, the compiler does the following:

1. If the argument ends in *.c* it's a C source file; compile into a *.o* object code file.

2. If the argument ends in *.s*, it's assembly language; assemble into a *.o* file.

3. If the argument ends in *.o*, do nothing; save for the linking step later.

4. If the argument ends in some other suffix, print an error message and exit.*

---

*For the purposes of this example. We know this isn't strictly true in real life.

5. Link all .o object code files into an executable file called *a.out*. This file is usually renamed to something more descriptive.

Step 3 allows object code files that have already been compiled (or assembled) to be re-used to build other executables. For example, an object code file that implements an interface to a CD-ROM drive could be useful in any program that reads from CD-ROMs.

Figure 5-1 should make the compilation process clearer; it shows how the compiler processes the C source files *a.c* and *b.c*, the assembly language file *c.s*, and the already-compiled object code file *d.o*. In other words, it shows how the compiler handles the command **cc a.c b.c c.s d.o**.

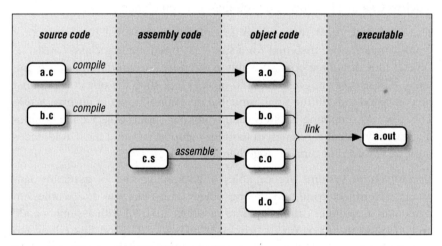

Figure 5-1: Files produced by a C compiler

Here is how we would begin to implement this behavior in a shell script. Assume that the variable **filename** holds the argument in question, and that *ccom* is the name of the program that actually compiles a C source file into object code. Assume further that *ccom* and *as* (assembler) take arguments for the names of the source and object files:

```
if [[ $filename = *.c ]]; then
    objname=${filename%.c}.o
    ccom $filename $objname
elif [[ $filename = *.s ]]; then
    objname=${filename%.s}.o
    as $filename $objname
```

```
elif [[ $filename != *.o ]]; then
    print "error: $filename is not a source or object file."
    return 1
fi
further processing...
```

Recall from the previous chapter that the expression ${filename%.c}.o deletes *.c* from **filename** and appends *.o*; ${filename%.s}.o does the analogous thing for files ending in *.s.*

The "further processing" is the link step, which we will see when we complete this example later in the chapter.

File Attribute Checking

The other kind of operator that can be used in conditional expressions checks a file for certain properties. There are 21 such operators. We will cover those of most general interest here; the rest refer to arcana like sticky bits, sockets, and file descriptors, and thus are of interest only to systems hackers. Refer to Appendix B for the complete list. Table 5-2 lists those that we will examine.

Table 5-2: File Attribute Operators

Operator	True if ...
-a *file*	*file* exists
-d *file*	*file* is a directory
-f *file*	*file* is a regular file (i.e., not a directory or other special type of file)
-r *file*	You have read permission on *file*
-s *file*	*file* exists and is not empty
-w *file*	You have write permission on *file*
-x *file*	You have execute permission on *file*, or directory search permission if it is a directory
-O *file*	You own *file*
-G *file*	Your group ID is the same as that of *file*
file1 -nt *file2*	*file1* is newer than *file2***
file1 -ot *file2*	*file1* is older than *file2*

* Specifically, the –nt and –ot operators compare *modification times* of two files.

Before we get to an example, you should know that conditional expressions inside [[and]] can also be combined using the logical operators && and ||, just as we saw with plain shell commands above, in the section entitled "Combinations of Exit Statuses." It's also possible to combine shell commands with conditional expressions using logical operators, like this:

```
if command && [[ condition ]]; then
    ...
```

Chapter 7, *Input/Output and Command-line Processing*, contains an example of this combination.

You can also negate the truth value of a conditional expression by preceding it with an exclamation point (!), so that ! *expr* evaluates to true only if *expr* is false. Furthermore, you can make complex logical expressions of conditional operators by grouping them with parentheses.*

Here is how we would use two of the file operators to embellish (yet again) our *pushd* function. Instead of having **cd** determine whether the argument given is a valid directory—i.e., by returning with a bad exit status if it's not—we can do the checking ourselves. Here is the code:

```
function pushd {                    # push current directory onto stack
    dirname=$1
    if [[ -d $dirname && -x $dirname ]]; then
        cd $dirname
        DIRSTACK="$dirname ${DIRSTACK:-$PWD}"
        print "$DIRSTACK"
    else
        print "still in $PWD."
    fi
}
```

The conditional expression evaluates to true only if the argument **$1** is a directory (**-d**) *and* the user has permission to change to it (**-x**).† Notice that this conditional also handles the case where the argument is missing: **$dirname** is null, and since the null string isn't a valid directory name, the conditional will fail.

---

*It turns out that this is true outside of the [[/]] construct as well. As we will see in Chapter 8, *Process Handling*, the construct (*statement list*) runs the statement list in a subshell, whose exit status is that of the last statement in the list. However, there is no equivalent of the negation (!) operator outside of the [[/]] construct, although there will be in future releases.

†Remember that the same permission flag that determines execute permission on a regular file determines search permission on a directory. This is why the -x operator checks both things depending on file type.

Here is a more comprehensive example of the use of file operators.

Task 5-1

> Write a script that prints essentially the same information as **ls -l** but in a more user-friendly way.

Although this task requires relatively long-winded code, it is a straightforward application of many of the file operators:

```
if [[ ! -a $1 ]]; then
    print "file $1 does not exist."
    return 1
fi
if [[ -d $1 ]]; then
    print -n "$1 is a directory that you may "
    if [[ ! -x $1 ]]; then
        print -n "not "
    fi
    print "search."
elif [[ -f $1 ]]; then
    print "$1 is a regular file."
else
    print "$1 is a special type of file."
fi
if [[ -O $1 ]]; then
    print 'you own the file.'
else
    print 'you do not own the file.'
fi
if [[ -r $1 ]]; then
    print 'you have read permission on the file.'
fi
if [[ -w $1 ]]; then
    print 'you have write permission on the file.'
fi
if [[ -x $1 && ! -d $1 ]]; then
    print 'you have execute permission on the file.'
fi
```

We'll call this script *fileinfo*. Here's how it works:

- The first conditional tests if the file given as argument does *not* exist (the exclamation point is the "not" operator; the spaces around it are required). If the file does not exist, the script prints an error message and exits with error status.

- The second conditional tests if the file is a directory. If so, the first *print* prints part of a message; remember that the **-n** option tells *print* not to print a LINEFEED at the end. The inner conditional checks if you do *not* have search permission on the directory. If you don't have search permission, the word "not" is added to the partial message. Then, the message is completed with "search." and a LINEFEED.

- The **elif** clause checks if the file is a regular file; if so, it prints a message.

- The **else** clause accounts for the various special file types on recent UNIX systems, such as sockets, devices, FIFO files, etc. We assume that the casual user isn't interested in details of these.

- The next conditional tests to see if the file is owned by you (i.e., if its owner ID is the same as your login ID). If so, it prints a message saying that you own it.

- The next two conditionals test for your read and write permission on the file.

- The last conditional checks if you can execute the file. It checks to see if you have execute permission and that the file is *not* a directory. (If the file were a directory, execute permission would really mean directory search permission.)

As an example of *fileinfo*'s output, assume that you do an **ls -l** of your current directory and it contains these lines:

```
-rwxr-xr-x   1 billr    other       594 May 28 09:49 bob
-rw-r--r--   1 billr    other     42715 Apr 21 23:39 custom.tbl
drwxr-xr-x   2 billr    other        64 Jan 12 13:42 exp
-r--r--r--   1 root     other       557 Mar 28 12:41 lpst
```

custom.tbl and *lpst* are regular text files, *exp* is a directory, and *bob* is a shell script. Typing **fileinfo bob** produces this output:

```
bob is a regular file.
you own the file.
you have read permission on the file.
you have write permission on the file.
you have execute permission on the file.
```

Typing **fileinfo custom.tbl** results in this:

```
custom.tbl is a regular file.
you own the file.
you have read permission on the file.
you have write permission on the file.
```

Typing **fileinfo exp** results in this:

```
exp is a directory that you may search.
you own the file.
you have read permission on the file.
you have write permission on the file.
```

Finally, typing **fileinfo lpst** produces this:

```
lpst is a regular file.
you do not own the file.
you have read permission on the file.
```

Chapter 7, *Input/Output and Command-line Processing*, contains an example of the **-nt** test operator.

Integer Conditionals

The shell also provides a set of *arithmetic* tests. These are different from *character string* comparisons like < and >, which compare *lexicographic* values of strings, not numeric values. For example, "6" is greater than "57" lexicographically, just as "p" is greater than "ox," but of course the opposite is true when they're compared as integers.

The integer comparison operators are summarized in Table 5-3. FORTRAN programmers will find their syntax slightly familiar.

Table 5-3: Arithmetic Test Operators

Test	Comparison
-lt	Less than
-le	Less than or equal
-eq	Equal
-ge	Greater than or equal
-gt	Greater than
-ne	Not equal

You'll find these to be of the most use in the context of the integer variables we'll see in the next chapter. They're necessary if you want to combine integer tests with other types of tests within the same conditional expression.

However, the shell has a separate syntax for conditional expressions that involve integers only. It's considerably more efficient, so you should use it in preference to the arithmetic test operators listed above. Again, we'll cover the shell's integer conditionals in the next chapter.

for

The most obvious enhancement we could make to the previous script is the ability to report on multiple files instead of just one. Tests like **-a** and **-d** only take single arguments, so we need a way of calling the code once for each file given on the command line.

The way to do this—indeed, the way to do many things with the Korn shell—is with a looping construct. The simplest and most widely applicable of the shell's looping constructs is the **for** loop. We'll use **for** to enhance *fileinfo* soon.

The **for** loop allows you to repeat a section of code a fixed number of times. During each time through the code (known as an *iteration*), a special variable called a *loop variable* is set to a different value; this way each iteration can do something slightly different.

The **for** loop is somewhat, but not entirely, similar to its counterparts in conventional languages like C and Pascal. The chief difference is that the shell's **for** loop doesn't let you specify a number of times to iterate or a range of values over which to iterate; instead, it only lets you give a fixed list of values. In other words, you can't do anything like this Pascal-type code, which executes *statements* 10 times:

```
for x := 1 to 10 do
begin
    statements...
end
```

(You need the **while** construct, which we'll see soon, to construct this type of loop. You also need the ability to do integer arithmetic, which we will see in Chapter 6, *Command-line Options and Typed Variables.*)

However, the **for** loop is ideal for working with arguments on the command line and with sets of files (e.g., all files in a given directory). We'll look at an example of each of these. But first, we'll show the syntax for the **for** construct:

```
for name [in list]
do
    statements that can use $name...
done
```

The *list* is a list of names. (If **in** *list* is omitted, the list defaults to "$@", i.e., the quoted list of command-line arguments, but we'll always supply the **in** *list* for the sake of clarity.) In our solutions to the following task, we'll show two simple ways to specify lists.

Task 5-2

> You work in an environment with several computers in a local network. Write a shell script that tells you who is logged in to each machine on the network.

The command *finger*(1) can be used (among other things) to find the names of users logged into a remote system; the command **finger** @*system-name* does this. Its output depends on the version of UNIX, but it looks something like this:

```
[motet.early.com]
Trying 127.146.63.17...
-User-     --Full name--        -What- Idle TTY -Console Location-
hildy      Hildegard von Bingen  ksh   2d5h p1  jem.cal (Telnet)
mikes      Michael Schultheiss   csh   1:21 r4  ncd2.cal (X display 0)
orlando    Orlando di Lasso      csh     28 r7  maccala (Telnet)
marin      Marin Marais          mush  1:02 pb  mussell.cal (Telnet)
johnd      John Dowland          tcsh    17 p0  nugget.west.nobis. (X Window)
```

In this output, *motet.early.com* is the full network name of the remote machine.

Assume the systems in your network are called *fred*, *bob*, *dave*, and *pete*. Then the following code would do the trick:

```
for sys in fred bob dave pete
do
    finger @$sys
    print
done
```

This works no matter which of the systems you are currently logged into. It prints output for each machine similar to the above, with blank lines in between.

A slightly better solution would be to store the names of the systems in an environment variable. This way, if systems are added to your network and you need a list of their names in more than one script, you need change them in only one place. If a variable's value is several words separated by blanks (or TABS), **for** will treat it as a list of words.

Here is the improved solution. First, put lines in your *.profile* or environment file that define the variable **SYSNAMES** and make it an environment variable:

```
SYSNAMES="fred bob dave pete"
export SYSNAMES
```

Then, the script can look like this:

```
for sys in $SYSNAMES
do
     finger @$sys
     print
done
```

The foregoing illustrated a simple use of **for**, but it's much more common to use **for** to iterate through a list of command-line arguments. To show this, we can enhance the *fileinfo* script above to accept multiple arguments. First, we write a bit of "wrapper" code that does the iteration:

```
for filename in "$@" ; do
     finfo $filename
     print
done
```

Next, we make the original script into a function called *finfo:**

```
function finfo {
     if [[ ! -a $1 ]]; then
         print "file $1 does not exist."
         return 1
     fi
     ...
}
```

The complete script consists of the **for** loop code and the above function, in either order; good programming style dictates that the function definition should go first.

The *fileinfo* script works as follows: in the **for** statement, `"$@"` is a list of all positional parameters. For each argument, the body of the loop is run with **filename** set to that argument. In other words, the function *fileinfo* is called once for each value of **$filename** as its first argument (**$1**). The call to *print* after the call to *fileinfo* merely prints a blank line between sets of information about each file.

---

*A function can have the same name as a script; however, this isn't good programming practice.

Given a directory with the same files as the previous example, typing **fileinfo** * would produce the following output:

```
bob is a regular file.
you own the file.
you have read permission on the file.
you have write permission on the file.
you have execute permission on the file.

custom.tbl is a regular file.
you own the file.
you have read permission on the file.
you have write permission on the file.

exp is a directory that you may search.
you own the file.
you have read permission on the file.
you have write permission on the file.

lpst is a regular file.
you do not own the file.
you have read permission on the file.
```

Here is a programming task that exploits the other major use of **for**.

<hr>

Task 5-3

Your UNIX system has the ability to transfer files from an MS-DOS system, but it leaves the DOS filenames intact. Write a script that translates the filenames in a given directory from DOS format to a more UNIX-friendly format.

DOS filenames have the format *FILENAME.EXT. FILENAME* can be up to eight characters long; *EXT* is an extension that can be up to three characters. The dot is required even if the extension is null; letters are all uppercase. We want to do the following:

1. Translate letters from uppercase to lowercase.
2. If the extension is null, remove the dot.

The first tool we will need for this job is the UNIX *tr*(1) utility, which translates characters on a one-to-one basis. Given the arguments *charset1* and *charset2*, it will translate characters in the standard input that are members of *charset1* into corresponding characters in *charset2*. The two sets are ranges of characters enclosed in square brackets ([] in standard regular-expression form in the manner of *grep, awk, ed,* etc.). More to the point, **tr [A-Z] [a-z]** takes its standard input, converts uppercase letters to lowercase, and writes the converted text to the standard output.

That takes care of the first step in the translation process. We can use a Korn shell string operator to handle the second. Here is the code for a script we'll call *dosmv*:

```
for filename in ${1:+$1/}* ; do
    newfilename=$(print $filename | tr [A-Z] [a-z])
    newfilename=${newfilename%.}
    print "$filename -> $newfilename"
    mv $filename $newfilename
done
```

The * in the **for** construct is *not* the same as **$***. It's a wildcard, i.e., all files in a directory.

This script accepts a directory name as argument, the default being the current directory. The expression **${1:+$1/}** evaluates to the argument (**$1**) with a slash appended if the argument is supplied, or the null string if it isn't supplied. So the entire expression **${1:+$1/}*** evaluates to all files in the given directory, or all files in the current directory if no argument is given.

Therefore, **filename** takes on the value of each filename in the list. **filename** gets translated into **newfilename** in two steps. (We could have done it in one, but readability would have suffered.) The first step uses *tr* in a pipeline within a command substitution construct. Our old friend **print** makes the value of **filename** the standard input to *tr*. *tr*'s output becomes the value of the command substitution expression, which is assigned to **newfilename**. Thus, if **$filename** were *DOSFILE.TXT*, **newfilename** would become *dosfile.txt*.

The second step uses one of the shell's pattern-matching operators, the one that deletes the shortest match it finds at the end of the string. The pattern here is **.**, which means a dot at the end of the string.* This means that the expression **${newfilename%.}** will delete a dot from **$newfilename** only if it's at the end of the string; otherwise the expression will leave **$newfilename** intact. For example, if **$newfilename** is *dosfile.txt*, it will be untouched, but if it's *dosfile.*, the expression will change it to *dosfile* without the final dot. In either case, the new value is assigned back to *newfilename*.

---

*UNIX regular expression mavens should remember that this is shell wildcard syntax, in which dots are not operators and therefore do not need to be backslash-escaped.

The last statement in the **for** loop body does the file renaming with the standard UNIX *mv*(1) command. Before that, a **print** command simply informs the user of what's happening.

There is one little problem with the solution on the previous page: if there are any files in the given directory that *aren't* DOS files (in particular, if there are files whose names don't contain uppercase letters and don't contain a dot), then the conversion will do nothing to those filenames and *mv* will be called with two identical arguments. *mv* will complain with the message: **mv: filename and** *filename* **are identical.** We can solve this problem by letting *grep* determine whether each file has a DOS filename or not. The *grep* regular expression:

```
[^a-z]\{1,8\}\.[^a-z]\{0,3\}
```

is adequate (for these purposes) for matching DOS-format filenames.* The character class [**^a-z**] means "any character *except* a lowercase letter."† So the entire regular expression means: "Between 1 and 8 non-lowercase letters, followed by a dot, followed by 0 to 3 non-lowercase letters."

When *grep* runs, it normally prints all of the lines in its standard input that match the pattern you give it as argument. But we only need it to test whether or not the pattern is matched. Luckily, *grep's* exit status is "well-behaved": it's 0 if there is a match in the input, 1 if not. Therefore, we can use the exit status to test for a match. We also need to discard *grep's* output; to do this, we redirect it to the special file */dev/null*, which is colloquially known as the "bit bucket."‡ Any output directed to */dev/null* effectively disappears. Thus, the command line:

```
print "$filename" | grep '[^a-z]\{1,8\}\.[^a-z]\{0,3\}' > /dev/null
```

prints nothing and returns exit status 0 if the filename is in DOS format, 1 if not.

---

*As with the **lsd** function in Chapter 4, *Basic Shell Programming*, older BSD-derived versions of UNIX don't support the "repeat count" operator within *grep*. You must use this instead:

```
[^a-z][^a-z]?[^a-z]?[^a-z]?[^a-z]?[^a-z]?[^a-z]?[^a-z]?\.[^a-z]?[^a-z]?[^a-z]?
```

†To be completely precise, this class also excludes NEWLINEs.

‡Some Berkeley-derived versions of UNIX have a –s ("silent") option to *grep* that suppresses standard output, thereby making redirection to */dev/null* unnecessary.

Now we can modify our *dosmv* script to incorporate this code:

```
dos_regexp='[^a-z]\{1,8\}\.[^a-z]\{0,3\}'
for filename in ${1:+$1/}* ; do
    if print $filename | grep $dos_regexp > /dev/null; then
        newfilename=$(print $filename | tr [A-Z] [a-z])
        newfilename=${newfilename%.}
        print "$filename -> $newfilename"
        mv $filename $newfilename
    fi
done
```

For readability reasons, we use the variable **dos_regexp** to hold the DOS filename-matching regular expression.

If you are familiar with an operating system other than DOS and UNIX, you may want to test your script-writing prowess at this point by writing a script that translates filenames from that system's format into UNIX format. Use the above script as a guideline.

In particular, if you know DEC's VAX/VMS operating system, here's a programming challenge:

1. Write a script called *vmsmv* that is similar to *dosmv* but works on VAX/VMS filenames instead of DOS filenames. Remember that VAX/VMS filenames end with semicolons and version numbers.

2. Modify your script so that if there are several versions of the same file, it renames only the latest version (with the highest version number).

3. Modify further so that your script erases old versions of files.

The first of these is a relatively straightforward modification of *dosmv*. Number 2 is difficult; here's a strategy hint:

*   Develop a regular expression that matches VAX/VMS filenames (you need this for No. 1 anyway).

*   Get a list of base names (sans version numbers) of files in the given directory by piping *ls* through *grep* (with the above regular expression), *cut*, and *sort -u*. Use *cut* with a semicolon as "field separator"; make sure that you quote the semicolon so that the shell doesn't treat it as a statement separator. *sort -u* removes duplicates after sorting. Use command substitution to save the resulting list in a variable.

*   Use a **for** loop on the list of base names. For each name, get the highest version number of the file (just the number, not the whole name). Do this with another pipeline: pipe *ls* through *cut*, *sort -n*, and *tail -1*. *sort -n* sorts in numerical (not lexicographical) order; *tail -N*

outputs the last *N* lines of its input. Again, use command substitution to capture the output of this pipeline in a variable.

- Append the highest version number to the base name; this is the file to rename in UNIX format.

Once you have completed No. 2, you can do No. 3 by adding a single line of code to your script; see if you can figure out how.

case

The next flow control construct we will cover is **case**. While the **case** statement in Pascal and the similar **switch** statement in C can be used to test simple values like integers and characters, the Korn shell's **case** construct lets you test strings against patterns that can contain wildcard characters. Like its conventional language counterparts, **case** lets you express a series of if-then-else type statements in a concise way.

The syntax of **case** is as follows:

```
case expression in
    pattern1 )
        statements ;;
    pattern2 )
        statements ;;
    ...
esac
```

Any of the *patterns* can actually be several patterns separated by pipe characters (|). If *expression* matches one of the patterns, its corresponding statements are executed. If there are several patterns separated by pipe characters, the expression can match any of them in order for the associated statements to be run. The patterns are checked in order until a match is found; if none is found, nothing happens.

This rather ungainly syntax should become clearer with an example. An obvious choice is to revisit our solution to Task 4-2, the front-end for the C compiler. Earlier in this chapter, we wrote some code, that processed input files according to their suffixes (*.c .s,* or *.o* for C, assembly, or object code, respectively).

We can improve upon this solution in two ways.

First, we can use **for** to allow multiple files to be processed at one time; second, we can use **case** to streamline the code:

```
for filename in $*; do
    case $filename in
        *.c )
            objname=${filename%.c}.o
            ccom $filename $objname ;;
        *.s )
            objname=${filename%.s}.o
            as $filename $objname ;;
        *.o ) ;;
        *   )
            print "error: $filename is not a source or object file."
            return 1 ;;
    esac
done
```

The **case** construct in this code handles four cases. The first two are similar to the **if** and first **elif** cases in the code earlier in this chapter; they call the compiler or the assembler if the filename ends in *.c* or *.s* respectively.

After that, the code is a bit different. Recall that if the filename ends in *.o* nothing is to be done (on the assumption that the relevant files will be linked later). If the filename does not end in *.o* there is an error. We handle this with the case ***.o**), which has no statements. There is nothing wrong with a "case" for which the script does nothing.

The final case is *****, which is a catchall for whatever didn't match the other cases. (In fact, a ***** case is analogous to a **default** case in C and an **otherwise** case in some Pascal-derived languages.)

The surrounding **for** loop processes all command-line arguments properly. This leads to a further enhancement: now that we know how to process all arguments, we should be able to write the code that passes all of the object files to the linker (the program *ld*) at the end. We can do this by building up a string of object file names, separated by spaces, and hand that off to the linker when we've processed all of the input files. We initialize the string to null and append an object file name each time one is created, i.e., during each iteration of the **for** loop. The code for this is simple, requiring only minor additions:

```
objfiles=""
for filename in $*; do
    case $filename in
        *.c )
            objname=${filename%.c}.o
            ccom $filename $objname ;;
```

```
        *.s )
            objname=${filename%.s}.o
            as $filename $objname ;;
        *.o )
            objname=$filename ;;
        *   )
            print "error: $filename is not a source or object file."
            return 1 ;;
    esac
    objfiles="$objfiles $objname"
done
ld $objfiles
```

The first line in this version of the script initializes the variable **objfiles** to null.* We added a line of code in the *.o case to set **objname** equal to **$filename**, because we already know it's an object file. Thus, the value of **objname** is set in every case—except for the error case, in which the routine prints a message and bails out.

The last line of code in the **for** loop body appends a space and the latest **$objname** to **objfiles**. Calling this script with the same arguments as in Figure 5.1 would result in **$objfiles** being equal to " a.o b.o c.o d.o" when the **for** loop finishes (the leading space doesn't matter). This list of object filenames is given to *ld* as a single argument, but the shell divides it up into multiple file names properly.

We'll return to this example once more in Chapter 6, *Command-line Options and Typed Variables*, when we discuss how to handle dash options on the command line. Meanwhile, here is a new task whose initial solution will use **case**.

Task 5-4

You are a system administrator,† and you need to set up the system so that users' **TERM** environment variables reflect correctly what type of terminal they are on. Write some code that does this.

The code for the solution to this task should go into the file */etc/profile*, which is the master startup file that is run for each user *before* his or her *.profile*.

---

*This isn't strictly necessary, because all variables are assumed to be null if not explicitly initialized (unless the **nounset** option is turned on). It just makes the code easier to read.

†Our condolences.

For the time being, we will assume that you have a traditional mainframe-style setup, in which terminals are hard-wired to the computer. This means that you can determine which (physical) terminal is being used by the line (or *tty*) it is on. This is typically a name like */dev/ttyNN*, where *NN* is the line number. You can find your tty with the command *tty*(1), which prints it on the standard output.

Let's assume that your system has ten lines plus a system console line (*/dev/console*), with the following terminals:

- Lines tty01, tty03, and tty04 are Givalt GL35a's (*terminfo* name "gl35a").
- Line tty07 is a Tsoris T-2000 ("t2000").
- Line tty08 and the console are Shande 531s ("s531").
- The rest are Vey VT99s ("vt99").

Here is the code that does the job:

```
case $(tty) in
    /dev/tty0[134]               ) TERM=gl35a ;;
    /dev/tty07                   ) TERM=t2000 ;;
    /dev/tty08 | /dev/console )    TERM=s531  ;;
    *                            ) TERM=vt99  ;;
esac
```

The value that **case** checks is the result of command substitution. Otherwise, the only thing new about this code is the pipe character after */dev/tty08*. This means that */dev/tty08* and */dev/console* are alternate patterns for the case that sets **TERM** to "s531".

Note that it is *not* possible to put alternate patterns on separate lines unless you use backslash continuation characters at the end of all but the last line, i.e., the line:

```
    /dev/tty08 | /dev/console ) TERM=s531  ;;
```

could be changed to the slightly more readable:

```
    /dev/tty08 | \
    /dev/console   ) TERM=s531  ;;
```

The backslash must be at the end of the line. If you omit it, or if there are characters (even blanks) following it, the shell complains with a syntax error message.

This problem is actually better solved using a file that contains a table of lines and terminal types. We'll see how to do it this way in Chapter 7.

select

All of the flow-control constructs we have seen so far are also available in the Bourne shell, and the C shell has equivalents with different syntax. Our next construct, **select**, is new for the Korn shell; moreover, it has no analog in conventional programming languages.

select allows you to generate simple menus easily. It has concise syntax, but it does quite a lot of work. The syntax is:

```
select name [in list]
do
    statements that can use $name...
done
```

This is the same syntax as **for** except for the keyword **select**. And like **for**, you can omit the in *list* and it will default to "$@", i.e., the list of quoted command-line arguments.

Here is what **select** does:

- Generates a menu of each item in *list*, formatted with numbers for each choice
- Prompts the user for a number
- Stores the selected choice in the variable *name* and the selected number in the built-in variable **REPLY**
- Executes the statements in the body
- Repeats the process forever (but see below for how to exit)

Once again, an example should help make this process clearer. Assume you need to write the code for Task 5-4, but your life is not as simple. You don't have terminals hardwired to your computer; instead, your users communicate through a terminal server. This means, among other things, that the tty number does *not* determine the type of terminal.

Therefore, you have no choice but to prompt the user for his or her terminal type at login time. To do this, you can put the following code in */etc/profile* (assume you have the same choice of terminal types):

```
PS3='terminal? '
select term in gl35a t2000 s531 vt99; do
    if [[ -n $term ]]; then
        TERM=$term
        print TERM is $TERM
        break
```

```
        else
            print 'invalid.'
        fi
done
```

If you run this code, you will see this menu:

```
1) gl35a
2) t2000
3) s531
4) vt99
terminal?
```

The built-in shell variable **PS3** contains the prompt string that **select** uses; its default value is the not particularly useful "#? ". So the first line of the above code sets it to a more relevant value.

The **select** statement constructs the menu from the list of choices. If the user enters a valid number (from 1 to 4), then the variable **term** is set to the corresponding value; otherwise it is null. (If the user just presses RETURN, the shell prints the menu again.)

The code in the loop body checks if **term** is non-null. If so, it assigns **$term** to the environment variable **TERM** and prints a confirmation message; then the **break** statement exits the **select** loop. If **term** is null, the code prints an error message and repeats the prompt (but not the menu).

The **break** statement is the usual way of exiting a **select** loop. Actually (like its analog in C), it can be used to exit any surrounding control structure we've seen so far (except **case**, where the double-semicolons act like **break**) as well as the **while** and **until** we will see soon. We haven't introduced **break** until now because it is considered bad coding style to use it to exit a loop. However, it is necessary for exiting **select** when the user makes a valid choice.*

Let's refine our solution by making the menu more user-friendly, so that the user doesn't have to know the *terminfo* name of his or her terminal. We do this by using quoted character strings as menu items and then using **case** to determine the termcap name:

```
print 'Select your terminal type:'
PS3='terminal? '
```

---

*A user can also type CTRL-D (for end-of-input) to get out of a **select** loop. This gives the user a uniform way of exiting, but it doesn't help the shell programmer much.

```
select term in \
    'Givalt GL35a' \
    'Tsoris T-2000' \
    'Shande 531' \
    'Vey VT99'
do
    case $REPLY in
        1 ) TERM=gl35a ;;
        2 ) TERM=t2000 ;;
        3 ) TERM=s531 ;;
        4 ) TERM=vt99 ;;
        * ) print 'invalid.' ;;
    esac
    if [[ -n $term ]]; then
        print TERM is $TERM
        break
    fi
done
```

This code looks a bit more like a menu routine in a conventional program, though **select** still provides the shortcut of converting the menu choices into numbers. We list each of the menu choices on its own line for reasons of readability, but once again we need continuation characters to keep the shell from complaining about syntax.

Here is what the user will see when this code is run:

```
Select your terminal type:
1) Givalt GL35a
2) Tsoris T-2000
3) Shande 531
4) Vey VT99
terminal?
```

This is a bit more informative than the previous code's output.

When the body of the **select** loop is entered, **$term** equals one of the four strings (or is null if the user made an invalid choice), while the built-in variable **REPLY** contains the number the user selects. We need a **case** statement to assign the correct value to **TERM**; we use the value of **REPLY** as the **case** selector.

Once the **case** statement is finished, the **if** checks to see if a valid choice was made, as in the previous solution. If the choice was valid, then **TERM** has already been assigned, so the code just prints a confirmation message and exits the **select** loop. If it wasn't valid, the **select** loop repeats the prompt and goes through the process again.

while and until

The remaining two flow control constructs the Korn shell provides are **while** and **until**. These are similar; they both allow a section of code to be run repetitively while (or until) a certain condition holds true. They also resemble analogous constructs in Pascal (**while/do** and **repeat/until**) and C (**while** and **do/until**).

while and **until** are actually most useful when combined with features we will see in the next chapter, such as integer arithmetic, input/output of variables, and command-line processing. Yet we can show a useful example even with the machinery we have covered so far.

The syntax for **while** is:

```
while condition
do
    statements...
done
```

For **until**, just substitute **until** for **while** in the above example. As with **if**, the *condition* is really a list of *statements* that are run; the exit status of the last one is used as the value of the condition. You can use a conditional with [[and]] here, just as you can with **if**.

Note that the *only* difference between **while** and **until** is the way the condition is handled. In **while**, the loop executes as long as the condition is true; in **until**, it runs as long as the condition is false. So far, so familiar. BUT: the **until** condition is checked at the *top* of the loop, *not* at the bottom as it is in analogous constructs in C and Pascal.

The result is that you can convert any **until** into a **while** by simply negating the condition. The only place where **until** might be better is something like this:

```
until command; do
    statements...
done
```

The meaning of this is essentially, "Do *statements* until *command* runs correctly." This is not, in our opinion, a likely contingency. Therefore we will use **while** throughout the rest of this book.

Here is a task that is a good candidate for **while**.

Implement a simplified version of the shell's built-in **whence** command.

By "simplified," we mean that we will implement only the part that checks all of the directories in your **PATH** for the command you give as argument (we won't implement checking for aliases, built-in commands, etc.).

We can do this by picking off the directories in **PATH** one by one, using one of the shell's pattern-matching operators, and seeing if there is a file with the given name in the directory that you have permission to execute. Here is the code:

```
path=$PATH:
dir=${path%%:*}
while [[ -n $path ]]; do
    if [[ -x $dir/$1 && ! -d $dir/$1 ]]; then
        print "$dir/$1"
        return
    fi
    path=${path#*:}
    dir=${path%%:*}
done
return 1
```

The first line of this code saves **$PATH** in **path**, our own temporary copy. We append a colon to the end so that every directory in **$path** ends in a colon (in **$PATH**, colons are used only *between* directories); subsequent code depends on this being the case.

The next line picks the first directory off of **$path** by using the operator that deletes the longest match to the pattern given. In this case, we delete the longest match to the pattern **:***, i.e., a colon followed by anything. This gives us the first directory in **$path**, which we store in the variable **dir**.

The condition in the **while** loop checks if **$path** is non-null. If it is not null, it constructs the full pathname **$dir/$1** and sees if there is a file by that name for which you have execute permission (and that is not a directory). If so, it prints the full pathname and exits the routine with a 0 ("OK") exit status.

If a file is not found, then this code is run:

```
path=${path#*:}
dir=${path%%:*}
```

The first of these uses another shell string operator: this one deletes the shortest match to the pattern given from the front of the string. By now, this type of operator should be familiar. This line deletes the front directory from **$path** and assigns the result back to **path**. The second line is the same as before the **while**: it finds the (new) front directory in **$path** and assigns it to **dir**. This sets up the loop for another iteration.

Thus, the code loops through all of the directories in **PATH**. It exits when it finds a matching executable file or when it has "eaten up" the entire **PATH**. If no matching executable file is found, it prints nothing and exits with an error status.

We can enhance this script a bit by taking advantage of the UNIX utility *file*(1). *file* examines files given as arguments and determines what type they are, based on the file's *magic number* and various heuristics (educated guesses). A magic number is a field in the header of an executable file that the linker sets to identify what type of executable it is.

If *filename* is an executable program (compiled from C or some other language), then typing **file** *filename* produces output similar to this:

filename: ELF 32-bit LSB executable 80386 Version 1

However, if *filename* is not an executable program, it will examine the first few lines and try to guess what kind of information the file contains. If the file contains text (as opposed to binary data), *file* will look for indications that it is English, shell commands, C, FORTRAN, *troff*(1) input, and various other things. *file* is wrong sometimes, but it is mostly correct.

We can just substitute *file* for *print* to print a more informative message in our script:

```
path=$PATH
dir=${path%%:*}
while [[ -n $path ]]; do
    if [[ -x $dir/$1 && ! -d $dir/$1 ]]; then
        file $dir/$1
        return
    fi
    path=${path#*:}
    dir=${path%%:*}
done
return 1
```

Assume that *fred* is an executable file in the directory */usr/bin*, and that *bob* is a shell script in */usr/local/bin*. Then typing **file fred** produces this output:

```
/usr/bin/fred: ELF 32-bit LSB executable 80386 Version 1
```

And typing **file bob** has this result:

```
/usr/local/bin/bob: commands text
```

Before we end this chapter, we have two final notes. First, notice that the statement **dir=${path%%:*}** appears in two places, before the start of the loop and as the last statement in the loop's body. Some diehard C hackers are offended by this Pascal-like coding technique. Certain features of the C language allow programmers to create loops of the form:

```
while iterative-step; condition; do
    ...
done
```

This is the same as the form of the script above: the *iterative-step* runs just before the *condition* each time around the loop.

We can write our script this way:

```
path=$PATH
while dir=${path%%:*}; [[ -n $path ]]; do
    if [[ -x $dir/$1 && ! -d $dir/$1 ]]; then
        file $dir/$1
        return
    fi
    path=${path#*:}
done
return 1
```

Although this example doesn't show great programming style, it does make the code smaller—hence its popularity with C programmers. Make sure you understand that our script is functionally identical to the previous script.

Finally, just to show how little difference there is between **while** and **until**, we note that the line

```
until [[ ! -n $path ]]; do
```

can be used in place of

```
while [[ -n $path ]]; do
```

with identical results.

We'll see additional examples of **while** in the next chapter.

6

Command-line Options and Typed Variables

You should have a healthy grasp of shell programming techniques now that you have gone through the previous chapters. What you have learned up to this point enables you to write many nontrivial, useful shell scripts and functions.

Still, you may have noticed some remaining gaps in the knowledge you need to write shell code that behaves like the UNIX commands you are used to. In particular, if you are an experienced UNIX user, it might have occurred to you that none of the example scripts shown so far have the ability to handle *options* (preceded by a dash (-)) on the command line. And if you program in a conventional language like C or Pascal, you will have noticed that the only type of data that we have seen in shell variables is character strings; we haven't seen how to do arithmetic, for example.

These capabilities are certainly crucial to the shell's ability to function as a useful UNIX programming language. In this chapter, we will show how the Korn shell supports these and related features.

Command-line Options

We have already seen many examples of the *positional parameters* (variables called 1, 2, 3, etc.) that the shell uses to store the command-line arguments to a shell script or function when it runs. We have also seen related variables like * (for the string of all arguments) and # (for the number of arguments).

Indeed, these variables hold all of the information on the user's command-line. But consider what happens when options are involved. Typical UNIX commands have the form *command [–options] args*, meaning that there can be 0 or more options. If a shell script processes the command **fred bob pete**, then **$1** is "bob" and **$2** is "pete". But if the command is **fred -o bob pete**, then **$1** is -o, **$2** is "bob", and **$3** is "pete".

You might think you could write code like this to handle it:

```
if [[ $1 = -o ]]; then
    code that processes the -o option
    1=$2
    2=$3
fi

normal processing of $1 and $2...
```

But this code has several problems. First, assignments like **1=$2** are illegal because positional parameters are read-only. Even if they were legal, another problem is that this kind of code imposes limitations on how many arguments the script can handle—which is very unwise. Furthermore, if this command had several possible options, the code to handle all of them would get very messy very quickly.

shift

Luckily, the shell provides a way around this problem. The command **shift** performs the function of:

```
1=$2
2=$3
...
```

for every argument, regardless of how many there are. If you supply a numeric argument to **shift**, it will shift the arguments that many times over; for example, **shift 3** has this effect:

```
1=$4
2=$5
...
```

This leads immediately to some code that handles a single option (call it -o) and arbitrarily many arguments:

```
if [[ $1 = -o ]]; then
    process the -o option
    shift
fi
normal processing of arguments...
```

After the **if** construct, **$1**, **$2**, etc., are set to the correct arguments.

We·can use **shift** together with the programming features we have seen so far to implement simple option schemes. However, we will need additional help when things get more complex. The **getopts** built-in command, which we will introduce later, provides this help.

shift by itself gives us enough power to implement the *-N* option to the *highest* script we saw in Chapter 4, *Basic Shell Programming* (Task 4-1). Recall that this script takes an input file that lists artists and the number of albums you have by them. It sorts the list and prints out the *N* highest numbers, in descending order. The code that does the actual data processing is:

```
filename=$1
howmany=${2:-10}
sort -nr $filename | head -$howmany
```

Our original syntax for calling this script was **highest** *filename* [*-N*], where *N* defaults to 10 if omitted. Let's change this to a more conventional UNIX syntax, in which options are given before arguments: **highest** [*-N*] *filename*. Here is how we would write the script with this syntax:

```
if [[ $1 = -+([0-9]) ]]; then
    howmany=$1
    shift
elif [[ $1 = -* ]]; then
    print 'usage: highest [-N] filename'
    return 1
else
    howmany="-10"
fi

filename=$1
sort -nr $filename | head -$howmany
```

In this code, the option is considered to be supplied if **$1** matches the pattern -+([0-9]). This uses one of the Korn shell's regular expression operators, which we saw in Chapter 4. Notice that we didn't surround the pattern with quotes (even double quotes); if we did, the shell would interpret it literally, not as a pattern. This pattern means "A dash followed by one or more digits." If **$1** matches, then we assign it to the variable **howmany**.

If **$1** doesn't match, we test to see if it's an option at all, i.e., if it matches the pattern -*. If it does, then it's invalid; we print an error message and exit with error status. If we reach the final (**else**) case, we assume that **$1** is a filename and treat it as such in the ensuing code. The rest of the script processes the data as before.

We can extend what we have learned so far to a general technique for handling multiple options. For the sake of concreteness, assume that our script is called *bob* and we want to handle the options −**a**, −**b**, and −**c**:

```
while [[ $1 = -* ]]; do
    case $1 in
      -a ) process option -a ;;
      -b ) process option -b ;;
      -c ) process option -c ;;
      *  ) print 'usage: bob [-a] [-b] [-c] args...'
           return 1
    esac
    shift
done

normal processing of arguments...
```

This code checks **$1** repeatedly as long as it starts with a dash (−). Then the **case** construct runs the appropriate code depending on which option **$1** is. If the option is invalid—i.e., if it starts with a dash but isn't −**a**, −**b**, or −**c**—then the script prints a usage message and returns with an error exit status. After each option is processed, the arguments are shifted over. The result is that the positional parameters are set to the actual arguments when the **while** loop finishes.

Notice that this code is capable of handling options of arbitrary length, not just one letter (e.g., −**fred** instead of −**a**).

Options with Arguments

We need to add one more ingredient to make option processing really useful. Recall that many commands have options that take their *own* arguments. For example, the *cut* command, on which we relied heavily in Chapter 4, accepts the option −**d** with an argument that determines the field delimiter (if it is not the default TAB). To handle this type of option, we just use another **shift** when we are processing the option.

Assume that, in our *bob* script, the option −**b** requires its own argument. Here is the modified code that will process it:

```
while [[ $1 = -* ]]; do
    case $1 in
      -a ) process option -a ;;
      -b ) process option -b
           $2 is the option's argument
           shift ;;
      -c ) process option -c ;;
```

```
     *  ) print 'usage: bob [-a] [-b barg] [-c] args...'
        return 1
   esac
   shift
done
```

normal processing of arguments...

getopts

So far, we have a complete, though still constrained, way of handling command-line options. The above code does not allow a user to combine arguments with a single dash, e.g., **–abc** instead of **–a –b –c**. It also doesn't allow one to specify arguments to options without a space in between, e.g., **–barg** in addition to **–b arg**.*

The shell provides a built-in way to deal with multiple complex options without these constraints. The built-in command **getopts**† can be used as the condition of the **while** in an option-processing loop. Given a specification of which options are valid and which require their own arguments, it sets up the body of the loop to process each option in turn.

getopts takes two arguments. The first is a string that can contain letters and colons. Each letter is a valid option; if a letter is followed by a colon, the option requires an argument. **getopts** picks options off the command line and assigns each one (without the leading dash) to a variable whose name is **getopts'** second argument. As long as there are options left to process, **getopts** will return exit status 0; when the options are exhausted, it returns exit status 1, causing the **while** loop to exit.

getopts does a few other things that make option processing easier; we'll encounter them as we examine how to use **getopts** in the preceding example:

```
while getopts ":ab:c" opt; do
    case $opt in
      a  ) process option -a ;;
      b  ) process option -b
           $OPTARG is the option's argument ;;
      c  ) process option -c ;;
```

---

*Although most UNIX commands allow this, it is actually contrary to the Command Syntax Standard Rules in *intro*(1) of the *User's Manual*.

†**getopts** replaces the external command *getopt(1)*, used in Bourne shell programming; **getopts** is better integrated into the shell's syntax and runs more efficiently. C programmers will recognize **getopts** as very similar to the standard library routine *getopt(3)*.

```
      \? ) ) print 'usage: bob [-a] [-b barg] [-c] args...'
            return 1
      esac
done
shift $(($OPTIND - 1))
```

normal processing of arguments...

The call to **getopts** in the **while** condition sets up the loop to accept the options -a, -b, and -c, and specifies that -b takes an argument. (We will explain the : that starts the option string in a moment.) Each time the loop body is executed, it will have the latest option available, without a dash (-), in the variable **opt**.

If the user types an invalid option, **getopts** normally prints an unfortunate error message (of the form **cmd: getopts: o bad option(s)**) and sets **opt** to ?. However—now here's an obscure kludge—if you begin the option letter string with a colon, **getopts** won't print the message.* We recommend that you specify the colon and provide your own error message in a case that handles ?, as above.

We have modified the code in the **case** construct to reflect what **getopts** does. But notice that there are no more **shift** statements inside the **while** loop: **getopts** does not rely on **shift**s to keep track of where it is. It is unnecessary to shift arguments over until **getopts** is finished, i.e., until the **while** loop exits.

If an option has an argument, **getopts** stores it in the variable **OPTARG**, which can be used in the code that processes the option.

The one **shift** statement left is after the **while** loop. **getopts** stores in the variable **OPTIND** the number of the next argument to be processed; in this case, that's the number of the first (non-option) command-line argument. For example, if the command line were **bob -ab pete**, then **$OPTIND** would be "2". If it were **bob -a -b pete**, then **$OPTIND** would be "3".

The expression **$(($OPTIND - 1))** is an arithmetic expression (as we'll see later in this chapter) equal to **$OPTIND** minus 1. This value is used as the argument to **shift**. The result is that the correct number of arguments are shifted out of the way, leaving the "real" arguments as **$1**, **$2**, etc.

---

*Evidently this was deemed necessary because you can't redirect **getopts**' standard error output to */dev/null*; the result is (usually) a core dump.

Before we continue, now is a good time to summarize everything that **getopts** does:

1. Its first argument is a string containing all valid option letters. If an option requires an argument, a colon follows its letter in the string. An initial colon causes **getopts** not to print an error message when the user gives an invalid option.

2. Its second argument is the name of a variable that will hold each option letter (without any leading dash) as it is processed.

3. If an option takes an argument, the argument is stored in the variable **OPTARG**.

4. The variable **OPTIND** contains a number equal to the next command-line argument to be processed. After **getopts** is done, it equals the number of the first "real" argument.

The advantages of **getopts** are that it minimizes extra code necessary to process options and fully supports the standard UNIX option syntax (as specified in *intro(1)* of the *User's Manual*).

As a more concrete example, let's return to our C compiler front end (Task 4-2). So far, we have given our script the ability to process C source files (ending in *.c*), assembly code files (*.s*), and object code files (*.o*). Here is the latest version of the script:

```
objfiles=""
for filename in "$@"; do
    case $filename in
        *.c )
            objname=${filename%.c}.o
            compile $filename $objname ;;
        *.s )
            objname=${filename%.s}.o
            assemble $filename $objname ;;
        *.o )
            objname=$filename ;;
        *   )
            print "error: $filename is not a source or object file."
            return 1 ;;
    esac
    objfiles="$objfiles $objname"
done
ld $objfiles
```

Now we can give the script the ability to handle options. To know what options we'll need, we'll have to discuss further what compilers do.

More About C Compilers

The C compiler on a typical modern UNIX system (ANSI C on System V Release 4) has roughly 30 different command-line options, but we'll limit ourselves to the most widely-used ones.

Here's what we'll implement. All compilers provide the ability to eliminate the final linking step, i.e., the call to the linker *ld*. This is useful for compiling C code into object code files that will be linked later, and for taking advantage of the compiler's error checking separately before trying to link. The –c option suppresses the link step, producing only the compiled object code files.

C compilers are also capable of including lots of extra information in an object code file that can be used by a debugger (though it is ignored by the linker and the running program). If you don't know what a debugger is, see Chapter 9, *Debugging Shell Programs*. The debugger needs lots of information about the original C code to be able to do its job; the option –g directs the compiler to include this information in its object-code output.

If you aren't already familiar with UNIX C compilers, you may have thought it strange when you saw in the last chapter that the linker puts its output (the executable program) in a file called *a.out*. This convention is a historical relic that no one has bothered to change. Although it's certainly possible to change the executable's name with the *mv* command, the C compiler provides the option –o *filename*, which uses *filename* instead of *a.out*.

Another option we will support here has to do with *libraries*. A library is a collection of object code, *some* of which is to be included in the executable at link time. (This is in contrast to a precompiled object code file, *all* of which is linked in.) Each library includes a large amount of object code that supports a certain type of interface or activity; typical UNIX systems have libraries for things like networking, math functions, and graphics.

Libraries are extremely useful as building blocks that help programmers write complex programs without having to "reinvent the wheel" every time. The C compiler option –l *name* tells the linker to include whatever code is necessary from the library *name** in the executable it builds. One particular library called *c* (the file *libc.a*) is always included. This is known as the C

---

*This is actually a file called *lib*name.*a* in a standard library directory such as */lib*.

runtime library; it contains code for C's standard input and output capability, among other things.

Finally, it is possible for a good C compiler to do certain things that make its output object code smaller and more efficient. Collectively, these things are called *optimization*. You can think of an *optimizer* as an extra step in the compilation process that looks back at the object-code output and changes it for the better. The option –O invokes the optimizer.

Table 6-1 summarizes the options we will build into our C compiler front end.

Table 6-1: Popular C Compiler Options

Option	Meaning
–c	Produce object code only; do not invoke the linker
–g	Include debugging information in object code files
–l *lib*	Include the library *lib* when linking
–o *exefile*	Produce the executable file *exefile* instead of the default *a.out*
–O	Invoke the optimizer

You should also bear in mind this information about the options:

- The options –o and –l *lib* are merely passed on to the linker (*ld*), which processes them on its own.

- The –l *lib* option can be used multiple times to link in multiple libraries.

- The –g option is passed to the *ccom* command (the program that does the actual C compilation).

- We will assume that the optimizer is a separate program called *optimize* that accepts an object file as argument and optimizes it "in place," i.e., without producing a separate output file.

Here is the code for the script *occ* that includes option processing:

```
# initialize option-related variables
do_link=true
debug=""
link_libs="-l c"
exefile=""
opt=false

# process command-line options
while getopts ":cgl:o:O" opt; do
    case $opt in
        c )    do_link=false ;;
```

```
        g )     debug="-g" ;;
        l )     link_libs="$link_libs -l $OPTARG" ;;
        o )     exefile="-o $OPTARG" ;;
        O )     opt=true ;;
        \? )     print 'usage: occ [-cgO] [-l lib] [-o file] files...'
                return 1 ;;
    esac
done
shift $(($OPTIND - 1))

# process the input files
objfiles=""
for filename in "$@"; do
    case $filename in
        *.c )
            objname=${filename%.c}.o
            ccom $debug $filename $objname
            if [[ $opt = true ]]; then
                optimize $objname
            fi ;;
        *.s )
            objname=${filename%.s}.o
            as $filename $objname ;;
        *.o )
            objname=$filename ;;
        *    )
            print "error: $filename is not a source or object file."
            return 1 ;;
    esac
    objfiles="$objfiles $objname"
done

if [[ $do_link = true ]]; then
    ld $exefile $link_libs $objfiles
fi
```

Let's examine the option-processing part of this code. The first several lines initialize variables that we will use later to store the status of each of the options. We use "true" and "false" for truth values for readability; they are just strings and otherwise have no special meaning. The initializations reflect these assumptions:

1. We will want to link.

2. We will not want the compiler to generate space-consuming debugger information.

3. The only object-code library we will need is *c*, the standard C runtime library that is automatically linked in.

4. The executable file that the linker creates will be the linker's default file, *a.out.*

5. We will not want to invoke the optimizer.

The **while**, **getopts**, and **case** constructs process the options in the same way as the previous example. Here is what the code that handles each option does:

- If the **–c** option is given, the **do_link** flag is set to "false," which will cause the **if** condition at the end of the script to be false, meaning that the linker will not run.

- If **–g** is given, the **debug** variable is set to "–g". This is passed on the command line to the compiler.

- Each **–l** *lib* that is given is appended to the variable **link_libs**, so that when the **while** loop exits, **$link_libs** is the entire string of –l options. This string is passed to the linker.

- If **–o** *file* is given, the **exefile** variable is set to "-o *file*". This string is passed to the linker.

- If **–O** is specified, the **opt** flag will be set. This specification causes the conditional **if [[$opt = true]]** to be true, which means that the optimizer will run.

The remainder of the code is a modification of the **for** loop we have already seen; the modifications are direct results of the above option processing and should be self-explanatory.

Integer Variables and Arithmetic

The expression **$(($OPTIND – 1))** in the last example gives a clue as to how the shell can do integer arithmetic. As you might guess, the shell interprets words surrounded by **$((** and **))** as arithmetic expressions. Variables in arithmetic expressions do *not* need to be preceded by dollar signs, though it is not wrong to do so.

Arithmetic expressions are evaluated inside double quotes, like tildes, variables, and command substitutions. We're *finally* in a position to state the definitive rule about quoting strings: When in doubt, enclose a string in single quotes, unless it contains tildes or any expression involving a dollar sign, in which case you should use double quotes.

For example, the *date*(1) command on System V-derived versions of UNIX accepts arguments that tell it how to format its output. The argument **+%j** tells it to print the day of the year, i.e., the number of days since December 31st of the previous year.

We can use **+%j** to print a little holiday anticipation message:

```
print "Only $(( (365-$(date +%j)) / 7 )) weeks until the New Year!"
```

We'll show where this fits in the overall scheme of command-line processing in Chapter 7, *Input/Output and Command-line Processing*.

The arithmetic expression feature is built in to the Korn shell's syntax, and was available in the Bourne shell (most versions) only through the external command *expr*(1). Thus it is yet another example of a desirable feature provided by an external command (i.e., a syntactic kludge) being better integrated into the shell. [[/]] and **getopts** are also examples of this design trend.

Korn shell arithmetic expressions are equivalent to their counterparts in the C language.* Precedence and associativity are the same as in C. Table 6-2 shows the arithmetic operators that are supported. Although some of these are (or contain) special characters, there is no need to backslash-escape them, because they are within the **$((...))** syntax.

Table 6-2: Arithmetic Operators

Operator	Meaning
+	Plus
−	Minus
*	Times
/	Division (with truncation)
%	Remainder
<<	Bit-shift left
>>	Bit-shift right
&	Bitwise and
|	Bitwise or
~	Bitwise not
^	Bitwise exclusive or

Parentheses can be used to group subexpressions. The arithmetic expression syntax also (like C) supports relational operators as "truth values" of 1

---

*The assignment forms of these operators are also permitted. For example, **$((x += 2))** adds 2 to **x** and stores the result back in **x**.

for true and 0 for false. Table 6-3 shows the relational operators and the logical operators that can be used to combine relational expressions.

Table 6-3: Relational Operators

Operator	Meaning
<	Less than
>	Greater than
<=	Less than or equal
>=	Greater than or equal
==	Equal
!=	Not equal
&&	Logical and
||	Logical or

For example, $((3 > 2))$ has the value 1; $(((3 > 2) || (4 <= 1)))$ also has the value 1, since at least one of the two subexpressions is true.

The shell also supports base N numbers, where N can be up to 36. The notation $B\#N$ means "N base B". Of course, if you omit the $B\#$, the base defaults to 10.

Arithmetic Conditionals

Another construct, closely related to $((\ldots))$, is $((\ldots))$ (without the leading dollar sign). We use this for evaluating arithmetic condition tests, just as [[...]] is used for string, file attribute, and other types of tests.

$((\ldots))$ evaluates relational operators differently from $((\ldots))$ so that you can use it in **if** and **while** constructs. Instead of producing a textual result, it just sets its exit status according to the truth of the expression: 0 if true, 1 otherwise. So, for example, $((3 > 2))$ produces exit status 0, as does $(((3 > 2) || (4 <= 1)))$, but $(((3 > 2) \&\& (4 <= 1)))$ has exit status 1 since the second subexpression isn't true.

You can also use numerical values for truth values within this construct. It's like the analogous concept in C, which means that it's somewhat counterintuitive to non-C programmers: a value of 0 means *false* (i.e., returns exit status 1), and a non-0 value means *true* (returns exit status 0), e.g., $((14))$ is true. See the code for the *kshdb* debugger in Chapter 9, *Debugging Shell Programs*, for two more examples of this.

Arithmetic Variables and Assignment

The ((...)) construct can also be used to define integer variables and assign values to them. The statement:

```
(( intvar=expression ))
```

creates the integer variable *intvar* (if it doesn't already exist) and assigns to it the result of *expression*.

That syntax isn't intuitive, so the shell provides a better equivalent: the built-in command **let**. The syntax is:

```
let intvar=expression
```

It is not necessary (because it's actually redundant) to surround the expression with $((and)) in a **let** statement. As with any variable assignment, there must not be any space on either side of the equal sign (=). It is good practice to surround expressions with quotes, since many characters are treated as special by the shell (e.g., *, #, and parentheses); furthermore, you must quote expressions that include whitespace (spaces or TABs). See Table 6-4 for examples.

Table 6-4: Sample Integer Expression Assignments

Assignment let x=	Value $x
1+4	5
'1 + 4'	5
'(2+3) * 5'	25
'2 + 3 * 5'	17
'17 / 3'	5
'17 % 3'	2
'1<<4'	16
'48>>3'	6
'17 & 3'	1
'17	3'	19
'17 ^ 3'	18

Here is a small task that makes use of integer arithmetic.

Task 6-1

> Write a script called *pages* that, given the name of a text file, tells how many pages of output it contains. Assume that there are 66 lines to a page but provide an option allowing the user to override that.

We'll make our option –*N*, a la *head*. The syntax for this single option is so simple that we need not bother with **getopts**. Here is the code:

```
if [[ $1 = -+([0-9]) ]]; then
    let page_lines=${1#-}
    shift
else
    let page_lines=66
fi
let file_lines="$(wc -l < $1)"

let pages=file_lines/page_lines
if (( file_lines % page_lines > 0 )); then
    let pages=pages+1
fi

print "$1 has $pages pages of text."
```

Notice that we use the integer conditional ((**file_lines % page_lines > 0**)) rather than the [[. . .]] form.

At the heart of this code is the UNIX utility *wc(1)*, which counts the number of lines, words, and characters (bytes) in its input. By default, its output looks something like this:

```
    8      34    161  bob
```

wc's output means that the file *bob* has 8 lines, 34 words, and 161 characters. *wc* recognizes the options –l, –w, and –c, which tell it to print only the number of lines, words, or characters, respectively.

wc normally prints the name of its input file (given as argument). Since we want only the number of lines, we have to do two things. First, we give it input from file redirection instead, as in **wc -l < bob** instead of **wc -l bob**. This produces the number of lines preceded by a single space (which would normally separate the filename from the number).

Unfortunately, that space complicates matters: the statement **let file_lines=$(wc -l < $1)** becomes "let file_lines= *N*" after command substitution; the space after the equal sign is an error. That leads to the second modification, the quotes around the command substitution expression. The statement **let file_lines=**" *N*" is perfectly legal, and **let** knows how to remove the leading space.

The first **if** clause in the *pages* script checks for an option and, if it was given, strips the dash (–) off and assigns it to the variable **page_lines**. *wc* in the command substitution expression returns the number of lines in the file whose name is given as argument.

The next group of lines calculates the number of pages and, if there is a remainder after the division, adds 1. Finally, the appropriate message is printed.

As a bigger example of integer arithmetic, we will complete our emulation of the C shell's *pushd* and *popd* functions (Task 4-8). Remember that these functions operate on **DIRSTACK**, a stack of directories represented as a string with the directory names separated by spaces. The C shell's *pushd* and *popd* take additional types of arguments, which are:

- **pushd +n** takes the *n*th directory in the stack (starting with 0), rotates it to the top, and **cd**s to it.
- **pushd** without arguments, instead of complaining, swaps the two top directories on the stack and **cd**s to the new top.
- **popd +n** takes the *n*th directory in the stack and just deletes it.

The most useful of these features is the ability to get at the *n*th directory in the stack. Here are the latest versions of both functions:

```
function pushd { # push current directory onto stack
    dirname=$1
    if [[ -d $dirname && -x $dirname ]]; then
        cd $dirname
        DIRSTACK="$dirname ${DIRSTACK:-$PWD}"
        print "$DIRSTACK"
    else
        print "still in $PWD."
    fi
}

function popd {  # pop directory off the stack, cd to new top
    if [[ -n $DIRSTACK ]]; then
        DIRSTACK=${DIRSTACK#* }
        cd ${DIRSTACK%% *}
        print "$PWD"
    else
        print "stack empty, still in $PWD."
    fi
}
```

To get at the *n*th directory, we use a **while** loop that transfers the top directory to a temporary copy of the stack *n* times. We'll put the loop into a function called *getNdirs* that looks like this:

```
function getNdirs{
    stackfront=''
    let count=0
    while (( count < $1 )); do
        stackfront="$stackfront ${DIRSTACK%% *}"
        DIRSTACK=${DIRSTACK#* }
        let count=count+1
    done
}
```

The argument passed to *getNdirs* is the *n* in question. The variable **stackfront** is the temporary copy that will contain the first *n* directories when the loop is done. **stackfront** starts as null; **count**, which counts the number of loop iterations, starts as 0.

The first line of the loop body appends the top of the stack (**${DIRSTACK%% *}**) to **stackfront**; the second line deletes the top from the stack. The last line increments the counter for the next iteration. The entire loop executes *N* times, for values of **count** from 0 to *N*-1.

When the loop finishes, the last directory in **$stackfront** is the *N*th directory. The expression **${stackfront##* }** extracts this directory. Furthermore, **DIRSTACK** now contains the "back" of the stack, i.e., the stack *without* the first *n* directories. With this in mind, we can now write the code for the improved versions of *pushd* and *popd*:

```
function pushd {
  if [[ $1 = ++([0-9]) ]]; then
        # case of pushd +n: rotate n-th directory to top
        let num=${1#+}
        getNdirs $num

        newtop=${stackfront##* }
        stackfront=${stackfront%$newtop}

        DIRSTACK="$newtop $stackfront $DIRSTACK"
        cd $newtop

  elif [[ -z $1 ]]; then
        # case of pushd without args; swap top two directories
        firstdir=${DIRSTACK%% *}
        DIRSTACK=${DIRSTACK#* }
        seconddir=${DIRSTACK%% *}
        DIRSTACK=${DIRSTACK#* }
```

```
                DIRSTACK="$seconddir $firstdir $DIRSTACK"
                cd $seconddir

        else
            cd $dirname
            # normal case of pushd dirname
            dirname=$1
            if [[ -d $dirname && -x $dirname ]]; then
                DIRSTACK="$dirname ${DIRSTACK:-$PWD}"
                print "$DIRSTACK"
            else
                print still in "$PWD."
            fi
        fi
}


function popd {      # pop directory off the stack, cd to new top
    if [[ $1 = ++([0-9]) ]]; then
            # case of popd +n: delete n-th directory from stack
            let num=${1#+}
            getNdirs $num

            stackfront=${stackfront% *}
            DIRSTACK="$stackfront $DIRSTACK"

    else
        # normal case of popd without argument
        if [[ -n $DIRSTACK ]]; then
            DIRSTACK=${DIRSTACK#* }
            cd ${DIRSTACK%% *}
            print "$PWD"
        else
            print "stack empty, still in $PWD."
        fi
    fi
}
```

These functions have grown rather large; let's look at them in turn. The **if** at the beginning of *pushd* checks if the first argument is an option of the form +*N*. If so, the first body of code is run. The first **let** simply strips the plus sign (+) from the argument and assigns the result—as an integer—to the variable **num**. This, in turn, is passed to the *getNdirs* function.

The next two assignment statements set **newtop** to the *N*th directory—i.e., the last directory in **$stackfront**—and delete that directory from **stackfront**. The final two lines in this part of *pushd* put the stack back together again in the appropriate order and **cd** to the new top directory.

The **elif** clause tests for no argument, in which case *pushd* should swap the top two directories on the stack. The first four lines of this clause assign the top two directories to **firstdir** and **seconddir**, and delete these from the stack. Then, as above, the code puts the stack back together in the new order and **cd**s to the new top directory.

The **else** clause corresponds to the usual case, where the user supplies a directory name as argument.

popd works similarly. The **if** clause checks for the +*N* option, which in this case means delete the *N*th directory. A **let** extracts the *N* as an integer; the *getNdirs* function puts the first *n* directories into **stackfront**. Then the line **stackfront=${stackfront% *}** deletes the last directory (the *N*th directory) from **stackfront**. Finally, the stack is put back together with the *N*th directory missing.

The **else** clause covers the usual case, where the user doesn't supply an argument.

Before we leave this subject, here are a few exercises that should test your understanding of this code:

1. Add code to *pushd* that exits with an error message if the user supplies no argument and the stack contains fewer than two directories.

2. Verify that when the user specifies +*N* and *N* exceeds the number of directories in the stack, both *pushd* and *popd* use the last directory as the *N*th directory.

3. Modify the *getNdirs* function so that it checks for the above condition and exits with an appropriate error message if true.

4. Change *getNdirs* so that it uses *cut* (with command substitution), instead of the **while** loop, to extract the first *N* directories. This uses less code but runs more slowly because of the extra processes generated.

Arrays

So far we have seen two types of variables: character strings and integers. The third type of variable the Korn shell supports is an *array*. As you may know, an array is like a list of things; you can refer to specific elements in an array with integer *indices*, so that *a[i]* refers to the *i*th element of array *a*.

The Korn shell provides an array facility that, while useful, is much more limited than analogous features in conventional programming languages. In particular, arrays can be only one-dimensional (i.e., no arrays of arrays), and they are limited to 1024 elements. Indices can start at 0.

There are two ways to assign values to elements of an array. The first is the most intuitive: you can use the standard shell variable assignment syntax with the array index in brackets ([]). For example:

```
nicknames[2]=bob
nicknames[3]=ed
```

puts the values **bob** and **ed** into the elements of the array **nicknames** with indices 2 and 3, respectively. As with regular shell variables, values assigned to array elements are treated as character strings unless the assignment is preceded by **let**.

The second way to assign values to an array is with a variant of the **set** statement, which we saw in Chapter 3, *Customizing Your Environment*. The statement:

```
set -A aname val1 val2 val3 ...
```

creates the array *aname* (if it doesn't already exist) and assigns *val1* to *aname[0]*, *val2* to *aname[1]*, etc. As you would guess, this is more convenient for loading up an array with an initial set of values.

To extract a value from an array, use the syntax ${*aname*[*i*]}. For example, ${**nicknames**[2]} has the value "bob". The index *i* can be an arithmetic expression—see above. If you use * in place of the index, the value will be all elements, separated by spaces. Omitting the index is the same as specifying index 0.

Now we come to the somewhat unusual aspect of Korn shell arrays. Assume that the only values assigned to **nicknames** are the two we saw above. If you type **print "${nicknames[*]}"**, you will see the output:

```
bob ed
```

In other words, **nicknames[0]** and **nicknames[1]** don't exist. Furthermore, if you were to type:

```
nicknames[9]=pete
nicknames[31]=ralph
```

and then type **print "${nicknames[*]}"**, the output would look like this:

```
bob ed pete ralph
```

This is why we said "the elements of **nicknames** with indices 2 and 3" earlier, instead of "the 2nd and 3rd elements of **nicknames**". Any array elements with unassigned values just don't exist; if you try to access their values, you will get null strings.

You can preserve whatever whitespace you put in your array elements by using "${*aname*[@]}" (with the double quotes) instead of ${*aname*[*]}, just as you can with "$@" instead of $*.

The shell provides an operator that tells you how many elements an array has defined: ${#*aname*[*]}. Thus ${#nicknames[*]} has the value 4. Note that you need the [*] because the name of the array alone is interpreted as the 0th element. This means, for example, that ${#nicknames} equals the length of **nicknames**[0] (see Chapter 4, *Basic Shell Programming*). Since **nicknames**[0] doesn't exist, the value of ${#nicknames} is 0, the length of the null string.

To be quite frank, we feel that the Korn shell's array facility is of little use to shell programmers. This is partially because it is so limited, but mainly because shell programming tasks are much more often oriented toward character strings and text than toward numbers. If you think of an array as a mapping from integers to values (i.e., put in a number, get out a value), then you can see why arrays are "number-dominated" data structures.

Nevertheless, we can find useful things to do with arrays. For example, here is a cleaner solution to Task 5-4, in which a user can select his or her terminal type (**TERM** environment variable) at login time. Recall that the "user-friendly" version of this code used **select** and a **case** statement:

```
print 'Select your terminal type:'
PS3='terminal? '
select term in
    'Givalt GL35a' \
    'Tsoris T-2000' \
    'Shande 531' \
    'Vey VT99'
do
    case $REPLY in
        1 ) TERM=gl35a ;;
        2 ) TERM=t2000 ;;
        3 ) TERM=s531 ;;
        4 ) TERM=vt99 ;;
        * ) print "invalid." ;;
    esac
    if [[ -n $term ]]; then
        print "TERM is $TERM"
        break
    fi
done
```

We can eliminate the entire **case** construct by taking advantage of the fact that the **select** construct stores the user's number choice in the variable **REPLY**. We just need a line of code that stores all of the possibilities for

TERM in an array, in an order that corresponds to the items in the **select** menu. Then we can use **$REPLY** to index the array. The resulting code is:

```
set -A termnames gl35a t2000 s531 vt99
print 'Select your terminal type:'
PS3='terminal? '
select term in
    'Givalt GL35a' \
    'Tsoris T-2000' \
    'Shande 531' \
    'Vey VT99'
do
    if [[ -n $term ]]; then
        TERM=${termnames[REPLY-1]}
        print "TERM is $TERM"
        break
    fi
done
```

This code sets up the array **termnames** so that **${termnames[0]}** is "gl35a", **${termnames[1]}** is "t2000", etc. The line **TERM=${termnames[REPLY-1]}** essentially replaces the entire **case** construct by using **REPLY** to index the array.

Notice that the shell knows to interpret the text in an array index as an arithmetic expression, as if it were enclosed in ((and)), which in turn means that variable need not be preceded by a dollar sign ($). We have to subtract 1 from the value of **REPLY** because array indices start at 0, while **select** menu item numbers start at 1.

typeset

The final Korn shell feature that relates to the kinds of values that variables can hold is the **typeset** command. If you are a programmer, you might guess that **typeset** is used to specify the *type* of a variable (integer, string, etc.); you'd be partially right.

typeset is a rather *ad hoc* collection of things that you can do to variables that restrict the kinds of values they can take. Operations are specified by options to **typeset**; the basic syntax is:

```
typeset -o varname[=value]
```

Options can be combined; multiple *varnames* can be used. If you leave out *varname*, the shell prints a list of variables for which the given option is turned on.

The options available break down into two basic categories:

1. String formatting operations, such as right- and left-justification, truncation, and letter case control.

2. Type and attribute functions that are of primary interest to advanced programmers.

Local Variables in Functions

typeset without options has an important meaning: if a **typeset** statement is inside a function definition, then the variables involved all become *local* to that function (in addition to any properties they may take on as a result of **typeset** options). The ability to define variables that are local to "subprogram" units (procedures, functions, subroutines, etc.) is necessary for writing large programs, because it helps keep subprograms independent of the main program and of each other.

If you just want to declare a variable local to a function, use **typeset** without any options. For example:

```
function afunc {
    typeset diffvar
    samevar=funcvalue
    diffvar=funcvalue
    print "samevar is $samevar"
    print "diffvar is $diffvar"
}

samevar=globvalue
diffvar=globvalue
print "samevar is $samevar"
print "diffvar is $diffvar"
afunc
print "samevar is $samevar"
print "diffvar is $diffvar"
```

This code will print the following:

```
samevar is globvalue
diffvar is globvalue
samevar is funcvalue
diffvar is funcvalue
samevar is funcvalue
diffvar is globvalue
```

Figure 6-1 shows this graphically.

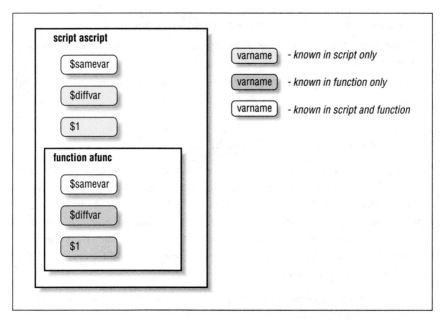

Figure 6-1: Local variables in functions

You will see several additional examples of local variables within functions in Chapter 9, *Debugging Shell Programs.*

String Formatting Options

Now let's look at the various options to **typeset**. Table 6-5 lists the string formatting options; the first three take an optional numeric argument.

Table 6-5: Typeset String Formatting Options

Option	Operation
-Ln	Left-justify. Remove leading blanks; if n is given, fill with blanks or truncate on right to length n.
-Rn	Right-justify. Remove trailing blanks; if n is given, fill with blanks or truncate on left to length n.
-Zn	Same as above, except add leading 0's instead of blanks if needed.
-l	Convert letters to lowercase.
-u	Convert letters to uppercase.

Here are a few simple examples. Assume that the variable **alpha** is assigned the letters of the alphabet, in alternating case, surrounded by three blanks on each side:

```
alpha="   aBcDeFgHiJkLmNoPqRsTuVwXyZ   "
```

Table 6-6 shows some **typeset** statements and their resulting values (assuming that each of the statements are run "independently").

Table 6-6: Examples of typeset String Formatting Options

Statement	Value of v
typeset –L v=$alpha	`"aBcDeFgHiJkLmNoPqRsTuVwXyZ   "`
typeset –L10 v=$alpha	`"aBcDeFgHiJ"`
typeset –R v=$alpha	`"   aBcDeFgHiJkLmNoPqRsTuVwXyZ"`
typeset –R16 v=$alpha	`"kLmNoPqRsTuVwXyZ"`
typeset –l v=$alpha	`"   abcdefghijklmnopqrstuvwxyz   "`
typeset –uR5 v=$alpha	`"VWXYZ"`
typeset –Z8 v="123.50"	`"00123.50"`

When you run **typeset** on an existing variable, its effect is *cumulative* with whatever **typeset**s may have been used previously. This has the obvious exceptions:

- A **typeset –u** undoes a **typeset –l**, and vice versa.
- A **typeset –R** undoes a **typeset –L**, and vice versa.
- **typeset –Z** has no effect if **typeset –L** has been used.

You can turn off **typeset** options explicitly by typing **typeset +o**, where *o* is the option you turned on before. Of course, it is hard to imagine scenarios where you would want to turn multiple **typeset** formatting options on and off over and over again; you usually set a **typeset** option on a given variable only once.

An obvious application for the **–L** and **–R** options is one in which you need fixed-width output. The most ubiquitous source of fixed-width output in the UNIX system is reflected in the following programming task.

Task 6-2

Pretend that *ls* doesn't do multicolumn output; write a shell script that does it.

For the sake of simplicity, we'll assume further that our version of UNIX is derived from AT&T System V, in which filenames are (*still!*) limited to 14 characters.

Our solution to this task relies on many of the concepts we have seen earlier in this chapter. It also relies on the fact that **set -A** (for constructing arrays) can be combined with command substitution in an interesting way: each word (separated by blanks, TABs, or NEWLINESs) becomes an element of the array. For example, if the file *bob* contains 50 words, then after the statement:

```
set -A fred $(< bob)
```

the array **fred** has 50 elements.

Our strategy is to get the names of all files in the given directory into an array variable. We use a **while** loop that mimics a **for** loop, as we saw earlier in this chapter, to get each filename into a variable whose length has been set to 14. We print that variable in five-column format, with two spaces between each column (for a total of 80 columns), using a counter to keep track of columns. Here is the code:

```
set -A filenames $(ls $1)
typeset -L14 fname
let count=0
let numcols=5

while (( $count < ${#filenames[*]} )); do
    fname=${filenames[count]}
    print -n "$fname  "
    let count="count + 1"
    if (( count % numcols == 0 )); then
        print            # NEWLINE
    fi
done

if (( count % numcols != 0 )); then
    print
fi
```

The first line sets up the array **filenames** to contain all files in the directory given by the first argument (the current directory by default). The **typeset** statement sets up the variable **fname** to have a fixed width of 14 characters.

The next line initializes a counter that counts elements in the array. **numcols** is the number of columns per line.

The **while** loop iterates once for every element in **filenames**. In the body of the loop, the first line assigns the next array element to the fixed-width variable. The **print** statement prints the latter followed by two spaces; the **-n** option suppresses **print**'s final NEWLINE.

The **let** statements increments the counter. Then there is the **if** statement, which determines when to start the next line. It checks the *remainder* of **$count** divided by **$numcols**—remember that dollar signs aren't necessary within a $((...)) construct—and if the result is 0, it's time to output a NEWLINE via a **print** statement without arguments. Notice that even though **$count** increases by 1 with every iteration of the loop, the remainder goes through a cycle of 1, 2, 3, 4, 0, 1, 2, 3, 4, 0, ...

After the loop, an **if** construct outputs a final NEWLINE if necessary, i.e., if the **if** within the loop didn't just do it.

We can also use **typeset** options to clean up the code for our *dosmv* function (Task 5-3), which translates filenames in a given directory from MS-DOS to UNIX format. The code for the function is:

```
dos_regexp='[^a-z]\{1,8\}\.[^a-z]\{0,3\}'
for filename in ${1:+$1/}* ; do
    if print "$filename" | grep $dos_regexp > /dev/null; then
        newfilename=$(print $filename | tr [A-Z] [a-z])
        newfilename=${newfilename%.}
        print "$filename -> $newfilename"
        mv $filename $newfilename
    fi
done
```

We can replace the call to *tr* in the **for** loop with one to **typeset -l** before the loop:

```
typeset -l newfilename
dos_regexp='[^a-z]\{1,8\}\.[^a-z]\{0,3\}'
for filename in ${1:+$1/}* ; do
    if print "$filename" | grep $dos_regexp > /dev/null; then
        newfilename=${filename%.}
        print "$filename -> $newfilename"
        mv $filename $newfilename
    fi
done
```

This way, the translation to lowercase letters is done automatically each time a value is assigned to **newfilename**. Not only is this code cleaner, but it is also more efficient because the extra processes created by *tr* and command substitution are eliminated.

Type and Attribute Options

The other options to **typeset** are of more use to advanced shell programmers who are "tweaking" large scripts. These options are listed in Table 6-7.

Table 6-7: Typeset Type and Attribute Options

Option	Operation
-i*n*	Represent the variable internally as an integer; improves efficiency of arithmetic. If *n* is given, it is the base used for output.
-r	Make the variable read-only: forbid assignment to it and disallow it from being **unset**.*
-x	Export; same as **export** command.
-f	Refer to function names only; see "Function Options" below.

* The built-in command **readonly** does the same thing.

–i is the most useful of these. You can put it in a script when you are done writing and debugging it to make arithmetic run a bit faster, though the speedup will be apparent only if your script does a *lot* of arithmetic. The more readable **integer** is a built-in alias for **typeset –i**, so that **integer x=5** is the same as **typeset –i x=5**.

The –r option is useful for setting up "constants" in shell scripts; constants are like variables except that you can't change their values once they have been initialized. Constants allow you to give names to values even if you don't want them changed; it is considered good programming practice to use constants in large programs.

The solution to Task 6-2 contains a good candidate for **typeset –r**: the variable **numcols**, which specifies the number of columns in the output. Since **numcols** is an integer, we could also use the –i option, i.e., replace **let numcols=5** with **typeset –ri numcols=5**. If we were to try assigning another value to **numcols**, the shell would respond with the error message **ksh: numcols: is read only**.

–r is also useful for system administrators who set up shell variables in
/etc/profile, the system-wide Korn shell initialization file. For example, if
you wanted to tighten system security, one step you might take is to prevent the **PATH** environment variable from being changed. This helps prevent computer crackers from installing bogus executables. The statement
typeset –r PATH does the trick.

These options are also useful without arguments, i.e., to see which variables exist that have those options turned on.

Function Options

The **–f** option has various suboptions, all of which relate to functions.
These are listed in Table 6-8.

Table 6-8: Typeset Function Options

Option	Operation
–f	With no arguments, prints all function definitions.
–f *fname*	Prints the definition of function *fname*.
+f	Prints all function names.
–ft	Turns on trace mode for named function(s). (Chapter 9)
+ft	Turns off trace mode for named function(s). (Chapter 9)
–fu	Defines given name(s) as autoloaded function(s). (Chapter 4)

Two of these have built-in aliases that are more mnemonic: **functions** is an
alias for **typeset –f** and **autoload** is an alias for **typeset –fu**.

Finally, if you type **typeset** without *any* arguments, you will see a list of *all*
currently-defined variables (in no discernable order), preceded by appropriate keywords if they have one or more **typeset** options turned on. For
example, typing **typeset** in an uncustomized shell gives you a listing of the
shell's built-in variables and their attributes that looks like this:*

```
export HZ
export PATH
integer ERRNO
integer OPTIND
function LINENO
export LOGNAME
export MAIL
```

---

*For some reason, this list excludes **PS1** and a few others.

```
function SECONDS
integer PPID
PS3
PS2
export TERMCAP
OPTARG
function RANDOM
export SHELL
integer TMOUT
export HOME
export _
FCEDIT
export TERM
export PWD
export TZ
integer MAILCHECK
```

7

Input/Output and Command-line Processing

The past few chapters have gone into detail about various shell programming techniques, mostly focused on the flow of data and control through shell programs. In this chapter, we'll switch the focus to two related topics. The first is the shell's mechanisms for doing file-oriented input and output. We'll present information that expands on what you already know about the shell's basic I/O redirectors.

Second, we'll "zoom in" and talk about I/O at the line and word level. This is a fundamentally different topic, since it involves moving information between the domains of files/terminals and shell variables. **print** and command substitution are two ways of doing this that we've seen so far.

Our discussion of line and word I/O will lead into a more detailed explanation of how the shell processes command lines. This information is necessary so that you can understand exactly how the shell deals with *quotation*, and so that you can appreciate the power of an advanced command called **eval**, which we will cover at the end of the chapter.

I/O Redirectors

In Chapter 1, *Korn Shell Basics*, you learned about the shell's basic I/O redirectors, >, <, and |. Although these are enough to get you through 95% of your UNIX life, you should know that the Korn shell supports a total of 16 I/O redirectors. Table 7-1 lists them, including the three we've already seen. Although some of the rest are useful, others are mainly for systems programmers. We will wait until the next chapter to discuss the last three, which, along with >|, are not present in most Bourne shell versions.

Table 7-1: I/O Redirectors

Redirector	Function
> *file*	Direct standard output to *file*
< *file*	Take standard input from *file*
cmd1 | *cmd2*	Pipe; take standard output of *cmd1* as standard input to *cmd2*
>> *file*	Direct standard output to *file*; append to *file* if it already exists
>| *file*	Force standard output to *file* even if **noclobber** set
<> *file*	Use *file* as both standard input and standard output
<< *label*	Here-document; see text
n> *file*	Direct file descriptor *n* to *file*
n< *file*	Set *file* as file descriptor *n*
>&*n*	Duplicate standard output to file descriptor *n*
<&*n*	Duplicate standard input from file descriptor *n*
<&-	Close the standard input
>&-	Close the standard output
|&	Background process with I/O from parent shell
>&p	Direct background process' standard output to the parent shell's standard output
<&p	Direct parent shell's standard input to background process' standard input

Notice that some of the redirectors in Table 7-1 contain a digit *n*, and that their descriptions contain the term *file descriptor*; we'll cover that in a little while.

The first two new redirectors, >> and >|, are simple variations on the standard output redirector >. The >> appends to the output file (instead of overwriting it) if it already exists; otherwise it acts exactly like >. A common use of >> is for adding a line to an initialization file (such as *.profile* or *.mailrc*) when you don't want to bother with a text editor. For example:

```
cat >> .mailrc
alias fred frederick@longmachinename.longcompanyname.com
^D
```

As we saw in Chapter 1, *Korn Shell Basics*, *cat* without an argument uses standard input as its input. This allows you to type the input and end it with CTRL-D on its own line. The **alias** line will be appended to the file *.mailrc* if it already exists; if it doesn't, the file is created with that one line.

Recall from Chapter 3, *Customizing Your Environment*, that you can prevent the shell from overwriting a file with > *file* by typing **set –o noclobber**. **>|** overrides **noclobber**—it's the "Do it anyway, dammit!" redirector.

The redirector <> is mainly meant for use with device files (in the */dev* directory), i.e., files that correspond to hardware devices such as terminals and communication lines. Low-level systems programmers can use it to test device drivers; otherwise, it's not very useful. But if you use a windowing system like X, you can try the following to see how it works:

1. Create two terminal windows (e.g., *xterms*).

2. In one of them, type **who am i** to find out the name of the window's "pseudo-device." This will be the second word in the output.

3. In the other, type **cat <> /dev/***pty*, where *pty* is the name you found in the last step.

4. Back in the first window, type some characters. You will see them appear in *alternate* windows.

5. Type CTRL-C in both windows to end the process.

Here-documents

The **<<** *label* redirector essentially forces the input to a command to be the shell's standard input, which is read until there is a line that contains only *label*. The input in between is called a *here-document*. Here-documents aren't very interesting when used from the command prompt. In fact, it's the same as the normal use of standard input except for the label. We could have used a here-document in the previous example of >>, like this (EOF, for "end of file," is an often-used label):

```
cat >> .mailrc << EOF
alias fred frederick@longmachinename.longcompanyname.com
EOF
```

Here-documents are meant to be used from within shell scripts; they let you specify "batch" input to programs. A common use of here-documents is with simple text editors like *ed(1)*. Here is a programming task that uses a here-document in this way:

Task 7-1

The **s** *file* command in *mail(1)* saves the current message in *file*. If the message came over a network (such as the Internet), then it has several header lines prepended that give information about network routing. Write a shell script that deletes the header lines from the file.

We can use *ed* to delete the header lines. To do this, we need to know something about the syntax of mail messages; specifically, that there is always a blank line between the header lines and the message text. The *ed* command 1,/^[]*$/d does the trick: it means, "Delete from line 1 until the first blank line." We also need the *ed* commands **w** (write the changed file) and **q** (quit). Here is the code that solves the task:

```
ed $1 << EOF
1,/^[]*$/d
w
q
EOF
```

The shell does parameter (variable) substitution and command substitution on text in a here-document, meaning that you can use shell variables and commands to customize the text. Here is a simple task for system administrators that shows how this works:

Task 7-2

Write a script that sends a mail message to a set of users saying that a new version of a certain program has been installed in a certain directory.

You can get a list of all users on the system in various ways; perhaps the easiest is to use *cut* to extract the first field of */etc/passwd*, the file that contains all user account information.* Fields in this file are separated by colons (:).

Given such a list of users, the following code does the trick:

```
pgmname=$1
for user in $(cut -f1 -d: /etc/passwd); do
    mail $user << EOF
Dear $user,

A new version of $pgmname has been installed in $(whence pgmname).

Regards,

Your friendly neighborhood sysadmin.
EOF
done
```

---

*There are a few possible problems with this; for example, */etc/passwd* usually contains information on "accounts" that aren't associated with people, like **uucp**, **lp**, and **daemon**. We'll ignore such problems for the purpose of this example.

The shell will substitute the appropriate values for the name of the program and its directory.

The redirector << has two variations. First, you can prevent the shell from doing parameter and command substitution by surrounding the *label* in single or double quotes. In the above example, if you used the line **mail $user << 'EOF'**, then **$pgmname** and **$(whence pgmname)** would remain untouched.

The second variation is <<-, which deletes leading TABs (but not blanks) from the here-document and the label line. This allows you to indent the here-document's text, making the shell script more readable:

```
pgmname=$1
for user in $(cut -f1 -d: /etc/passwd); do
    mail $user <<- EOF
        Dear user,

        A new version of $pgmname has been installed in $(whence pgmname).

        Regards,

        Your friendly neighborhood sysadmin.
EOF
done
```

Of course, you need to choose your *label* so that it doesn't appear as an actual input line.

File Descriptors

The next few redirectors in Table 7-1 depend on the notion of a *file descriptor*. Like the device files used with <>, this is a low-level UNIX I/O concept that is of interest only to systems programmers—and then only occasionally. File descriptors are historical relics that really should be banished from the realm of shell use.* You can get by with a few basic facts about them; for the whole bloody story, look at the entries for *read()*, *write()*, *fcntl()*, and others in Section 2 of the UNIX manual.

File descriptors are integers starting at 0 that index an array of file information within a process. When a process starts, it usually has three file descriptors open. These correspond to the three *standards*: standard input (file descriptor 0), standard output (1), and standard error (2). If a process

---

*The C shell's set of redirectors contains no mention of file descriptors whatsoever.

opens UNIX files for input or output, they are assigned to the next available file descriptors, starting with 3.

By far the most common use of file descriptors with the Korn shell is in saving standard error in a file. For example, if you want to save the error messages from a long job in a file so that they don't scroll off the screen, append *2> file* to your command. If you also want to save standard output, append *> file1 2> file2*.

This leads to another programming task.

Task 7-3

> You want to start a long job in the background (so that your terminal is freed up) and save both standard output and standard error in a single log file. Write a script that does this.

We'll call this script *start*. The code is very terse:

```
"$@" > logfile 2>&1 &
```

This line executes whatever command and parameters follow **start**. (The command cannot contain pipes or output redirectors.) It sends the command's standard output to *logfile*.

Then, the redirector **2>&1** says, "send standard error (file descriptor 2) to the same place as standard output (file descriptor 1)." **2>&1** is actually a combination of two redirectors in Table 7-1: *n> file* and *>&n*. Since standard output is redirected to *logfile*, standard error will go there too. The final **&** puts the job in the background so that you get your shell prompt back.

As a small variation on this theme, we can send both standard output and standard error into a *pipe* instead of a file: *command 2>&1 | ...* does this. (Make sure you understand why.) Here is a script that sends both standard output and standard error to the logfile (as above) and to the terminal:

```
"$@" 2>&1 | tee logfile &
```

The command *tee*(1) takes its standard input and copies it to standard output *and* the file given as argument.

These scripts have one shortcoming: you must remain logged in until the job completes. Although you can always type **jobs** (see Chapter 1, *Korn Shell Basics*) to check on progress, you can't leave your office for the day unless you want to risk a breach of security or waste electricity. We'll see how to solve this problem in the next chapter.

The other file-descriptor-oriented redirectors (e.g., <&*n*) are usually used for reading input from (or writing output to) more than one file at the same time. We'll see an example later in this chapter. Otherwise, they're mainly meant for systems programmers, as are <&- (force standard input to close) and >&- (force standard output to close).

Before we leave this topic, we should just note that 1> is the same as >, and 0< is the same as <. If you understand this, then you probably know all you need to know about file descriptors.

String I/O

Now we'll zoom back in to the string I/O level and examine the **print** and **read** statements, which give the shell I/O capabilities that are more analogous to those of conventional programming languages.

print

As we've seen countless times in this book, **print** simply prints its arguments to standard output. You should use it instead of the **echo** command, whose functionality differs from system to system.* Now we'll explore the command in greater detail.

print escape sequences

print accepts a number of options, as well as several *escape sequences* that start with a backslash.† These are similar to the escape sequences recognized by **echo** and the C language; they are listed in Table 7-2.

These sequences exhibit fairly predictable behavior, except for \f on some displays, it causes a screen clear, while on others it causes a line feed. It ejects the page on most printers. \v is somewhat obsolete; it usually causes a line feed.

---

*Specifically, there is a difference between System V and BSD versions. The latter accepts options similar to those of **print**, while the former accepts C language-style escape sequences.

†You must use a double backslash if you don't surround the string that contains them with quotes; otherwise, the shell itself "steals" a backslash before passing the arguments to **print**.

Table 7-2: print Escape Sequences

Sequence	Character printed
\a	ALERT or CTRL-G
\b	BACKSPACE or CTRL-H
\c	Omit final NEWLINE
\f	FORMFEED or CTRL-L
\n	NEWLINE (not at end of command) or CTRL-J
\r	RETURN (ENTER) or CTRL-M
\t	TAB or CTRL-I
\v	VERTICAL TAB or CTRL-K
\0n	ASCII character with octal (base-8) value n, where n is 1 to 3 digits
\\	Single backslash

The \0n sequence is even more device-dependent and can be used for complex I/O, such as cursor control and special graphics characters.

Options to print

print also accepts a few dash options; we've already seen **-n** for omitting the final NEWLINE. The options are listed in Table 7-3.

Table 7-3: print Options

Option	Function
-n	Omit the final newline (same as the \c escape sequence)
-r	Raw; ignore the escape sequences listed above
-p ·	Print on pipe to coroutine; see next chapter
-s	Print to command history file. See Chapter 2.
-un	Print to file descriptor n

Notice that some of these are redundant: **print -n** is the same as **print** with c at the end of a line; **print -un** ... is equivalent to **print** ... **>&n** (though the former is more efficient).

However, **print -s** is *not* the same as **print** ... **>> $HISTFILE**. The latter command renders the **vi** and **emacs** editing modes temporarily inoperable; you must use **print -s** if you want to print to your history file.

Printing to your history file is useful if you want to edit something that the shell expands when it processes a command line; for example, a complex environment variable such as **PATH**. If you enter the command **print –s PATH=$PATH** and then press **CTRL-P** in emacs-mode (or **ESC k** in vi-mode), you will see something like this:

```
$ PATH=/bin:/usr/bin:/etc:/usr/ucb:/usr/local/bin:/home/billr/bin
```

That is, the shell expands the variable (and would expand anything else, like command substitutions, wildcards, etc.) before it writes the line to the history file. Your cursor will be at the end of the line (or at the beginning of the line in vi-mode), and you can edit your **PATH** without having to type in the whole thing again.

read

The other half of the shell's string I/O facilities is the **read** command, which allows you to read values *into* shell variables. The basic syntax is:

```
read var1 var2...
```

There are a few options, which we will cover in the section "Options to read," below. This statement takes a line from the standard input and breaks it down into words delimited by any of the characters in the value of the environment variable **IFS** (see Chapter 4, *Basic Shell Programming*; these are usually a space, a TAB, and NEWLINE). The words are assigned to variables *var1*, *var2*, etc. For example:

```
$ read fred bob
dave pete
$ print "$fred"
dave
$ print "$bob"
pete
```

If there are more words than variables, then excess words are assigned to the last variable. If you omit the variables altogether, the entire line of input is assigned to the variable **REPLY**.

You may have identified this as the "missing ingredient" in the shell programming capabilities we have seen thus far. It resembles input statements in conventional languages, like its namesake in Pascal. So why did we wait this long to introduce it?

Actually, **read** is sort of an "escape hatch" from traditional shell programming philosophy, which dictates that the most important unit of data to process is a *text file*, and that UNIX utilities such as *cut*, *grep*, *sort*, etc., should be used as building blocks for writing programs.

read, on the other hand, implies line-by-line processing. You could use it to write a shell script that does what a pipeline of utilities would normally do, but such a script would inevitably look like:

```
while (read a line) do
    process the line
    print the processed line
end
```

This type of script is usually much slower than a pipeline; furthermore, it has the same form as a program someone might write in C (or some similar language) that does the same thing much *much* faster. In other words, if you are going to write it in this line-by-line way, there is no point in writing a shell script. (The author has gone for years without writing a script with **read** in it.)

Reading lines from files

Nevertheless, shell scripts with **read** are useful for certain kinds of tasks. One is when you are reading data from a file small enough so that efficiency isn't a concern (say a few hundred lines or less), and it's *really necessary* to get bits of input into shell variables.

One task that we have already seen fits this description: Task 5-4, the script that a system administrator could use to set a user's **TERM** environment variable according to which terminal line he or she is using. The code in Chapter 5, *Flow Control*, used a **case** statement to select the correct value for **TERM**.

This code would presumably reside in */etc/profile*, the system-wide initialization file that the Korn shell runs before running a user's *.profile*. If the terminals on the system change over time—as surely they must—then the code would have to be changed. It would be better to store the information in a file and change just the file instead.

Assume we put the information in a file whose format is typical of such UNIX "system configuration" files: each line contains a device name, a TAB, and a **TERM** value. If the file, which we'll call */etc/terms*, contained the same data as the **case** statement in Chapter 5, *Flow Control*, it would look like this:

```
console          s531
tty01            gl35a
tty03            gl35a
tty04            gl35a
tty07            t2000
tty08            s531
```

We can use **read** to get the data from this file, but first we need to know how to test for the end-of-file condition. Simple: **read**'s exit status is 1 (i.e., non-0) when there is nothing to read. This leads to a clean **while** loop:

```
TERM=vt99          # assume this as a default
line=$(tty)
while read dev termtype; do
    if [[ $dev = $line ]]; then
        TERM=$termtype
        print "TERM set to $TERM."
        break
    fi
done
```

The **while** loop reads each line of the input into the variables **dev** and **termtype**. In each pass through the loop, the **if** looks for a match between **$dev** and the user's tty (**$line**, obtained by command substitution from the *tty* command). If a match is found, **TERM** is set, a message is printed, and the loop exits; otherwise **TERM** remains at the default setting of **vt99**.

We're not quite done, though: this code reads from the standard input, not from */etc/terms*! We need to know how to redirect input to *multiple commands*. It turns out that there are a few ways of doing this.

I/O Redirection and multiple commands

One way to solve the problem is with a *subshell*, as we'll see in the next chapter. This involves creating a separate process to do the reading. However, it is usually more efficient to do it in the same process; the Korn shell gives us three ways of doing this.

The first, which we have seen already, is with a function:

```
function findterm {
    TERM=vt99          # assume this as a default
    line=$(tty)
    while read dev termtype; do
        if [[ $dev = $line ]]; then
            TERM=$termtype
```

```
             print "TERM set to $TERM."
             break;
        fi
    done
}

findterm < /etc/terms
```

A function acts like a script in that it has its own set of standard I/O descriptors, which can be redirected in the line of code that calls the function. In other words, you can think of this code as if *findterm* were a script and you typed **findterm < /etc/terms** on the command line. The **read** statement takes input from */etc/terms* a line at a time, and the function runs correctly.

The second way is by putting the I/O redirector at the end of the loop, like this:

```
TERM=vt99        # assume this as a default
line=$(tty)
while read dev termtype; do
    if [[ $dev = $line ]]; then
        TERM=$termtype
        print "TERM set to $TERM."
        break;
    fi
done < /etc/terms
```

You can use this technique with any flow-control construct, including **if ... fi, case ... esac, select ... done,** and **until ... done.** This makes sense because these are all *compound statements* that the shell treats as single commands for these purposes. This technique works fine—the **read** command reads a line at a time—as long as all of the input is done within the compound statement.

Code blocks

But if you want to redirect I/O to or from an arbitrary group of commands without creating a separate process, you need to use a construct that we haven't seen yet. If you surround some code with { and }, the code will behave like a function that has no name. This is another type of compound statement. In accordance with the equivalent concept in the C language, we'll call this a *block* of code.*

---

*LISP programmers may prefer to think of this as an *anonymous function* or *lambda-function.*

What good is a block? In this case, it means that the code within the curly brackets ({}) will take standard I/O descriptors just as we described in the last block of code. This construct is appropriate for the current example because the code needs to be called only once, and the entire script is not really large enough to merit breaking down into functions. Here is how we use a block in the example:

```
{
    TERM=vt99         # assume this as a default
    line=$(tty)
    while read dev termtype; do
        if [[ $dev = $line ]]; then
            TERM=$termtype
            print "TERM set to $TERM."
            break;
        fi
    done
} < /etc/terms
```

To help you understand how this works, think of the curly brackets and the code inside them as if they were one command, i.e.:

```
{ TERM=vt99; line=$(tty); while ... } < /etc/terms
```

Configuration files for system administration tasks like this one are actually fairly common; a prominent example is */etc/hosts*, which lists machines that are accessible in a TCP/IP network. We can make */etc/terms* more like these standard files by allowing comment lines in the file that start with #, just as in shell scripts. This way */etc/terms* can look like this:

```
#
# System Console is a Shande 531s
console     s531
#
# Prof. Subramaniam's line has a Givalt GL35a
tty01 gl35a
...
```

We can handle comment lines in two ways. First, we could modify the **while** loop so that it ignores lines beginning with #. We would take advantage of the fact that the equal sign (=) under [[/]] does pattern matching, not just equality testing:

```
if [[ $dev != \#* && $dev = $line ]]; then
    ...
```

The pattern is #*, which matches any string beginning with #. We must precede # with a backslash so that the shell doesn't treat the rest of the line as a comment. Also, remember from Chapter 5, *Flow Control*, that the **&&**

combines the two conditions so that *both* must be true for the entire condition to be true.

This would certainly work, but the more usual way to filter out comment lines is to use a pipeline with *grep*. We give *grep* the regular expression ^[^#], which matches anything except lines beginning with #. Then we change the call to the block so that it reads from the output of the pipeline instead of directly from the file.*

```
grep "^[^#]" /etc/terms | {
    TERM=vt99
    ...
}
```

We can also use **read** to improve our solution to Task 6-2, in which we emulate the multicolumn output of *ls*. In the solution in the previous chapter, we assumed that (as in System V-derived versions of UNIX) filenames are limited to 14 characters, and we used 14 as a fixed column width. We'll improve the solution so that it allows *any* filename length (as in BSD-derived UNIX versions) and uses the length of the longest filename (plus 2) as the column width.

We will need to pass the output of *ls* twice through the list of files we want to display in multicolumn format. In the first pass, we will find the longest filename and use that to set the number of columns as well as their width; the second pass will do the actual output. Here is a block of code for the first pass:

```
ls "$@" | {
    let width=0
    while read fname; do
        if (( ${#fname} > $width )); then
            let width=${#fname}
        fi
    done
    let width="$width + 2"
    let numcols="${COLUMNS:-80} / $width"
}
```

This code looks a bit like an exercise from a first-semester programming class. The **while** loop goes through the input looking for files with names that are longer than the longest found so far; if a longer one is found, its length is saved as the new longest length.

---

*Unfortunately, using **read** with input from a pipe is often very inefficient, because of issues in the design of the shell that aren't relevant here.

After the loop finishes, we add 2 to the width to allow for space between columns. Then we divide the width of the terminal by the column width to get the number of columns; the shell's integer division operator truncates remainders, which is just what we want. Recall from Chapter 3, *Customizing Your Environment*, that the built-in variable **COLUMNS** often contains the display width; the construct **${COLUMNS:-80}** gives a default of 80 if this variable is not set.

The results of the block are the variables **width** and **numcols**. These are global variables, so they are accessible by the rest of the code inside our (eventual) script. In particular, we need them in our second pass through the filenames. The code for this resembles the code to our original solution; all we need to do is replace the fixed column width and number of columns with the variables:

```
set -A filenames $(ls $@)
typeset -L$width fname
let count=0

while (( $count < ${#filenames[*]} )); do
    fname=${filenames[$count]}
    print "$fname  \\c"
    let count="count + 1"
    if [[ $((count % numcols)) = 0 ]]; then
        print            # output a NEWLINE
    fi
done

if [[ $((count % numcols)) != 0 ]]; then
    print
fi
```

The entire script consists of both pieces of code.

Reading User Input

The other type of task to which **read** is suited is prompting a user for input. Think about it: we have hardly seen any such scripts so far in this book. In fact, the only ones were the modified solutions to Task 5-4, which involved **select**.

As you've probably figured out, **read** can be used to get user input into shell variables. We can use **print** to prompt the user, like this:

```
print -n 'terminal? '
read TERM
print "TERM is $TERM"
```

Here is what this looks like when it runs:

```
terminal? vt99
TERM is vt99
```

However, shell convention dictates that prompts should go to standard *error*, not standard output. (Recall that **select** prompts to standard error.) We could just use file descriptor 2 with the output redirector we saw earlier in this chapter:

```
print -n 'terminal? ' >&2
read TERM
print TERM is $TERM
```

However, this has various disadvantages. The shell provides a better way of doing the same thing: if you follow the first variable name in a **read** statement with a question mark (?) and a string, the shell will use that string as a prompt. In other words:

```
read TERM?'terminal? '
print "TERM is $TERM"
```

does the same as the above. This looks a bit nicer; also, the shell knows not to generate the prompt if the input is redirected to come from a file, and this scheme allows you to use vi- or emacs-mode on your input line.

We'll flesh out this simple example by showing how Task 5-4 would be done if **select** didn't exist. Compare this with the code in Chapter 5, *Flow Control*:

```
print 'Select your terminal type:'
done=false
while [[ $done = false ]]; do
    done=true          # assume user will make a valid choice
    {
        print '1) gl35a'
        print '2) t2000'
        print '3) s531'
        print '4) vt99'
    } >&2
    read REPLY?'terminal? '

    case $REPLY in
        1 ) TERM=gl35a ;;
```

```
        2 )  TERM=t2000 ;;
        3 )  TERM=s531 ;;
        4 )  TERM=vt99 ;;
        * )  print 'invalid.'
                   done=false ;;
     esac
done
print 'TERM is $TERM'
```

The **while** loop is necessary so that the code repeats if the user makes an invalid choice.

This is roughly twice as many lines of code as the first solution in Chapter 5—but exactly as many as the later, more user-friendly version! This shows that **select** saves you code only if you don't mind using the same strings to *display* your menu choices as you use inside your script.

However, **select** has other advantages, including the ability to construct multicolumn menus if there are many choices, and better handling of null user input.

Options to read

read takes a set of options that are similar to those for **print**. Table 7-4 lists them.

Table 7-4: read Options

Option	Function
-r	Raw; do not use \ as line continuation character.
-p	Read from pipe to coroutine; see next chapter.
-s	Save input in command history file. See Chapter 2.
-u*n*	Read from file descriptor *n*.

read lets you input lines that are longer than the width of your display device by providing backslash (\) as a continuation character, just as in shell scripts. The -r option to **read** overrides this, in case your script reads from a file that may contain lines that happen to end in backslashes.

read -r also preserves any other escape sequences the input might contain. For example, if the file *fred* contains this line:

```
A line with a\n escape sequence
```

Then **read -r fredline** will include the backslash in the variable **fredline**, whereas without the **-r**, **read** will "eat" the backslash. As a result:

```
$ read -r fredline < fred
$ print "$fredline"
A line with a
 escape sequence
$
```

However:

```
$ read fredline < fred
$ print "$fredline"
A line with an escape sequence
$
```

The **-s** option helps you if you are writing a highly interactive script and you want to provide the same command-history capability as the shell itself has. For example, say you are writing a new version of *mail* as a shell script. Your basic command loop might look like this:

```
while read -s cmd; do
     # process the command
done
```

Using **read -s** allows the user to retrieve previous commands to *your program* with the emacs-mode CTRL-P command or the vi-mode ESC k command. The *kshdb* debugger in Chapter 9, *Debugging Shell Programs*, uses this feature.

Finally, the **-u***N* option is useful in scripts that read from more than one file at the same time. Here's an example of this that also uses the *n*< I/O redirector that we saw earlier in this chapter.

Task 7-4

Write a script that prints the contents of two files side by side.

We'll format the output so the two output columns are fixed at 30 characters wide. Here is the code:

```
typeset -L30 f1 f2
while read -u3 f1 && read -u4 f2; do
     print "$f1$f2"
done 3<$1 4<$2
```

read -u3 reads from file descriptor 3, and **3<$1** directs the file given as first argument to be input on that file descriptor; the same is true for the second argument and file descriptor 4. Remember that file descriptors 0, 1, and 2 are already used for standard I/O. We use file descriptors 3 and 4 for our two input files; it's best to start from 3 and work upwards to the shell's limit, which is 9.

The **typeset** command and the quotes around the argument to **print** ensure that the output columns are 30 characters wide and that all whitespace in the lines from the file is preserved. The **while** loop reads one line from each file until at least one of them runs out of input.

Assume the file *dave* contains the following:

```
DAVE
Height: 5'10"
Weight: 175 lbs.
Hair: brown
Eyes: brown
```

And the file *shirley* contains this:

```
SHIRLEY
Height: 5'6"
Weight: 142 lbs.
Hair: blonde
Eyes: blue
```

If the script is called *twocols*, then **twocols dave shirley** produces this output:

```
DAVE                          SHIRLEY
Height: 5'10"                 Height: 5'6"
Weight: 175 lbs.              Weight: 142 lbs.
Hair: brown                   Hair: blonde
Eyes: brown                   Eyes: blue
```

Command-line Processing

We've seen how the shell uses **read** to process input lines: it deals with single quotes (`' '`), double quotes (`" "`), and backslashes (`\`); it separates lines into words, according to delimiters in the environment variable **IFS**; and it assigns the words to shell variables. We can think of this process as a subset of the things the shell does when processing *command lines*.

We've touched upon command-line processing (see Figure 7-1) throughout this book; now is a good time to make the whole thing explicit.* Each line that the shell reads from the standard input or a script is called a *pipeline*, it contains one or more *commands* separated by zero or more pipe characters (|). For each pipeline it reads, the shell breaks it up into commands, sets up the I/O for the pipeline, then does the following for each command:

1. Splits the command into *tokens* that are separated by the fixed set of *metacharacters*: SPACE, TAB, NEWLINE, ; , (,), <, >, | , and &. Types of tokens include *words*, *keywords*, I/O redirectors, and semicolons.

2. Checks the first token of each command to see if it is a *keyword* with no quotes or backslashes. If it's an opening keyword (if and other control-structure openers, **function**, {, (, ((, or [[), then the command is actually a *compound command*. The shell sets things up internally for the compound command, reads the next command, and starts the process again. If the keyword isn't a compound command opener (e.g., is a control-structure "middle" like **then**, **else**, or **do**, an "end" like **fi** or **done**, or a logical operator), the shell signals a syntax error.

3. Checks the first word of each command against the list of *aliases*. If a match is found, it substitutes the alias' definition and *goes back to Step 1*; otherwise it goes on to Step 4. This scheme allows *recursive* aliases; see Chapter 3, *Customizing Your Environment*. It also allows aliases for keywords to be defined, e.g., **alias aslongas=while** or **alias procedure=function**.

4. Substitutes the user's home directory ($HOME) for *tilde* if it is at the beginning of a word.† Substitutes *user*'s home directory for ~*user*.

5. Performs *parameter (variable) substitution* for any expression that starts with a dollar sign ($).

6. Does *command substitution* for any expression of the form $(*string*).

7. Evaluates *arithmetic expressions* of the form $((*string*)).

8. Takes the parts of the line that resulted from parameter, command, and arithmetic substitution and splits them into words again. This time it uses the characters in $IFS as delimiters instead of the set of metacharacters in Step 1.

---

*Even this explanation is slightly simplified to elide the most petty details, e.g., "middles" and "ends" of compound commands, special characters within [[. . .]] and ((. . .)) constructs, etc. The last word on this subject is the reference book, *The KornShell Command and Programming Language*, by Morris Bolsky and David Korn, published by Prentice-Hall.

†Two obscure variations on this: the shell substitutes the current directory ($PWD) for ~+ and the previous directory ($OLDPWD) for ~-.

9. Performs *filename generation*, a.k.a. *wildcard expansion*, for any occurrences of *, ?, and [/] pairs. It also processes the regular expression operators that we saw in Chapter 4, *Basic Shell Programming*.

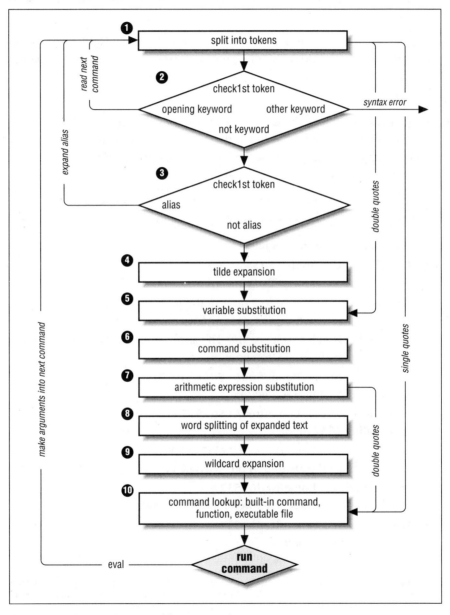

Figure 7-1: Steps in Command-line Processing

10. Uses the first word as a command by looking up its source according to the rest of the list in Chapter 4, i.e., as a *built-in* command, then as a *function*, then as a file in any of the directories in **$PATH**.

11. Runs the command after setting up I/O redirection and other such things.

That's a lot of steps—and it's not even the whole story! But before we go on, an example should make this process clearer. Assume that the following command has been run:

```
alias ll="ls -l"
```

Further assume that a file exists called *.hist537* in user **fred**'s home directory, which is */home/fred*, and that there is a double-dollar-sign variable **$$** whose value is **2537** (we'll see what this special variable is in the next chapter).

Now let's see how the shell processes the following command:

```
ll $(whence cc) ~fred/.*$(($$%1000))
```

Here is what happens to this line:

1. **ll $(whence cc) ~fred/.*$(($$%1000))**
   Splitting the input into words.

2. **ll** is not a keyword, so step 2 does nothing.

3. **ls -l $(whence cc) ~fred/.*$(($$%1000))**
   Substituting **ls -l** for its alias "ll". The shell then repeats steps 1 through 3; step 2 splits the **ls -l** into two words.*

4. **ls -l $(whence cc) /home/fred/.*$(($$%1000))**
   Expanding ~fred into */home/fred*.

5. **ls -l $(whence cc) /home/fred/.*$((2537%1000))**
   Substituting **2537** for **$$**.

6. **ls -l /usr/bin/cc /home/fred/.*$((2537%1000))**
   Doing command substitution on "whence cc".

7. **ls -l /usr/bin/cc /home/fred/.*537**
   Evaluating the arithmetic expression **2537%1000**.

8. **ls -l /usr/bin/cc /home/fred/.*537**
   This step does nothing.

---

*Some of the shell's built-in aliases, however, seem to make it through single quotes: **true** (an alias for **:**, a "do-nothing" command that always returns exit status 0), **false** (an alias for **let 0**, which always returns exit status 1), and **stop** (an alias for **kill -STOP**).

9. **ls** –l **/usr/bin/cc /home/fred/.hist537**

    Substituting the filename for the wildcard expression **.*537**.

10. The command **ls** is found in */usr/bin*.

11. */usr/bin/ls* is run with the option –l and the two arguments.

Although this list of steps is fairly straightforward, it is not the whole story. There are still two ways to *subvert* the process: by quoting and by using the advanced command **eval**.

Quoting

You can think of quoting as a way of getting the shell to skip some of the 11 steps above. In particular:

- **Single quotes** (**' '**) bypass *everything* through Step 9—including aliasing.* All characters inside a pair of single quotes are untouched. You can't have single quotes inside single quotes—not even if you precede them with backslashes.†

- **Double quotes** (**" "**) bypass steps 1 through 4, plus steps 8 and 9. That is, they ignore pipe characters, aliases, tilde substitution, wildcard expansion, and splitting into words via delimiters (e.g., blanks) inside the double quotes. Single quotes inside double quotes have no effect. But double quotes do allow parameter substitution, command substitution, and arithmetic expression evaluation. You can include a double quote inside a double-quoted string by preceding it with a backslash (\). You must also backslash-escape **$**, ` (the archaic command substitution delimiter), and \ itself.

Table 7-5 contains some simple examples that show how these work; they assume that the statement **dave=bob** was run and that user **fred**'s home directory is */home/fred*.

If you are wondering whether to use single or double quotes in a particular shell programming situation, it is safest to use single quotes unless you specifically need parameter, command, or arithmetic substitution.

---

*However, as we saw in Chapter 1, *Korn Shell Basics*, **' \ ' '** (i.e., single quote, backslash, single quote, single quote) acts pretty much like a single quote in the middle of a single-quoted string; e.g., **' abc ' \ ' ' def'** evaluates to **abc ' def**.

Table 7-5: Examples of Quoting Rules

Expression	Value
$dave	bob
"$dave"	bob
\$dave	$dave
'$dave'	$dave
'$dave'	'bob'
˜fred	/home/fred
"˜fred"	˜fred
'˜fred'	˜fred

Here's a more advanced example of command-line processing that should give you deeper insight into the overall process.

Customize your primary prompt string so that it contains the current directory with tilde (˜) notation.

Recall from Chapter 4, *Basic Shell Programming*, that we found a simple way to set up the prompt string **PS1** so that it always contains the current directory:

```
PS1='($PWD)--> '
```

One problem with this setup is that the resulting prompt strings can get very long. One way to shorten them is to substitute tilde notation for users' home directories. This cannot be done with a simple string expression analogous to the above. The solution is somewhat complicated and takes advantage of the command-line processing rules.

The basic idea is to create a "wrapper" around the **cd** command, as we did in Chapter 5, *Flow Control*, that installs the current directory with tilde notation as the prompt string. Because **cd** is a built-in command, the wrapper must be an alias in order to override it. But the code we need to insert tilde notation is too complicated for an alias, so we'll use a function and then alias the function as **cd**.

We'll start with a function that, given a pathname as argument, prints its equivalent in tilde notation if possible:

```
function tildize {
    if [[ $1 = $HOME* ]]; then
        print "\~/${1#$HOME}"
        return 0
    fi
    awk 'BEGIN {FS=":"} {print $1, $6}' /etc/passwd
        while read user homedir; do
            if [[ $homedir != / && $1 = ${homedir}?(/*) ]]; then
                print "\~$user/${1#$homedir}"
                return 0
            fi
        done
    print "$1"
    return 1
}
```

The first **if** clause checks if the given pathname is under the user's home directory. If so, it substitutes tilde (~) for the home directory in the pathname and returns.

If not, we use the *awk* utility to extract the first and sixth fields of the file */etc/passwd*, which contain users IDs and home directories, respectively. In this case, *awk* acts like *cut*. The **BEGIN{FS=":"}** is analogous to -d:, which we saw in Chapter sbasshell, except that it prints the values on each line separated by blanks, not colons (:).

awk's output is fed into a **while** loop that checks the pathname given as argument to see if it contains some user's home directory. (The first part of the conditional expression eliminates "users" like **daemon** and **root**, whose home directories are root and therefore are contained in every full pathname.The second part matches home directories by themselves or with some other directory appended (the ?(/*) part.)) If a user's home directory is found, then ~*user* is substituted for the full home directory in the given pathname, the result is printed, and the function exits.

Finally, if the **while** loop exhausts all users without finding a home directory that is a prefix of the given pathname, then **tildize** simply echoes back its input.

Now that we have this function, you might think we could use it in a command substitution expression like this:

```
PS1='$(tildize $PWD)'
```

But this won't work, because the shell doesn't do command substitution when it evaluates the prompt string after every command. That's why we have to incorporate it into an alias that supersedes **cd**. The following code should go into your *.profile* or environment file, along with the definition of **tildize**:

```
PS1=$(tildize $PWD)

function _cd {
    "cd" "$@"
    es=$?
    PS1=$(tildize $PWD)
    return $es
}

alias cd=_cd
```

When you log in, this code will set **PS1** to the initial current directory (presumably your home directory). Then, whenever you enter a **cd** command, the alias runs the function **_cd**, which looks a lot like the "wrapper" in Chapter 5, *Flow Control.*

The first line in **_cd** runs the "real" **cd** by surrounding it in quotes—which makes the shell bypass alias expansion (Step 3 in the list). Then the shell resets the prompt string to the new current directory, or the old one if the **cd** failed for some reason.

Of course, the function **tildize** can be any code that formats the directory string. See the exercises at the end of this chapter for a couple of suggestions.

eval

We have seen that quoting lets you skip steps in command-line processing. Then there's the eval command, which lets you go through the process again. Performing command-line processing twice may seem strange, but it's actually very powerful: it lets you write scripts that create command strings on the fly and then pass them to the shell for execution. This means that you can give scripts "intelligence" to modify their own behavior as they are running.

The **eval** statement tells the shell to take **eval**'s arguments and run them through the command-line processing steps all over again. To help you understand the implications of **eval**, we'll start with a trivial example and work our way up to a situation in which we're constructing and running commands on the fly.

eval ls passes the string **ls** to the shell to execute; the shell prints list of files in the current directory. Very simple; there is nothing about the string **ls** that needs to be sent through the command-processing steps twice. But consider this:

```
listpage="ls | more"
$listpage
```

Instead of producing a paginated file listing, the shell will treat | and **more** as arguments to *ls*, and *ls* will complain that no files of those names exist. Why? Because the pipe character "appears" in step 5 when the shell evaluates the variable, *after* it has actually looked for pipe characters (in step 2). The variable's expansion isn't even parsed until step 8. As a result, the shell will treat | and **more** as arguments to *ls*, so that *ls* will try to find files called | and *more* in the current directory!

Now consider **eval $listpage** instead of just **$listpage**. When the shell gets to the last step, it will run the command **eval** with arguments **ls**, |, and **more**. This causes the shell to go back to Step 1 with a line that consists of these arguments. It finds | in Step 2 and splits the line into two commands, *ls* and *more*. Each command is processed in the normal (and in both cases trivial) way. The result is a paginated list of the files in your current directory.

Now you may start to see how powerful **eval** can be. It is an advanced feature that requires considerable programming cleverness to be used most effectively. It even has a bit of the flavor of artificial intelligence, in that it enables you to write programs that can "write" and execute other programs.* You probably won't use **eval** for everyday shell programming, but it's worth taking the time to understand what it can do.

As a more interesting example, we'll revisit Task 4-1, the very first task in the book. In it, we constructed a simple pipeline that sorts a file and prints out the first N lines, where N defaults to 10. The resulting pipeline was:

```
sort -nr $1 | head -${2:-10}
```

The first argument specified the file to sort; **$2** is the number of lines to print.

---

*You could actually do this without **eval**, by **printing** commands to a temporary file and then "sourcing" that file with . *filename*. But that is *much* less efficient.

Now suppose we change the task just a bit so that the default is to print the *entire file* instead of 10 lines. This means that we don't want to use *head* at all in the default case. We could do this in the following way:

```
if [[ -n $2 ]]; then
    sort -nr $1 | head -$2
else
    sort -nr $1
fi
```

In other words, we decide which pipeline to run according to whether or not **$2** is null. But here is a more compact solution:

```
eval sort -nr \$1 ${2:+"| head -\$2"}
```

The last expression in this line evaluates to the string **| head -\$2** if **$2** exists (is not null); if **$2** is null, then the expression is null too. We backslash-escape dollar signs (**\$**) before variable names to prevent unpredictable results if the variables' values contain special characters like **>** or **|**. The backslash effectively puts off the variables' evaluation until the **eval** command itself runs. So the entire line is either:

```
eval sort -nr \$1 | head -\$2
```

if **$2** is given or:

```
eval sort -nr \$1
```

if **$2** is null. Once again, we can't just run this command without **eval** because the pipe is "uncovered" after the shell tries to break the line up into commands. **eval** causes the shell to run the correct pipeline when **$2** is given.

Next, we'll revisit Task 7-3 from earlier in this chapter, the *start* script that lets you start a command in the background and save its standard output and standard error in a logfile. Recall that the one-line solution to this task had the restriction that the command could not contain output redirectors or pipes. Although the former doesn't make sense when you think about it, you certainly would want the ability to start a pipeline in this way.

eval is the obvious way to solve this problem:

```
eval "$@" > logfile 2>&1 &
```

The only restriction that this imposes on the user is that pipes and other such special characters be quoted (surrounded by quotes or preceded by backslashes).

Here's a way to apply **eval** in conjunction with various other interesting shell programming concepts.

Task 7-6

Implement the guts of the *make(1)* utility as a shell script.

make is known primarily as a programmer's tool, but it seems as though someone finds a new use for it every day. Without going into too much extraneous detail, *make* basically keeps track of multiple files in a particular project, some of which depend on others (e.g., a document depends on its word processor input file(s)). It makes sure that when you change a file, all of the other files that depend on it are processed.

For example, assume you're using the *troff* word processor to write a book. You have files for the book's chapters called *ch1.t*, *ch2.t*, and so on; the *troff* output for these files are *ch1.out*, *ch2.out*, etc. You run commands like **troff ch*N*.t > ch*N*.out** to do the processing. While you're working on the book, you tend to make changes to several files at a time.

In this situation, you can use *make* to keep track of which files need to be reprocessed, so that all you need to do is type **make**, and it will figure out what needs to be done. You don't need to remember to reprocess the files that have changed.

How does *make* do this? Simple: it compares the *modification times* of the input and output files (called *sources* and *targets* in *make* terminology), and if the input file is newer, then *make* reprocesses it.

You tell *make* which files to check by building a file called *makefile* that has constructs like this:

```
target : source1 source2 ...
    commands to make target
```

This essentially says, "For *target* to be up to date, it must be newer than all of the *sources*. If it's not, run the *commands* to bring it up to date." The *commands* are on one or more lines that must start with TABs: e.g., to make *ch7.out*:

```
ch7.out : ch7.t
    troff ch7.t > ch7.out
```

Now suppose that we write a shell function called **makecmd** that reads and executes a single construct of this form. Assume that the *makefile* is read from standard input. The function would look like the following code.

```
function makecmd {
    read target colon sources
    for src in $sources; do
        if [[ $src -nt $target ]]; then
            while read cmd && [[ $cmd = \t* ]]; do
                print "$cmd"
                eval ${cmd#\t}
            done
            break
        fi
    done
}
```

This function reads the line with the target and sources; the variable **colon** is just a placeholder for the :. Then it checks each source to see if it's newer than the target, using the **-nt** file attribute test operator that we saw in Chapter 5, *Flow Control.* If the source is newer, it reads, prints, and executes the commands until it finds a line that doesn't start with a TAB or it reaches end-of-file. (The real *make* does more than this; see the exercises at the end of this chapter.) After running the commands (which are stripped of the initial TAB), it breaks out of the **for** loop, so that it doesn't run the commands more than once.

The C Compiler as Pipeline

As a final example of **eval**, we'll revisit our old friend *occ*, the C compiler from the previous three chapters. Recall that the compiler does its work by calling separate programs to do the actual *compile* from C to object code (the *ccom* program), *optimization* of object code (*optimize*), *assembly* of assembler code files (*as*), and final *linking* of object code files into an executable program (*ld*). These separate programs use temporary files to store their outputs.

Now we'll assume that these components (except the linker) pass information in a *pipeline* to the final object code output. In other words, each component takes standard input and produces standard output instead of taking filename arguments. We'll also change an earlier assumption: instead of compiling a C source file directly to object code, *occ* compiles C to assembler code, which the assembler then assembles to object code. This lets us suppose that *occ* works like this:

```
ccom < filename.c | as | optimize > filename.o
```

Or, if you prefer:

```
cat filename.c | ccom | as | optimize > filename.o
```

To get this in the proper framework for **eval**, let's assume that the variables **srcname** and **objname** contain the names of the source and object files, respectively. Then our pipeline becomes:

```
cat $srcname | ccom | as | optimize > $objname
```

As we've already seen, this is equivalent to:

```
eval cat \$srcname | ccom | as | optimize > \$objname
```

Knowing what we do about **eval**, we can transform this into:

```
eval cat \$srcname " | ccom" " | as" " | optimize" > \$objname
```

and from that into:

```
compile=" | ccom"
assemble=" | as"
optimize=" | optimize"

eval cat \$srcname \$compile \$assemble \$optimize > \$objname
```

Now, consider what happens if you don't want to invoke the optimizer—which is the default case anyway. (Recall that the **−O** option invokes the optimizer.) We can do this:

```
optimize=""
if -O given then
    optimize=" | optimize"
fi
```

In the default case, **$optimize** evaluates to the empty string, causing the final pipeline to "collapse" into:

```
eval cat $srcname | ccom | as > $objname
```

Similarly, if you pass **occ** a file of assembler code (*filename.s*), you can collapse the compile step:*

```
assemble="| as"
if $srcname ends in .s then
    compile=""
fi
```

---

*Astute readers will notice that, according to this rationale, we would handle object-code input files (*filename.o*) with the pipeline **eval cat $srcname > $objname**, where the two names are the same. This will cause UNIX to destroy *filename.o* by truncating it to zero length. We won't worry about this here.

That results in this pipeline:

```
eval cat \$srcname | as > \$objname
```

Now we're ready to show the full "pipeline" version of **occ**. It's similar to the previous version, except that for each input file, it constructs and runs a pipeline as above. It processes the **-g** (debug) option and the link step in the same way as before. Here is the code:

```
# initialize option-related variables
do_link=true
debug=""
link_libs="-l c"
exefile=""

# initialize pipeline components
compile=" | ccom"
assemble=" | as"
optimize=""

# process command-line options
while getopts ":cgl:o:O" opt; do
    case $opt in
        c )     do_link=false ;;
        g )     debug="-g" ;;
        l )     link_libs="$link_libs -l $OPTARG" ;;
        o )     exefile="-o $OPTARG" ;;
        O )     optimize=" | optimize" ;;
        \? )    print 'usage: occ [-cgO] [-l lib] [-o file] files...'
                return 1 ;;
    esac
done
shift $(($OPTIND - 1))

# process the input files
for filename in "$@"; do
    case $filename in
      *.c )
          objname=${filename%.c}.o ;;
      *.s )
          objname=${filename%.s}.o
          compile="" ;;
      *.o )
          compile=""
          assemble="" ;;
      *  )
        print "error: $filename is not a source or object file."
        return 1 ;;
    esac

    # run a pipeline for each input file
    eval cat \$filename \$compile \$assemble \$optimize > \$objname
```

```
    objfiles=$objfiles" "$objname
done

if [[ $do_link = true ]]; then
    ld $exefile $link_libs $objfiles
fi
```

We could go on forever with increasingly complex examples of **eval**, but we'll settle for concluding the chapter with a few exercises. The last two are really more like items on the menu of food for thought; the very last one is particularly difficult.

1. Here are a couple of ways to enhance **occ**, our C compiler:

    a. Real-world C compilers accept the option –S, which tells the compiler to suppress the assembly step and leave the output in files of assembler code whose names end in *.s*. Modify **occ** so that it recognizes this option.

    b. The language C++ is an evolutionary successor to C; it includes advanced features like operator overloading, function argument type checking, and class definitions. (Don't worry if you don't know what these are.) Some C++ compilers use C as an "assembly language", i.e., they compile C++ source files to C code and then pass them to a C compiler for further processing.

        Assume that C++ source files have names ending in *.cc*, and that */lib/cfront* is the C++ compiler "front-end" that produces C code on its standard output. Modify *occ* so that it accepts C++ as well as C, assembler, and object code files.

2. The possibilities for customizing your prompt string are practically endless. Here are two enhancements to customization schemes that we've seen already:

    a. Enhance the current-directory-in-the-prompt scheme by limiting the prompt string's length to a number of characters that the user can define with an environment variable.

    b. On some UNIX systems, it's not possible to get a list of all users by looking at */etc/passwd*. For example, networks of Suns use the Network Information Service (NIS, a.k.a. "Yellow Pages"), which stores a protected password file for the entire network on one server machine, instead of having separate */etc/passwd* files on each machine.

        If such a machine is set up so that all login directories are under a common directory (e.g., */users*), you can get a list of all users by simply *ls*-ing that directory. Modify the **tildize** function so that it uses this technique; pay particular attention to execution speed.

3. The function **makecmd** in the solution to Task 7-6 represents an over-simplification of the real *make*'s functionality. *make* actually checks file dependencies *recursively*, meaning that a *source* on one line in a *makefile* can be a *target* on another line. For example, the book chapters in the example could themselves depend on some figures in separate files that were made with a graphics package.

   a. Write a function called **readtargets** that goes through the *makefile* and stores all of the targets in a variable or temp file.

   b. Instead of reading the *makefile* from standard input, read it into an array variable called **lines**. Use the variable **curline** as the "current line" index. Modify **makecmd** so that it reads lines from the array starting with the current line.

   c. **makecmd** merely checks to see if any of the sources are newer than the given target. It should really be a recursive routine that looks like this:

```
function makecmd {
    target=$1
    get sources for $target
    for each source src; do
        if $src is also a target in this makefile then
            makecmd $src
        fi
        if [[ $src -nt $target ]]; then
            run commands to make target
            return
        fi
    done
}
```

   Implement this.

   d. Write the "driver" script that turns the **makecmd** function into a full *make* program. This should make the target given as argument, or if none is given, the first target listed in the makefile.

   e. The above **makecmd** still doesn't do one important thing that the real *make* does: allow for "symbolic" targets that aren't files. These give *make* much of the power that makes it applicable to such an incredible variety of situations. Symbolic targets always have a modification time of 0, so that *make* always runs the commands to make them. Modify **makecmd** so that it allows for symbolic targets. (Hint: the crux of this problem is to figure out how to get a file's modification time. This is quite difficult.)

4. Finally, here are some problems that really test your knowledge of **eval** and the shell's command-line processing rules. Solve these and you're a true Korn shell hacker!

   a. Advanced shell programmers sometimes use a little trick that includes **eval**: using the *value* of a variable as the *name* of another variable. In other words, you can give a shell script control over the *names* of variables to which it assigns values. How would you do this?

      (Hint: if **$fred** equals "dave", and **$dave** is "bob", then you might think that you could type **print $$fred** and get the response **bob**. This doesn't actually work, but it's on the right track.)

   b. You could use the above technique together with other **eval** tricks to implement new control structures for the shell. For example, see if you can write a script that emulates the behavior of a **for** loop in a conventional language like C or Pascal, i.e., a loop that iterates a fixed number of times, with a loop variable that steps from 1 to the number of iterations (or, for C fans, 0 to iterations-1). Call your script **loop** to avoid clashes with the keywords **for** and **do**.

In this chapter:
- *Process IDs and Job Numbers*
- *Job Control*
- *Signals*
- *trap*
- *Coroutines*
- *Subshells*

8

Process Handling

The UNIX operating system built its reputation on a small number of concepts, all of which are simple yet powerful. We've seen most of them by now: standard input/output, pipes, text-filtering utilities, the tree-structured file system, and so on. UNIX also gained notoriety as the first small-computer operating system to give each user control over more than one process. We call this capability *user-controlled multitasking*.

If UNIX is the only operating system that you're familiar with, you might be surprised to learn that several other major operating systems have been sadly lacking in this area. For example, Microsoft's MS-DOS, for IBM PC compatibles, has no multitasking at all, let alone user-controlled multitasking. IBM's own VM/CMS system for large mainframes handles multiple users but gives them only one process each. DEC's VAX/VMS has user-controlled multitasking, but it is limited and difficult to use. The latest generation of small-computer operating systems, such as Apple's Macintosh OS System 7, IBM's OS/2 Version 2, and Microsoft's Windows NT, finally include user-controlled multitasking at the operating system level.*

But if you've gotten this far in this book, you probably don't think that multitasking is a big deal. You're probably used to the idea of running a process in the background by putting an ampersand (&) at the end of the command line. You have also seen the idea of a *subshell* in Chapter 4, *Basic Shell Programming*, when we showed how shell scripts run.

In this chapter, we will cover most of the Korn shell's features that relate to multitasking and process handling in general. We say "most" because some

---

*Programs like Apple's Multifinder and Microsoft Windows work *on top of* the operating system (Mac OS Version 6 and MS-DOS, respectively) to give the user limited multitasking.

of these features are, like the file descriptors we saw in the previous chapter, of interest only to low-level systems programmers.

We'll start out by looking at certain important primitives for identifying processes and for controlling them during login sessions and within shell scripts. Then we will move out to a higher-level perspective, looking at ways to get processes to communicate with each other. The Korn shell's *coroutine* facility is the most sophisticated interprocess communication scheme that we'll examine; we'll also look in more detail at concepts we've already seen, like pipes and subshells.

Don't worry about getting bogged down in low-level technical details about UNIX. We will provide only the technical information that is necessary to explain higher-level features, plus a few other tidbits designed to pique your curiosity. If you are interested in finding out more about these areas, refer to your UNIX Programmer's Manual or a book on UNIX internals that pertains to your version of UNIX.

We strongly recommend that you try out the examples in this chapter. The behavior of code that involves multiple processes is not as easy to understand on paper as most of the other examples in this book.

Process IDs and Job Numbers

UNIX gives all processes numbers, called *process IDs*, when they are created. You will notice that, when you run a command in the background by appending & to it, the shell responds with a line that looks like this:

```
$ fred &
[1]     2349
```

In this example, 2349 is the process ID for the **fred** process. The **[1]** is a *job number* assigned by the shell (not the operating system). What's the difference? Job numbers refer to background processes that are currently running under your shell, while process IDs refer to all processes currently running on the entire system, for all users. The term *job* basically refers to a command line that was invoked from your login shell.

If you start up additional background jobs while the first one is still running, the shell will number them 2, 3, etc. For example:

```
$ bob &
[2]     2367
$ dave &
[3]     2382
```

Clearly, 1, 2, and 3 are easier to remember than 2349, 2367, and 2382!

The shell includes job numbers in messages it prints when a background job completes, like this:

```
[1] + Done                    fred &
```

We'll explain what the plus sign means soon. If the job exits with non-zero status (see Chapter 5, *Flow Control*), the shell will include the exit status in parentheses:

```
[1] + Done(1)                 fred &
```

The shell prints other types of messages when certain abnormal things happen to background jobs; we'll see these later in this chapter.

Job Control

Why should you care about process IDs or job numbers? Actually, you could probably get along fine through your UNIX life without ever referring to process IDs (unless you use a windowing workstation—as we'll see soon). Job numbers are more important, however: you can use them with the shell commands for *job control.**

You already know the most obvious way of controlling a job: you can create one in the background with **&**. Once a job is running in the background, you can let it run to completion, bring it into the *foreground*, or send it a message called a *signal*.

Foreground and Background

The built-in command **fg** brings a background job into the foreground. Normally this means that the job will have control of your terminal or window and therefore will be able to accept your input. In other words, the job will begin to act as if you typed its command without the **&**.

If you have only one background job running, you can use **fg** without arguments, and the shell will bring that job into the foreground. But if you have several running in the background, the shell will pick the one that you put into the background most recently. If you want some other job put into the

---

*NOTE: If you have an older version of UNIX, it is possible that your system does not support job control. This is particularly true for many systems derived from Xenix, System III, or early versions of System V. On such systems, the Korn shell does not have the **fg** and **bg** commands, you can't type CTRL-Z to suspend a job, and the TSTP signal doesn't exist. The shell does, however, support everything else discussed here, including job numbers and the **jobs** and **kill** commands, if monitor mode is on. To ensure this, put the line **set –o monitor** in your *.profile* file.

foreground, you need to use the job's command name, preceded by a percent sign (%), or you can use its job number, also preceded by %, or its process ID without a percent sign. If you don't remember which jobs are running, you can use the command **jobs** to list them.

A few examples should make this clearer. Let's say you created three background jobs as above. Then if you type **jobs**, you will see this:

```
[1]   Running              fred &
[2] - Running              bob &
[3] + Running              dave &
```

jobs has a few interesting options. **jobs -l** also lists process IDs:

```
[1]   2349      Running         fred &
[2] - 2367      Running         bob &
[3] + 2382      Running         dave &
```

The **-p** option tells **jobs** to list *only* process IDs:

```
2349
2367
2382
```

This could be useful with command substitution; see Task 8-1 below. Finally, the **-n** option lists only those jobs whose status has changed since the shell last reported it—whether with a **jobs** command or otherwise.

If you type **fg** without an argument, the shell will put **dave** in the foreground, because it was put in the background most recently. But if you type **fg %bob** (or **fg %2**), **bob** will go in the foreground.

You can also refer to the job most recently put in the background by %+. Similarly, %i- refers to the background job invoked *next*-most-recently (**bob** in this case). That explains the plus and minus signs in the above: the plus sign shows the most recently invoked job; the minus sign shows the next-most-recently invoked job.*

If more than one background job has the same command, then %*command* will disambiguate by choosing the most recently invoked job (as you'd expect). If this isn't what you want, you need to use the job number instead of the command name. However, if the commands have different *arguments*, you can use %?*string* instead of %*command*. %?*string* refers to the

---

*This is analogous to ~+ and ~- as references to the currently and previous directory; see the footnote in Chapter 7, *Input/Output and Command-line Processing*. Also: %% is a synonym for %+.

job whose command contains the string. For example, assume you started these background jobs:

```
$ bob pete &
[1]    189
$ bob ralph &
[2]    190
$
```

Then you can use **%?pete** and **%?ralph** to refer to each of them, although actually **%?pe** and **%?ra** are sufficient to disambiguate.

Table 8-1 lists all of the ways to refer to background jobs. We have found that, given how infrequently people use job control commands, job numbers or command names are sufficient, and the other ways are superfluous.

Table 8-1: Ways to Refer to Background Jobs

Reference	Background job
%*N*	Job number *N*
%*string*	Job whose command begins with *string*
%?*string*	Job whose command contains *string*
%+	Most recently invoked background job
%%	Same as above
%–	Second-most recently invoked background job

Suspending a Job

Just as you can put background jobs into the foreground with **fg**, you can also put a foreground job into the background. This involves suspending a job, so that the shell regains control of your terminal.

To suspend a job, type CTRL-Z* while it is running. This is analogous to typing CTRL-C (or whatever your interrupt key is), except that you can

---

*This assumes that the CTRL-Z key is set up as your suspend key; just as with CTRL-C and interrupts, this is conventional but by no means required.

resume the job after you have stopped it. When you type CTRL-Z, the shell responds with a message like this:

```
[1] + Stopped                 command
```

Then it gives you your prompt back.

To resume a suspended job so that it continues to run in the foreground, just type **fg**. If, for some reason, you put other jobs in the background after you typed CTRL-Z, use **fg** with a job name or number. For example:

```
fred is running...
CTRL-Z
[1] + Stopped                 fred
$ bob &
[2]       bob &
$ fg %fred
fred resumes in the foreground...
```

The ability to suspend jobs and resume them in the foreground comes in very handy when you have a conventional terminal (as opposed to a windowing workstation) and you are using a text editor like *vi* on a file that needs to be processed. For example, if you are editing a file for the *troff* text processor, you can do the following:

```
$ vi myfile
edit the file... CTRL-Z
Stopped [1] vi
$ troff myfile
troff reports an error
$ fg
vi comes back up in the same place in your file
```

Programmers often use the same technique when debugging source code.

You will probably also find it useful to suspend a job and resume it in the background instead of the foreground. You may start a command in the foreground (i.e., normally) and find that it takes much longer than you expected—for example, a *grep*, *sort*, or database query. You need the command to finish, but you would also like control of your terminal back so that you can do other work. If you type CTRL-Z followed by **bg**, you will move the job to the background.*

---

*Be warned, however, that not all commands are "well-behaved" when you do this. Be especially careful with commands that run over a network on a remote machine; you may end up "confusing" the remote program.

Signals

We mentioned earlier that typing CTRL-Z to suspend a job is similar to typing CTRL-C to stop a job, except that you can resume the job later. They are actually similar in a deeper way: both are particular cases of the act of sending a *signal* to a process.

A signal is a message that one process sends to another when some abnormal event takes place or when it wants the other process to do something. Most of the time, a process send a signal to a subprocess it created. You're undoubtedly already comfortable with the idea that one process can communicate with another through an I/O pipeline; think of a signal as another way for processes to communicate with each other. (In fact, any textbook on operating systems will tell you that both are examples of the general concept of *interprocess communication,* or IPC.)*

Depending on the version of UNIX, there are two or three dozen types of signals, including a few that can be used for whatever purpose a programmer wishes. Signals have numbers (from 1 to the number of signals the system supports) and names; we'll use the latter. You can get a list of all the signals on your system, by name and number, by typing **kill –l**. Bear in mind, when you write shell code involving signals, that signal names are more portable to other versions of UNIX than signal numbers.

Control-key Signals

When you type CTRL-C, you tell the shell to send the INT (for "interrupt") signal to the current job; CTRL-Z sends TSTP (on most systems, for "terminal stop"). You can also send the current job a QUIT signal by typing CTRL-\ (control-backslash); this is sort of like a "stronger" version of CTRL-C.† You would normally use CTRL-\ when (and *only* when) CTRL-C doesn't work.

---

*Pipes and signals were the only IPC mechanisms in early versions of UNIX. More modern versions like System V and 4.x BSD have additional mechanisms, such as sockets, named pipes, and shared memory. Named pipes are accessible to shell programmers through the *mknod(1)* command, which is beyond the scope of this book.

†CTRL-\ can also cause the shell to leave a file called *core* in your current directory. This file contains an image of the process to which you sent the signal; a programmer could use it to help debug the program that was running. The file's name is a (very) old-fashioned term for a computer's memory. Other signals leave these "core dumps" as well; you should feel free to delete them unless a systems programmer tells you otherwise.

As we'll see soon, there is also a "panic" signal called KILL that you can send to a process when even CTRL-\ doesn't work. But it isn't attached to any control key, which means that you can't use it to stop the currently running process. INT, TSTP, and QUIT are the only signals you can use with control keys.*

You can customize the control keys used to send signals with options of the *stty*(1) command. These vary from system to system—consult your man page for the command—but the usual syntax is **stty** *signame char. signame* is a name for the signal that, unfortunately, is often not the same as the names we use here. Table 1-7 in Chapter 1, *Korn Shell Basics,* lists *stty* names for signals found on all versions of UNIX. *char* is the control character, which you can give in the same notation we use. For example, to set your INT key to CTRL-X on most systems, use:

```
stty intr ^X
```

Now that we've told you how to do this, we should add that we don't recommend it. Changing your signal keys could lead to trouble if someone else has to stop a runaway process on your machine.

Most of the other signals are used by the operating system to advise processes of error conditions, like a bad machine code instruction, bad memory address, or division by zero, or "interesting" events such as a user logging out or a timer ("alarm") going off. The remaining signals are used for esoteric error conditions that are of interest only to low-level systems programmers; newer versions of UNIX have more and more arcane signal types.

kill

You can use the built-in shell command **kill** to send a signal to any process you created—not just the currently running job. **kill** takes as argument the process ID, job number, or command name of the process to which you want to send the signal. By default, **kill** sends the TERM ("terminate") signal, which usually has the same effect as the INT signal that you send with CTRL-C. But you can specify a different signal by using the signal name (or number) as an option, preceded by a dash.

kill is so-named because of the nature of the default TERM signal, but there is another reason, which has to do with the way UNIX handles signals in

---

*Some BSD-derived systems have additional control-key signals.

general. The full details are too complex to go into here, but the following explanation should suffice.

Most signals cause a process that receives them to roll over and die; therefore if you send any one of these signals, you "kill" the process that receives it. However, programs can be set up to "trap" specific signals and take some other action. For example, a text editor would do well to save the file being edited before terminating when it receives a signal such as INT, TERM, or QUIT. Determining what to do when various signals come in is part of the fun of UNIX systems programming.

Here is an example of **kill**. Say you have a **fred** process in the background, with process ID 480 and job number 1, that needs to be stopped. You would start with this command:

```
$ kill %1
```

If you were successful, you would see a message like this:

```
[1] + Terminated              fred &
```

If you don't see this, then the TERM signal failed to terminate the job. The next step would be to try QUIT:

```
$ kill -QUIT %1
```

If that worked, you would see these messages:

```
fred[1]: 480 Quit(coredump)
[1] +  Done(131)              fred &
```

The 131 is the exit status returned by **fred**.* But if even QUIT doesn't work, the "last-ditch" method would be to use KILL:

```
$ kill -KILL %1
```

(Notice how this has the flavor of "yelling" at the runaway process.) This produces the message:

```
[1] + Killed                  fred &
```

It is impossible for a process to "trap" a KILL signal—the operating system should terminate the process immediately and unconditionally. If it doesn't, then either your process is in one of the "funny states" we'll see later in this chapter, or (far less likely) there's a bug in your version of UNIX.

---

*When a shell script is sent a signal, it exits with status 128+N, where N is the number of the signal it received (128 changes to 256 in future releases). In this case, **fred** is a shell script, and QUIT happens to be signal number 3.

Here's another example.

Write a script called **killalljobs** that kills all background jobs.

The solution to this task is simple, relying on **jobs -p**:

```
kill "$@" $(jobs -p)
```

You may be tempted to use the KILL signal immediately, instead of trying TERM (the default) and QUIT first. Don't do this. TERM and QUIT are designed to give a process the chance to "clean up" before exiting, whereas KILL will stop the process, wherever it may be in its computation. *Use KILL only as a last resort!*

You can use the **kill** command with any process you create, not just jobs in the background of your current shell. For example, if you use a windowing system, then you may have several terminal windows, each of which runs its own shell. If one shell is running a process that you want to stop, you can **kill** it from another window—but you can't refer to it with a job number because it's running under a different shell. You must instead use its process ID.

ps

This is probably the only situation in which a casual user would need to know the ID of a process. The command *ps*(1) gives you this information; however, it can give you lots of extra information that you must wade through as well.

ps is a complex command. It takes several options, some of which differ from one version of UNIX to another. To add to the confusion, you may need different options on different UNIX versions to get the same information! We will use options available on the two major types of UNIX systems, those derived from System V (such as most of the versions for Intel 386/486 PCs, as well as IBM's AIX and Hewlett-Packard's HP/UX) and BSD (DEC's Ultrix, SunOS). If you aren't sure which kind of UNIX version you have, try the System V options first.

You can invoke *ps* in its simplest form without any options. In this case, it will print a line of information about the current login shell and any processes running under it (i.e., background jobs). For example, if you invoked three background jobs, as we saw earlier in the chapter, *ps* on

System V-derived versions of UNIX would produce output that looks something like this:

```
PID TTY       TIME COMD
 146 pts/10  0:03 ksh
2349 pts/10  0:03 fred
2367 pts/10  0:17 bob
2389 pts/10  0:09 dave
2390 pts/10  0:00 ps
```

The output on BSD-derived systems looks like this:

```
PID TT STAT  TIME COMMAND
 146 10 S    0:03 /bin/ksh -i
2349 10 R    0:03 fred
2367 10 D    0:17 bob -f /dev/rmt0
2389 10 R    0:09 dave
2390 10 R    0:00 ps
```

(You can ignore the STAT column.) This is a bit like the **jobs** command. PID is the process ID; TTY (or TT) is the terminal (or pseudo-terminal, if you are using a windowing system) the process was invoked from; TIME is the amount of processor time (not real or "wall clock" time) the process has used so far; COMD (or COMMAND) is the command. Notice that the BSD version includes the command's arguments, if any; also notice that the first line reports on the parent shell process, and in the last line, *ps* reports on itself.

ps without arguments lists all processes started from the current terminal or pseudo-terminal. But since *ps* is not a shell command, it doesn't correlate process IDs with the shell's job numbers. It also doesn't help you find the ID of the runaway process in another shell window.

To get this information, use *ps* **-a** (for "all"); this lists information on a different set of processes, depending on your UNIX version.

System V

Instead of listing all of those that were started under a specific terminal, *ps* **-a** on System V-derived systems lists all processes associated with any terminal that aren't group leaders. For our purposes, a "group leader" is the parent shell of a terminal or window. Therefore, if you are using a windowing system, *ps* **-a** lists all jobs started in all windows (by all users), but not their parent shells.

Assume that, in the above example, you have only one terminal or window. Then *ps* **-a** will print the same output as plain *ps* except for the first line, since that's the parent shell. This doesn't seem to be very useful.

But consider what happens when you have multiple windows open. Let's say you have three windows, all running terminal emulators like *xterm* for the X Window System. You start background jobs **fred**, **dave**, and **bob** in windows with pseudo-terminal numbers 1, 2, and 3, respectively. This situation is shown in Figure 8-1.

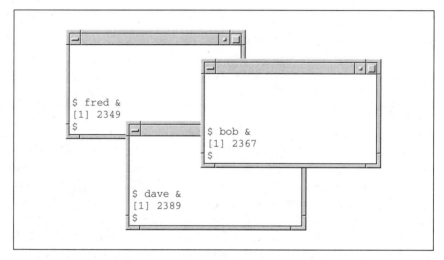

Figure 8-1: Background jobs in multiple windows

Assume you are in the uppermost window. If you type **ps**, you will see something like this:

```
PID TTY       TIME COMD
 146 pts/1    0:03 ksh
2349 pts/1    0:03 fred
2390 pts/1    0:00 ps
```

But if you type **ps -a**, you will see this:

```
PID TTY       TIME COMD
2349 pts/1    0:03 fred
2367 pts/2    0:17 bob
2389 pts/3    0:09 dave
2390 pts/1    0:00 ps
```

Now you should see how **ps -a** can help you track down a runaway process. If it's **dave**, you can type **kill 2389**. If that doesn't work, try **kill -QUIT 2389**, or in the worst case, **kill -KILL 2389**.

BSD

On BSD-derived systems, *ps* -a lists all jobs that were started on any terminal; in other words, it's a bit like concatenating the the results of plain *ps* for every user on the system. Given the above scenario, *ps* -a will show you all processes that the System V version shows, plus the group leaders (parent shells).

Unfortunately, *ps* -a (on any version of UNIX) will not report processes that are in certain pathological conditions where they "forget" things like what shell invoked them and what terminal they belong to. Such processes have colorful names ("zombies," "orphans") that are actually used in UNIX technical literature, not just informally by systems hackers. If you have a serious runaway process problem, it's possible that the process has entered one of these states.

Let's not worry about why or how a process gets this way. All you need to understand is that the process doesn't show up when you type **ps -a**. You need another option to *ps* to see it: on System V, it's *ps* -e ("everything"), whereas on BSD, it's *ps* -ax.

These options tell *ps* to list processes that either weren't started from terminals or "forgot" what terminal they were started from. The former category includes lots of processes that you probably didn't even know existed: these include basic processes that run the system and so-called *daemons* (pronounced "demons") that handle system services like mail, printing, network file systems, etc.

In fact, the output of *ps* -e or *ps* -ax is an excellent source of education about UNIX system internals, if you're curious about them. Run the command on your system and, for each line of the listing that looks interesting, invoke *man* on the process name or look it up in the Unix Programmer's Manual for your system.

User shells and processes are listed at the very bottom of *ps* -e or *ps* -ax output; this is where you should look for runaway processes. Notice that many processes in the listing have ? instead of a terminal. Either these aren't supposed to have one (such as the basic daemons) or they're runaways. Therefore it's likely that if *ps* -a doesn't find a process you're trying to kill, *ps* -e (or *ps* -ax) will list it with ? in the TTY (or TT) column. You can determine which process you want by looking at the COMD (or COMMAND) column.

trap

We've been discussing how signals affect the casual user; now let's talk a bit about how shell programmers can use them. We won't go into too much depth about this, because it's really the domain of systems programmers.

We mentioned above that programs in general can be set up to "trap" specific signals and process them in their own way. The **trap** built-in command lets you do this from within a shell script. **trap** is most important for "bullet-proofing" large shell programs so that they react appropriately to abnormal events—just as programs in any language should guard against invalid input. It's also important for certain systems programming tasks, as we'll see in the next chapter.

The syntax of **trap** is:

> **trap** *cmd sig1 sig2 ...*

That is, when any of *sig1*, *sig2*, etc., are received, run *cmd*, then resume execution. After *cmd* finishes, the script resumes execution just after the command that was interrupted.*

Of course, *cmd* can be a script or function. The *sigs* can be specified by name or by number. You can also invoke **trap** without arguments, in which case the shell will print a list of any traps that have been set, using symbolic names for the signals.

Here's a simple example that shows how **trap** works. Suppose we have a shell script called **loop** with this code:

```
while true; do
    sleep 60
done
```

This will just pause for 60 seconds (the *sleep*(1) command) and repeat indefinitely. **true** is a "do-nothing" command whose exit status is always 0.†
Try typing in this script. Invoke it, let it run for a little while, then type CTRL-C (assuming that is your interrupt key). It should stop, and you should get your shell prompt back.

---

*This is what *usually* happens. Sometimes the command currently running will abort (*sleep* acts like this, as we'll see soon); other times it will finish running. Further details are beyond the scope of this book.

†Actually, it's a built-in alias for **:**, the real shell "no-op."

Now insert the following line at the beginning of the script:

```
trap 'print \'You hit control-C!\'' INT
```

Invoke the script again. Now hit **CTRL-C**. The odds are overwhelming that you are interrupting the *sleep* command (as opposed to **true**). You should see the message "You hit control-C!", and the script will not stop running; instead, the *sleep* command will abort, and it will loop around and start another *sleep*. Hit **CTRL-** to get it to stop. Type **rm core** to get rid of the resulting core dump file.

Next, run the script in the background by typing **loop &**. Type **kill %loop** (i.e., send it the TERM signal); the script will terminate. Add TERM to the **trap** command, so that it looks like this:

```
trap 'print \'You hit control-C!\'' INT TERM
```

Now repeat the process: run it in the background and type **kill %loop**. As before, you will see the message and the process will keep on running. Type **kill -KILL %loop** to stop it.

Notice that the message isn't really appropriate when you use **kill**. We'll change the script so it prints a better message in the **kill** case:

```
trap 'print \'You hit control-C!\'' INT
trap 'print \'You tried to kill me!\'' TERM

while true; do
    sleep 60
done
```

Now try it both ways: in the foreground with CTRL-C and in the background with **kill**. You'll see different messages.

Traps and Functions

The relationship between traps and shell functions is straightforward, but it has certain nuances that are worth discussing. The most important thing to understand is that functions can have their own local traps; these aren't known outside of the function. In particular, the surrounding script doesn't know about them. Consider this code:

```
function settrap {
    trap 'print \'You hit control-C!\'' INT
}

settrap
while true; do
    sleep 60
done
```

If you invoke this script and hit your interrupt key, it will just exit. The trap on INT in the function is known only inside that function. On the other hand:

```
function loop {
    trap 'print \'How dare you!\'' INT
    while true; do
        sleep 60
    done
}

trap 'print \'You hit control-C!\'' INT
loop
```

When you run this script and hit your interrupt key, it will print "How dare you!". But how about this:

```
function loop {
    while true; do
        sleep 60
    done
}

trap 'print \'You hit control-C!\'' INT
loop
print 'exiting...'
```

This time the looping code is within a function, and the trap is set in the surrounding script. If you hit your interrupt key, it will print the message and then print "exiting . . . ". It will not repeat the loop as above.

Why? Remember that when the signal comes in, the shell aborts the current command, which in this case is a call to a function. The entire function aborts, and execution resumes at the next statement after the function call.

The advantage of traps that are local to functions is that they allow you to control a function's behavior separately from the surrounding code.

Yet you may want to define global traps inside functions. There is a rather kludgy way to do this; it depends on a feature that we introduce in the next chapter, which we call a "fake signal." Here is a way to set *trapcode* as a global trap for signal *SIG* inside a function:

```
trap "trap trapcode SIG" EXIT
```

This sets up the command **trap** *trapcode SIG* to run right after the function exits, at which time the surrounding shell script is in scope (i.e., is "in charge"). When that command runs, *trapcode* is set up to handle the *SIG* signal.

For example, you may want to reset the trap on the signal you just received, like this:

```
function trap_handler {
    trap "trap second_handler INT" EXIT
    print 'Interrupt: one more to abort.'
}

function second_handler {
    print 'Aborted.'
    exit
}

trap trap_handler INT
```

This code acts like the UNIX *mail* utility: when you are typing in a message, you must press your interrupt key twice to abort the process.

Speaking of *mail*, now we'll show a more practical example of traps.

Task 8-2

As part of an electronic mail system, write the shell code that lets a user compose a message.

The basic idea is to use *cat* to create the message in a temporary file and then hand the file's name off to a program that actually sends the message to its destination. The code to create the file is very simple:

```
msgfile=/tmp/msg$$
cat > $msgfile
```

Since *cat* without an argument reads from the standard input, this will just wait for the user to type a message and end it with the end-of-text character CTRL-D.

Process ID Variables and Temporary Files

The only thing new about this is **$$** in the filename expression. This is a special shell variable whose value is the process ID of the current shell.

To see how **$$** works, type **ps** and note the process ID of your shell process (*ksh*). Then type **print "$$"**; the shell will respond with that same number. Now type **ksh** to start a subshell, and when you get a prompt, repeat the process. You should see a different number, probably slightly higher than the last one.

A related built-in shell variable is ! (i.e., its value is $!), which contains the process ID of the most recently invoked background job. To see how this works, invoke any job in the background and note the process ID printed by the shell next to [1]. Then type **print "$!"**; you should see the same number.

The ! variable is useful in shell programs that involve multiple communicating processes, as we'll see later.

To return to our mail example: since all processes on the system must have unique process IDs, **$$** is excellent for constructing names of temporary files. We saw an example of this back in Chapter 2: we used the expression .hist$$ as a way of generating unique names for command history files so that several can be open at once, allowing multiple shell windows on a workstation to have their own history files. This expression generates names like .hist234. There are also examples of **$$** in Chapter 7, *Input/Output and Command-line Processing*, and Chapter 9, *Debugging Shell Programs*.

The directory */tmp* is conventionally used for temporary files. Many systems also have another directory, */usr/tmp*, for the same purpose. All files in these directories are usually erased whenever the computer is rebooted.

Nevertheless, a program should clean up such files before it exits, to avoid taking up unnecessary disk space. We could do this in our code very easily by adding the line **rm $msgfile** after the code that actually sends the message. But what if the program receives a signal during execution? For example, what if a user changes his or her mind about sending the message and hits CTRL-C to stop the process? We would need to clean up before exiting. We'll emulate the actual UNIX *mail* system by saving the message being written in a file called *dead.letter* in the current directory. We can do this by using **trap** with a command string that includes an **exit** command:

```
trap 'mv $msgfile dead.letter; exit' INT TERM
msgfile=/tmp/msg$$
cat > $msgfile
# send the contents of $msgfile to the specified mail address...
rm $msgfile
```

When the script receives an INT or TERM signal, it will remove the temp file and then exit. Note that the command string isn't *evaluated* until it needs to be run, so **$msgfile** will contain the correct value; that's why we surround the string in single quotes.

But what if the script receives a signal before **msgfile** is created—unlikely though that may be? Then **mv** will try to rename a file that doesn't exist. To fix this, we need to test for the existence of the file **$msgfile** before trying to delete it. The code for this is a bit unwieldy to put in a single command string, so we'll use a function instead:

```
function cleanup {
    if [[ -a $msgfile ]]; then
        mv $msgfile dead.letter
    fi
    exit
}

trap cleanup INT TERM

msgfile=/tmp/msg$$
cat > $msgfile
# send the contents of $msgfile to the specified mail address...
rm $msgfile
```

Ignoring Signals

Sometimes a signal comes in that you don't want to do anything about. If you give the null string (`" "` or `' '`) as the command argument to **trap**, then the shell will effectively ignore that signal. The classic example of a signal you may want to ignore is HUP (hangup), the signal the shell sends to all of your background processes when you log out.

HUP has the usual default behavior: it will kill the process that receives it. But there are bound to be times when you don't want a background job to terminate when you log out. For example, you may start a long compile or word processing job; you want to log out and come back later when you expect the job to be finished. Under normal circumstances, your background job will terminate when you log out. But if you run it in a shell environment where the HUP signal is ignored, the job will finish.

To do this, you could write a simple function that looks like this:

```
function ignorehup {
    trap "" HUP
    eval "$@"
}
```

We write this as a function instead of a script for reasons that will become clearer when we look in detail at subshells at the end of this chapter.

Actually, there is a UNIX command called *nohup* that does precisely this. The **start** script from the last chapter could include **nohup**:

```
eval nohup "$@" > logfile 2>&1 &
```

This prevents HUP from terminating your command and saves its standard and error output in a file. Actually, the following is just as good:

```
nohup "$@" > logfile 2>&1 &
```

If you understand why **eval** is essentially redundant when you use **nohup** in this case, then you have a firm grasp on the material in the previous chapter.

Resetting Traps

Another "special case" of the **trap** command occurs when you give a dash (-) as the command argument. This resets the action taken when the signal is received to the default, which usually is termination of the process.

As an example of this, let's return to Task 8-2, our mail program. After the user has finished sending the message, the temporary file is erased. At that point, since there is no longer any need to "clean up," we can reset the signal trap to its default state. The code for this, apart from function definitions, is:

```
trap abortmsg INT
trap cleanup TERM

msgfile=/tmp/msg$$
cat > $msgfile
# send the contents of $msgfile to the specified mail address...
rm $msgfile

trap - INT TERM
```

The last line of this code resets the handlers for the INT and TERM signals.

At this point you may be thinking that one could get seriously carried away with signal handling in a shell script. It is true that "industrial strength" programs devote considerable amounts of code to dealing with signals. But these programs are almost always large enough so that the signal-handling code is a tiny fraction of the whole thing. For example, you can bet that the real UNIX *mail* system is pretty darn bullet-proof.

However, you will probably never write a shell script that is complex enough, and that needs to be robust enough, to merit lots of signal handling. You may write a *prototype* for a program as large as *mail* in shell code, but prototypes by definition do not need to be bullet-proofed.

Therefore, you shouldn't worry about putting signal-handling code in every 20-line shell script you write. Our advice is to determine if there are any situations in which a signal could cause your program to do something seriously bad and add code to deal with those contingencies. What is "seriously bad"? Well, with respect to the above examples, we'd say that the case where HUP causes your job to terminate on logout *is* seriously bad, while the temporary file situation in our mail program is not.

The Korn shell has several new options to **trap** (with respect to the same command in most Bourne shells) that make it useful as an aid for debugging shell scripts. We'll cover these in the next chapter.

Coroutines

We've spent the last several pages on almost microscopic details of process behavior. Rather than continue our descent into the murky depths, we'll revert to a higher-level view of processes.

Earlier in this chapter, we covered ways of controlling multiple simultaneous jobs within an interactive login session; now we'll consider multiple process control within shell programs. When two (or more) processes are explicitly programmed to run simultaneously and possibly communicate with each other, we call them *coroutines*.

This is actually nothing new: a pipeline is an example of coroutines. The shell's pipeline construct encapsulates a fairly sophisticated set of rules about how processes interact with each other. If we take a closer look at these rules, we'll be better able to understand other ways of handling coroutines—most of which turn out to be simpler than pipelines.

When you invoke a simple pipeline, say **ls | more**, the shell invokes a series of UNIX primitive operations, a.k.a. *system calls*. In effect, the shell tells UNIX to do the following things; in case you're interested, we include in parentheses the actual system call used at each step:

1. Create two subprocesses, which we'll call P1 and P2 (the *fork* system call).
2. Set up I/O between the processes so that P1's standard output feeds into P2's standard input (*pipe*).
3. Start */bin/ls* in process P1 (*exec*).
4. Start */bin/more* in process P2 (*exec*).
5. Wait for both processes to finish (*wait*).

You can probably imagine how the above steps change when the pipeline involves more than two processes.

Now let's make things simpler. We'll see how to get multiple processes to run at the same time if the processes do not need to communicate. For example, we want the processes **dave** and **bob** to run as coroutines, without communication, in a shell script. Our initial solution would be this:

```
dave &
bob
```

Assume for the moment that **bob** is the last command in the script. The above will work—but only if **dave** finishes first. If **dave** is still running when the script finishes, then it becomes an *orphan*, i.e., it enters one of the "funny states" we mentioned earlier in this chapter. Never mind the details of orphanhood; just believe that you don't want this to happen, and if it does, you may need to use the "runaway process" method of stopping it, discussed earlier in this chapter.

wait

There is a way of making sure the script doesn't finish before **dave** does: the built-in command **wait**. Without arguments, **wait** simply waits until all background jobs have finished. So to make sure the above code behaves properly, we would add **wait**, like this:

```
dave &
bob
wait
```

Here, if **bob** finishes first, the parent shell will wait for **dave** to finish before finishing itself.

If your script has more than one background job and you need to wait for specific ones to finish, you can give **wait** the same type of job argument (with a percent sign) as you would use with **kill**, **fg**, or **bg**.

However, you will probably find that **wait** without arguments suffices for all coroutines you will ever program. Situations in which you would need to wait for specific background jobs are quite complex and beyond the scope of this book.

Advantages and Disadvantages of Coroutines

In fact, you may be wondering why you would ever need to program coroutines that don't communicate with each other. For example, why not just run **bob** after **dave** in the usual way? What advantage is there in running the two jobs simultaneously?

If you are running on a computer with one processor (CPU), then there is a performance advantage—but only if you have the **bgnice** option turned off (see Chapter 3, *Customizing Your Environment*), and even then only in certain situations.

Roughly speaking, you can characterize a process in terms of how it uses system resources in three ways: whether it is *CPU intensive* (e.g., does lots of number crunching), *I/O intensive* (does a lot of reading or writing to the disk), or *interactive* (requires user intervention).

We already know from Chapter 1, *Korn Shell Basics*, that it makes no sense to run an interactive job in the background. But apart from that, the more two or more processes differ with respect to these three criteria, the more advantage there is in running them simultaneously. For example, a number-crunching statistical calculation would do well when running at the same time as a long, I/O-intensive database query.

On the other hand, if two processes use resources in similar ways, it may even be less efficient to run them at the same time as it would be to run them sequentially. Why? Basically, because under such circumstances, the operating system often has to "time-slice" the resource(s) in contention.

For example, if both processes are "disk hogs," the operating system may enter a mode where it constantly switches control of the disk back and forth between the two competing processes; the system ends up spending at least as much time doing the switching as it does on the processes themselves. This phenomenon is known as *thrashing*; at its most severe, it can cause a system to come to a virtual standstill. Thrashing is a common problem; system administrators and operating system designers both spend lots of time trying to minimize it.

Parallelization

But if you have a computer with multiple CPUs (such as a Pyramid, Sequent, or Sun MP), you should be less concerned about thrashing. Furthermore, coroutines can provide dramatic increases in speed on this type of machine, which is often called a *parallel* computer; analogously, breaking up a process into coroutines is sometimes called *parallelizing* the job.

Normally, when you start a background job on a multiple-CPU machine, the computer will assign it to the next available processor. This means that the two jobs are actually—not just metaphorically—running at the same time.

In this case, the running time of the coroutines is essentially equal to that of the longest-running job plus a bit of overhead, instead of the sum of the run times of all processes (although if the CPUs all share a common disk drive, the possibility of I/O-related thrashing still exists). In the best case—all jobs having the same run time and no I/O contention—you get a speedup factor equal to the number of jobs.

Parallelizing a program is often not easy; there are several subtle issues involved and there's plenty of room for error. Nevertheless, it's worthwhile to know how to parallelize a shell script whether or not you have a parallel machine, especially since such machines are becoming more and more common.

We'll show how to do this—and give you an idea of some of the problems involved—by means of a simple task whose solution is amenable to parallelization.

Task 8-3

Write a utility that allows you to make multiple copies of a file at the same time.

We'll call this script *mcp*. The command **mcp** *filename dest1 dest2* ... should copy *filename* to all of the destinations given. The code for this should be fairly obvious:

```
file=$1
shift
for dest in "$@"; do
    cp $file $dest
done
```

Now let's say we have a parallel computer and we want this command to run as fast as possible. To parallelize this script, it's a simple matter of firing off the *cp* commands in the background and adding a **wait** at the end:

```
file=$1
shift
```

```
for dest in "$@"; do
    cp $file $dest &
done
wait
```

Simple, right? Well, there is one little problem: what happens if the user specifies duplicate destinations? If you're lucky, the file just gets copied to the same place twice. Otherwise, the identical *cp* commands will interfere with each other, possibly resulting in a file that contains two interspersed copies of the original file. In contrast, if you give the regular *cp* command two arguments that point to the same file, it will print an error message and do nothing.

To fix this problem, we would have to write code that checks the argument list for duplicates. Although this isn't too hard to do (see the exercises at the end of this chapter), the time it takes that code to run might offset any gain in speed from parallelization; furthermore, the code that does the checking detracts from the simple elegance of the script.

As you can see, even a seemingly trivial parallelization task has problems resulting from multiple processes having concurrent access to a given system resource (a file in this case). Such problems, known as *concurrency control* issues, become much more difficult as the complexity of the application increases. Complex concurrent programs often have much more code for handling the special cases than for the actual job the program is supposed to do!

Therefore it shouldn't surprise you that much research has been and is being done on parallelization, the ultimate goal being to devise a tool that parallelizes code automatically. (Such tools do exist; they usually work in the confines of some narrow subset of the problem.) Even if you don't have access to a multiple-CPU machine, parallelizing a shell script is an interesting exercise that should acquaint you with some of the issues that surround coroutines.

Coroutines with Two-way Pipes

Now that we have seen how to program coroutines that don't communicate with each other, we'll build on that foundation and discuss how to get them to communicate—in a more sophisticated way than with a pipeline. The Korn shell has a set of features that allow programmers to set up two-way communication between coroutines. These features aren't included in most Bourne shells.

If you start a background process by appending |& to a command instead of &, the Korn shell will set up a special two-way pipeline between the parent shell and the new background process. **read -p** in the parent shell reads a line of the background process' standard output; similarly, **print -p** in the parent shell feeds into the standard input of the background process. Figure 8-2 shows how this works.

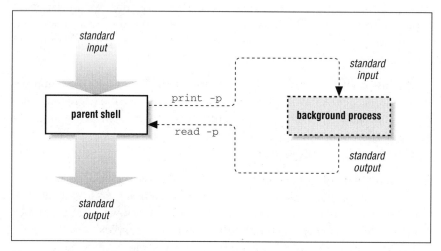

Figure 8-2: Coroutine I/O

This scheme has some intriguing possibilities. Notice the following things: first, the parent shell communicates with the background process independently of its own standard input and output. Second, the background process need not have any idea that a shell script is communicating with it in this manner. This means that the background process can be any pre-existing program that uses its standard input and output in normal ways.

Here's a task that shows a simple example:

Task 8-4

You would like to have an online calculator, but the existing UNIX utility *dc*(1) uses Reverse Polish Notation (RPN), *a la* Hewlett-Packard calculators. You'd rather have one that works like the $3.95 model you got with that magazine subscription. Write a calculator program that accepts standard algebraic notation.

The objective here is to write the program without re-implementing the calculation engine that *dc* already has—in other words, to write a program that translates algebraic notation to RPN and passes the translated line to *dc* to do the actual calculation.*

We'll assume that the function *alg2rpn*, which does the translation, already exists: given a line of algebraic notation as argument, it prints the RPN equivalent on the standard output. If we have this, then the calculator program (which we'll call *adc*) is very simple:

```
dc |&

while read line'?adc> '; do
    print -p "$(alg2rpn $line)"
    read -p answer
    print "     = $answer"
done
```

The first line of this code starts *dc* as a coroutine with a two-way pipe. Then the **while** loop prompts the user for a line and reads it until the user types **CTRL-D** for end-of-input. The loop body converts the line to RPN, passes it to *dc* through the pipe, reads *dc*'s answer, and prints it after an equal sign. For example:

```
$ adc
adc> 2 + 3
   = 5
adc> (7 * 8) + 54
   = 110
adc> ^D
$
```

Actually—as you may have noticed—it's not entirely necessary to have a two-way pipe with *dc*. You could do it with a standard pipe and let *dc* do its own output, like this:

```
{ while read line'?adc> '; do
      print "$(alg2rpn $line)"
  done
} | dc
```

The only difference from the above is the lack of equal sign before each answer is printed.

But: what if you wanted to make a fancy graphical user interface (GUI), like the *xcalc* program that comes with many X Window System installations? Then, clearly, *dc*'s own output would not be satisfactory, and you would need full control of your own standard output in the parent process. The user interface would have to capture *dc*'s output and display it in the

---

*The utility *bc*(1) actually provides similar functionality.

window properly. The two-way pipe is an excellent solution to this problem: just imagine that, instead of **print "** = **$answer"**, there is a call to a routine that displays the answer in the "readout" section of the calculator window.

All of this suggests that the two-way pipe scheme is great for writing shell scripts that interpose a software layer between the user (or some other program) and an existing program that uses standard input and output. In particular, it's great for writing new interfaces to old, standard UNIX programs that expect line-at-a-time, character-based user input and output. The new interfaces could be GUIs, or they could be network interface programs that talk to users over links to remote machines. In other words, the Korn shell's two-way pipe construct is designed to help develop very up-to-date software!

Two-way Pipes Versus Standard Pipes

Before we leave the subject of coroutines, we'll complete the circle by showing how the two-way pipe construct compares to regular pipelines. As you may have been able to figure out by now, it is possible to program a standard pipeline by using |& with **print –p**.

This has the advantage of reserving the parent shell's standard output for other use. The disadvantage is that the child process' standard output is directed to the two-way pipe: if the parent process doesn't read it with **read –p**, then it's effectively lost.

Subshells

Coroutines clearly represent the most complex relationship between processes that the Korn shell defines. To conclude this chapter, we will look at a much simpler type of interprocess relationship: that of a subshell with its parent shell. We saw in Chapter 3, *Customizing Your Environment*, that whenever you run a shell script, you actually invoke another copy of the shell that is a subprocess of the main, or *parent*, shell process. Now let's look at subshells in more detail.

Subshell Inheritance

The most important things you need to know about subshells are what characteristics they get, or *inherit,* from their parents. These are as follows:

- The current directory
- Environment variables
- Standard input, output, and error plus any other open file descriptors
- Any characteristics defined in the environment file (see Chapter 3, *Customizing Your Environment*)
- Signals that are ignored

The first three of these are inherited by all subprocesses, while the last is unique to subshells. Just as important are the things that a subshell does not inherit from its parent:

- Shell variables, except environment variables and those defined in the environment file
- Handling of signals that are not ignored

We covered some of this earlier (in Chapter 3, *Customizing Your Environment*), but these points are common sources of confusion, so they bear repeating.

Nested Subshells

Subshells need not be in separate scripts; you can also start a subshell within the same script (or function) as the parent. You do this in a manner very similar to the code blocks we saw in the last chapter. Just surround some shell code with parentheses (instead of curly brackets), and that code will run in a subshell. We'll call this a *nested* subshell.

For example, here is the calculator program, from above, with a subshell instead of a code block:

```
( while read line'?adc> '; do
      print "$(alg2rpn $line)"
  done
) | dc
```

The code inside the parentheses will run as a separate process. This is usually less efficient than a code block. The differences in functionality between subshells and code blocks are very few; they primarily pertain to issues of scope, i.e., the domains in which definitions of things like shell variables and signal traps are known. First, code inside a nested subshell obeys the above rules of subshell inheritance, except that it knows about variables defined in the surrounding shell; in contrast, think of blocks as code units that inherit *everything* from the outer shell. Second, variables and traps defined inside a code block are known to the shell code after the block, whereas those defined in a subshell are not.

For example, consider this code:

```
{
    fred=bob
    trap 'print \'You hit CTRL-C!\'' INT
}
while true; do
    print "\$fred is $fred"
    sleep 60
done
```

If you run this code, you will see the message **$fred is bob** every 60 seconds, and if you type CTRL-C, you will see the message, **You hit CTRL-C!**. You will need to type CTRL-\ to stop it (don't forget to remove the *core* file). Now let's change it to a nested subshell:

```
(
    fred=bob
    trap 'print \'You hit CTRL-C!\'' INT
)
while true; do
    print "\$fred is $fred"
    sleep 60
done
```

If you run this, you will see the message **$fred is**; the outer shell doesn't know about the subshell's definition of **fred** and therefore thinks it's null. Furthermore, the outer shell doesn't know about the subshell's trap of the INT signal, so if you hit CTRL-C, the script will terminate.

If a language supports code nesting, then it's considered desirable that definitions inside a nested unit have a scope limited to that nested unit. In other words, nested subshells give you better control than code blocks over the scope of variables and signal traps. Therefore we feel that you should use subshells instead of code blocks if they are to contain variable definitions or signal traps—unless efficiency is a concern.

This has been a long chapter, and it has covered a lot of territory. Here are some exercises that should help you make sure you have a firm grasp on the material. The last exercise is especially difficult for those without backgrounds in compilers, parsing theory, or formal language theory.

1. Write a shell script called *pinfo* that combines the **jobs** and *ps* commands by printing a list of jobs with their job numbers, corresponding process IDs, running times, and full commands.

2. Take the latest version of our C compiler shell script—or some other non-trivial shell script—and "bullet-proof" it with signal traps.

3. Take the *non-pipeline* version of our C compiler—or some other non-trivial shell script—and parallelize it as much as possible.

4. Write the code that checks for duplicate arguments to the *mcp* script. Bear in mind that different pathnames can point to the same file. (Hint: if **$i** is "1", then **eval 'print \${$i}'** prints the first command-line argument. Make sure you understand why.)

5. Redo the *findterms* program in the last chapter using a nested subshell instead of a code block.

6. (The following doesn't have that much to do with the material in this chapter *per se*, but it is a classic programming exercise:)

   Write the function *alg2rpn* used in *adc*. Here's how to do this: Arithmetic expressions in algebraic notation have the form *expr op expr*, where each *expr* is either a number or another expression (perhaps in parentheses), and *op* is +, –, ×, /, or % (remainder). In RPN, expressions have the form *expr expr op*. For example: the algebraic expression 2+3 is **2 3 +** in RPN; the RPN equivalent of **(2+3) × (9-5)** is **2 3 + 9 5 – ×**. The main advantage of RPN is that it obviates the need for parentheses and operator precedence rules (e.g., × is evaluated before +). The *dc* program accepts standard RPN, but each expression should have "p" appended to it: this tells *dc* to print its result, e.g., the first example above should be given to *dc* as **2 3 + p**.

   a. You need to write a routine that converts algebraic notation to RPN. This should be (or include) a function that calls itself (known as a *recursive* function) whenever it encounters a subexpression. It is especially important that this function keep track of where it is in the input string and how much of the string it "eats up" during its processing. (Hint: make use of the pattern matching operators discussed in Chapter 4, *Basic Shell Programming*, to ease the task of parsing input strings.)

   To make your life easier, don't worry about operator precedence for now; just convert to RPN from left to right. e.g., treat 3+4×5 as (3+4)×5 and 3×4+5 as (3×4)+5. This makes it possible for you to convert the input string on the fly, i.e., without having to read in the whole thing before doing any processing.

b. Enhance your solution to the previous exercise so that it supports operator precedence in the "usual" order: ×, /, % (remainder) +, −. e.g., treat **3+4×5** as **3+(4×5)** and **3×4+5** as **(3×4)+5**.

9
Debugging Shell Programs

We hope that we have convinced you that the Korn shell can be used as a serious UNIX programming environment. It certainly has enough features, control structures, etc. But another essential part of a programming environment is a set of powerful, integrated *support tools*. For example, there is a wide assortment of screen editors, compilers, debuggers, profilers, cross-referencers, etc., for languages like C and C++. If you program in one of these languages, you probably take such tools for granted, and you would undoubtedly cringe at the thought of having to develop code with, say, the *ed* editor and the *adb* machine-language debugger.

But what about programming support tools for the Korn shell? Of course, you can use any editor you like, including *vi* and *emacs*. And because the shell is an interpreted language, you don't need a compiler.* But there are no other tools available. The most serious problem is the lack of a debugger.

This chapter addresses that lack. The shell does have a few features that help in debugging shell scripts; we'll see these in the first part of the chapter. The Korn shell also has a couple of new features, not present in most Bourne shells, that make it possible to implement a full-blown debugging tool. We'll show these features; more importantly, we will present *kshdb*, a Korn shell debugger that uses them. *kshdb* is basic yet quite useable, and its implementation serves as an extended example of various shell programming techniques from throughout this book.

---

*Actually, if you are really concerned about efficiency, there are shell code compilers on the market; they convert shell scripts to C code that often runs quite a bit faster.

Basic Debugging Aids

What sort of functionality do you need to debug a program? At the most empirical level, you need a way of determining *what* is causing your program to behave badly, and *where* the problem is in the code. You usually start with an obvious *what* (such as an error message, inappropriate output, infinite loop, etc.), try to work backwards until you find a *what* that is closer to the actual problem (e.g., a variable with a bad value, a bad option to a command), and eventually arrive at the exact *where* in your program. Then you can worry about *how* to fix it.

Notice that these steps represent a process of starting with obvious information and ending up with often obscure facts gleaned through deduction and intuition. Debugging aids make it easier to deduce and intuit by providing relevant information easily or even automatically, preferably without modifying your code.

The simplest debugging aid (for any language) is the output statement, **print** in the shell's case. Indeed, old-timer programmers debugged their FORTRAN code by inserting **WRITE** cards into their decks. You can debug by putting lots of **print** statements in your code (and removing them later), but you will have to spend lots of time narrowing down not only *what* exact information you want but also *where* you need to see it. You will also probably have to wade through lots and lots of output to find the information you really want.

Set Options

Luckily, the shell has a few basic features that give you debugging functionality beyond that of **print**. The most basic of these are options to the **set -o** command (as covered in Chapter 3). These options can also be used on the command line when running a script, as Table 9-1 shows.

The **verbose** option simply echoes (to standard error) whatever input the shell gets. It is useful for finding the exact point at which a script is bombing. For example, assume your script looks like this:

```
fred
bob
dave
pete
ed
ralph
```

Table 9-1: Debugging Options

set –o Option	Command-line Option	Action
noexec	**–n**	Don't run commands; check for syntax errors only
verbose	**–v**	Echo commands before running them
xtrace	**–x**	Echo commands after command-line processing

None of these commands are standard UNIX programs, and they all do their work silently. Say the script crashes with a cryptic message like "segmentation violation." This tells you nothing about which command caused the error. If you type **ksh –v** *scriptname*, you might see this:

```
fred
bob
dave
segmentation violation
pete
ed
ralph
```

Now you know that **dave** is the probable culprit—though it is also possible that **dave** bombed because of something it expected **fred** or **bob** to do (e.g., create an input file) that they did incorrectly.

The **xtrace** option is more powerful: it echoes command lines after they have been through parameter substitution, command substitution, and the other steps of command-line processing (as listed in Chapter 7, *Input/Output and Command-line Processing*). For example:

```
$ set -o xtrace
$ fred=bob
+ fred=bob
$ print "$fred"
+ print bob
bob
$ ls -l $(whence emacs)
+ whence emacs
+ ls -l /usr/share/bin/emacs
-rwxr-xr-x  1 root     1593344 Apr  8  1991 /usr/share/bin/emacs
$
```

As you can see, **xtrace** starts each line it prints with **+**. This is actually customizable: it's the value of the built-in shell variable **PS4**. So if you set **PS4** to "**xtrace —> **" (e.g., in your *.profile* or environment file), then you'll get **xtrace** listings that look like this:

```
$ ls -l $(whence emacs)
xtrace--> whence emacs
xtrace--> ls -l /usr/share/bin/emacs
-rwxr-xr-x  1 root       1593344 Apr  8  1991 /usr/share/bin/emacs
$
```

An even better way of customizing **PS4** is to use a built-in variable we haven't seen yet: **LINENO**, which holds the number of the currently running line in a shell script. Put this line in your *.profile* or environment file:

```
PS4='line $LINENO: '
```

We use the same technique as we did with **PS1** in Chapter 3, *Customizing Your Environment*: using single quotes to postpone the evaluation of the string until each time the shell prints the prompt. This will print messages of the form **line** *N*: in your trace output. You could even include the name of the shell script you're debugging in this prompt by using the positional parameter **$0**:

```
PS4='$0 line $LINENO: '
```

As another example, say you are trying to track down a bug in a script called **fred** that contains this code:

```
dbfmq=$1.fmq
...
fndrs=$(cut -f3 -d' ' $dfbmq)
```

You type **fred bob** to run it in the normal way, and it hangs. Then you type **ksh -x fred bob**, and you see this:

```
+ dbfmq=bob.fmq
...
+ + cut -f3 -d
```

It hangs again at this point. You notice that *cut* doesn't have a filename argument, which means that there must be something wrong with the variable **dbfmq**. But it has executed the assignment statement **dbfmq=bob.fmq** properly... ah-*hah*! You made a typo in the variable name inside the command substitution construct.* You fix it, and the script works properly.

If the code you are trying to debug calls functions that are defined elsewhere (e.g., in your *.profile* or environment file), you can trace through these in the same way with an option to the **typeset** command. Just enter

---

*We should admit that if you turned on the **nounset** option at the top of this script, the shell would have flagged this error.

the command **typeset –ft** *functname*, and the named function will be traced whenever it runs. Type **typeset +ft** *functname* to turn tracing off.

The last option is **noexec**, which reads in the shell script, checks for syntax errors, but doesn't execute anything. It's worth using if your script is syntactically complex (lots of loops, code blocks, string operators, etc.) and the bug has side effects (like creating a large file or hanging up the system).

You can turn on these options with **set –o** in your shell scripts, and, as explained in Chapter 3, turn them off with **set +o** *option*. For example, if you're debugging a script with a nasty side effect, and you have localized it to a certain chunk of code, you can precede that chunk with **set –o noexec** (and, perhaps, close it with **set +o noexec**) to avoid the side effect.

Fake Signals

A more sophisticated set of debugging aids is the shell's three "fake signals," which can be used in **trap** statements to get the shell to act under certain conditions. Recall from the previous chapter that **trap** allows you to install some code that runs when a particular signal is sent to your script.

Fake signals act like real ones, but they are generated by the shell (as opposed to real signals, which the underlying operating system generates). They represent runtime events that are likely to be interesting to debuggers—both human ones and software tools—and can be treated just like real signals within shell scripts. The three fake signals and their meanings are listed in Table 9-2.

Table 9-2: Fake Signals

Fake Signal	When Sent
EXIT	The shell exits from a function or script
ERR	A command returns a non-0 exit status
DEBUG	After every statement

EXIT

The EXIT trap, when set, will run its code when the function or script within which it was set exits. Here's a simple example:

```
function func {
    print 'start of the function'
    trap 'print \'exiting from the function\'' EXIT
}

print 'start of the script'
trap 'print \'exiting from the script\'' EXIT
func
```

If you run this script, you will see this output:

```
start of the script
start of the function
exiting from the function
exiting from the script
```

In other words, the script starts by printing a message. Then it sets the trap for its own exit, then calls the function. The function does the same—prints a message and sets a trap for its exit. (Remember that functions can have their own local traps that supersede any traps set by the surrounding script.)

The function then exits, which causes the shell to send it the fake signal EXIT, which in turn runs the code **print 'exiting from the function'**. Then the script exits, and its own EXIT trap code is run.

An EXIT trap occurs no matter how the script or function exits—whether normally (by finishing the last statement), by an explicit **exit** or **return** statement, or by receiving a "real" signal such as INT or TERM. Consider the following inane number-guessing program:

```
trap 'print \'Thank you for playing!\'' EXIT

magicnum=$(($RANDOM%10+1))
print 'Guess a number between 1 and 10:'
while read guess'?number> '; do
    sleep 10
    if (( $guess == $magicnum )); then
        print 'Right!'
        exit
    fi
    print 'Wrong!'
done
```

This program picks a number between 1 and 10 by getting a random number (the built-in variable **RANDOM**), extracting the last digit (the remainder when divided by 10), and adding 1. Then it prompts you for a guess, and after 10 seconds, it will tell you if you guessed right.

If you did, the program will exit with the message, "Thank you for playing!", i.e., it will run the EXIT trap code. If you were wrong, it will prompt you again and repeat the process until you get it right. If you get bored with this little game and hit CTRL-C while waiting for it to tell you whether you were right, you will also see the message.

ERR

The fake signal ERR enables you to run code whenever a command in the surrounding script or function exits with non-zero status. Trap code for ERR can take advantage of the built-in variable ?, which holds the exit status of the previous command. It "survives" the trap and is accessible at the beginning of the trap-handling code.

A simple but effective use of this is to put the following code into a script you want to debug:

```
function errtrap {
    es=$?
    print "ERROR: Command exited with status $es."
}

trap errtrap ERR
```

The first line saves the non-zero exit status in the variable **es**. This code enables you to see which command in your script exits with error status and what the status is.

For example, if the shell can't find a command, it returns status 1. If you put the code in a script with a line of gibberish (like "lskdjfafd"), the shell will respond with:

```
scriptname[N]: lskdjfafd:  not found
ERROR: command exited with status 1.
```

N is the number of the line in the script that contains the bad command. In this case, the shell prints the line number as part of its own error-reporting mechanism, since the error was a command that the shell could not find. But if the non-0 exit status comes from another program, the shell won't report the line number. For example:

```
function errtrap {
    es=$?
    print "ERROR: Command exited with status $es."
}
```

```
trap errtrap ERR

function bad {
    return 17
}

bad
```

This will only print, **ERROR: Command exited with status 17**.

It would obviously be an improvement to include the line number in this error message. The built-in variable LINENO exists, but if you use it inside a function, it evaluates to the line number in the function, not in the overall file. In other words, if you used $LINENO in the **print** statement in the **errtrap** routine, it would always evaluate to 2.

To get around this problem, we simply pass $LINENO as an argument to the trap handler, surrounding it in single quotes so that it doesn't get evaluated until the fake signal actually comes in:

```
function errtrap {
    es=$?
    print "ERROR line $1: Command exited with status $es."
}

trap 'errtrap $LINENO' ERR
...
```

If you use this with the above example, the result is the message, **ERROR line 12: Command exited with status 17**. This is much more useful. We'll see a variation on this technique shortly.

This simple code is actually not a bad all-purpose debugging mechanism. It takes into account that a non-0 exit status does not necessarily indicate an undesirable condition or event: remember that every control construct with a conditional (**if**, **while**, etc.) uses a non-0 exit status to mean "false". Accordingly, the shell doesn't generate ERR traps when statements or expressions in the "condition" parts of control structures produce non-0 exit statuses.

But a disadvantage is that exit statuses are not as uniform (or even as meaningful) as they should be—as we explained in Chapter 5, *Flow Control*. A particular exit status need not say anything about the nature of the error or even that there was an error.

DEBUG

The final fake signal, DEBUG, causes the trap code to be run after every statement in the surrounding function or script. This has two possible uses. First is the use for humans, as a sort of a "brute force" method of tracking a certain element of a program's state that you notice is going awry.

For example, you notice that the value of a particular variable is running amok. The naive approach would be to put in lots of *print* statements to check the variable's value at several points. The DEBUG trap makes this easier by letting you do this:

```
function dbgtrap {
    print "badvar is $badvar"
}

trap dbgtrap DEBUG

...section of code in which problem occurs...

trap - DEBUG          # turn off DEBUG trap
```

This code will print the value of the wayward variable after every statement between the two **trap**s.

The second and far more important use of the DEBUG trap is as a primitive for implementing Korn shell debuggers. In fact, it would be fair to say that the DEBUG trap reduces the task of implementing a useful shell debugger from a large-scale software development project to a manageable exercise. Read on.

A Korn Shell Debugger

Commercially available debuggers give you much more functionality than the shell's **set** options and fake signals. The most advanced have fabulous graphical user interfaces, incremental compilers, symbolic evaluators, and other such amenities. But just about all modern debuggers—even the more modest ones—have features that enable you to "peek" into a program while it's running, to examine it in detail and in terms of its source language. Specifically, most debuggers let you do these things:

- Specify points at which the program stops execution and enters the debugger. These are called *breakpoints*.
- Execute only a bit of the program at a time, usually measured in source code statements. This ability is often called *stepping*.

- Examine and possibly change the state of the program (e.g., values of variables) in the middle of a run, i.e., when stopped at a breakpoint or after stepping.
- Do all of the above without having to change the source code.

Our debugger, called *kshdb*, has these features and a few more. Although it's a basic tool, without too many "bells and whistles", it is real.* The code is available from an anonymous FTP archive, as described in Appendix C; if you don't have access to the Internet, you can type or scan the code in. Either way, you can use *kshdb* to debug your own shell scripts, and you should feel free to enhance it. We'll suggest some enhancements at the end of this chapter.

Structure of the Debugger

The code for *kshdb* has several features worth explaining in some detail. The most important is the basic principle on which it works: it turns a shell script into a debugger for itself, by prepending debugger functionality to it; then it runs the new script.

The driver script

Therefore the code has two parts: the part that implements the debugger's functionality, and the part that installs that functionality into the script being debugged. The second part, which we'll see first, is the script called *kshdb*. It's very simple:

```
# kshdb -- Korn Shell debugger
# Main driver: constructs full script (with preamble) and runs it

print 'Korn Shell Debugger version 1.0\n'
_guineapig=$1
if [[ ! -r $1 ]]; then          # file not found or readable
    print "Cannot read $_guineapig." >&2
    exit 1
fi
shift

_tmpdir=/tmp
_libdir=.
_dbgfile=$_tmpdir/kshdb$$        # temp file for script being debugged (copy)
cat $_libdir/kshdb.pre $_guineapig > $_dbgfile
exec ksh $_dbgfile $_guineapig $_tmpdir $_libdir "$@"
```

---

*Unfortunately, *kshdb* won't work completely on SunOS versions 4.1.x and older.

kshdb takes as argument the name of the script being debugged, which for the sake of brevity we'll call the guinea pig. Any additional arguments will be passed to the guinea pig as its positional parameters.

If the argument is invalid (the file isn't readable), *kshdb* exits with error status. Otherwise, after an introductory message, it constructs a temporary filename in the way we saw in the last chapter. If you don't have (or don't have access to) */tmp* on your system, then you can substitute a different directory for **_tmpdir**.* Also, make sure that **_libdir** is set to the directory where the *kshdb.pre* and *kshdb.fns* files (which we'll see soon) reside. */usr/lib* is a good choice if you have access to it.

The *cat* statement builds the temp file: it consists of a file we'll see soon called *kshdb.pre*, which contains the actual debugger code, followed immediately by a copy of the guinea pig. Therefore the temp file contains a shell script that has been turned into a debugger for itself.

exec

The last line runs this script with **exec**, a statement we haven't seen yet. We've chosen to wait until now to introduce it because—as we think you'll agree—it can be dangerous. **exec** takes its arguments as a command line and runs the command in place of the current program, in the same process. In other words, the shell running the above script will *terminate immediately* and be replaced by **exec**'s arguments. The situations in which you would want to use **exec** are few, far between, and quite arcane—though this is one of them.†

In this case, **exec** just runs the newly-constructed shell script, i.e., the guinea pig with its debugger, in another Korn shell. It passes the new script three arguments—the names of the original guinea pig (**$_guineapig**), the temp directory (**$_tmpdir**), and the directory where *kshdb.pre* and *kshdb.fns* are kept—followed by the user's positional parameters, if any.

---

*All function names and variables (except those local to functions) in *kshdb* have names beginning with an underscore (_), to minimize the possibility of clashes with names in the guinea pig.

†**exec** can also be used with an I/O redirector only; this causes the redirector to take effect for the remainder of the script or login session. For example, the line **exec 2>errlog** at the top of a script directs standard error to the file *errlog* for the entire script.

The Preamble

Now we'll see the code that gets prepended to the script being debugged; we call this the *preamble*. It's kept in the following file *kshdb.pre*, which is also fairly simple.

```
# kshdb preamble
# prepended to shell script being debugged
# arguments:
# $1 = name of original guinea-pig script
# $2 = directory where temp files are stored
# $3 = directory where kshdb.pre and kshdb.fns are stored

_dbgfile=$0
_guineapig=$1
_tmpdir=$2
_libdir=$3
shift 3                       # move user's args into place

. $_libdir/kshdb.fns          # read in the debugging functions
_linebp=
_stringbp=
let _trace=0                  # initialize execution trace to off
let _i=1                      # read guinea-pig file into lines array
while read -r _lines[$_i]; do
    let _i=$_i+1
done < $_guineapig

trap _cleanup EXIT            # erase files before exiting
let _steps=1                  # no. of stmts to run after trap is set
LINENO=-1
trap '_steptrap $LINENO' DEBUG
:
```

The first few lines save the three fixed arguments in variables and shift them out of the way, so that the positional parameters (if any) are those that the user supplied on the command line as arguments to the guinea pig. Then, the preamble reads in another file, *kshdb.fns*, that contains the "meat" of the debugger as function definitions. We put this code in a separate file to minimize the size of the temp file. We'll examine *kshdb.fns* shortly.

Next, *kshdb.pre* initializes the two breakpoint lists to empty and execution tracing to off (see below), then reads the guinea pig into an array of lines. We do the latter so that the debugger can access lines in the script when performing certain checks, and so that the execution trace feature can print lines of code as they execute.

The real fun begins in the last group of code lines, where we set up the debugger to start working. We use two **trap** commands with fake signals. The first sets up a cleanup routine (which just erases the temporary file) to be called on EXIT, i.e., when the script terminates for any reason. The second, and more important, sets up the function **_steptrap** to be called after every statement.

_steptrap gets an argument that evaluates to the number of the line in the guinea pig that just ran. We use the same technique with the built-in variable **LINENO** that we saw earlier in the chapter, but with an added twist: if you assign a value to **LINENO**, it uses that as the next line number and increments from there. The statement **LINENO**=−1 re-starts line numbering so that the first line in the guinea pig is line 1.

After the DEBUG trap is set, the preamble ends with a "do-nothing" statement (:). The shell executes this statement and enters **_steptrap** for the first time. The variable **_steps** is set up so that **_steptrap** executes its last **elif** clause, as you'll see shortly, and enters the debugger. As a result, execution halts just before the first statement of the guinea pig is run, and the user sees a **kshdb>** prompt; the debugger is now in full operation.

Debugger Functions

The function **_steptrap** is the entry point into the debugger; it is defined in the file *kshdb.fns*, which is given in its entirety at the end of this chapter. Here is **_steptrap**:

```
# Here after each statement in script being debugged.
# Handle single-step and breakpoints.
function _steptrap {
    _curline=$1                          # arg is no. of line that just ran

    (( $_trace )) && _msg "$PS4 line $_curline: ${_lines[$_curline]}"

    if (( $_steps >= 0 )); then          # if in step mode
        let _steps="$_steps - 1"         # decrement counter
    fi

    # first check if line num or string breakpoint reached
    if _at_linenumbp || _at_stringbp; then
        _msg "Reached breakpoint at line $_curline"
        _cmdloop                         # breakpoint, enter debugger

    # if not, check whether break condition exists and is true
    elif [[ -n $_brcond ]] && eval $_brcond; then
        _msg "Break condition $_brcond true at line $_curline"
        _cmdloop

    # next, check if step mode and number of steps is up
    elif (( $_steps == 0 )); then        # if step mode and time to stop
        _msg "Stopped at line $_curline"
        _cmdloop                         # enter debugger
```

```
    fi
}
```

_steptrap starts by setting **_curline** to the number of the guinea pig line that just ran. If execution tracing is turned on, it prints the **PS4** execution trace prompt (a la **xtrace** mode), the line number, and the line of code itself.

Then it does one of two things: enter the debugger, the heart of which is the function **_cmdloop**, or just return so that the shell can execute the next statement. It chooses the former if a *breakpoint* or *break condition* (see below) has been reached, or if the user stepped into this statement.

Commands

We'll explain shortly how **_steptrap** determines these things; now we'll look at **_cmdloop**. It's a typical command loop, resembling a combination of the **case** statements we saw in Chapter 5, *Flow Control*, and the calculator loop we saw in the previous chapter.

```
# Debugger command loop.
# Here at start of debugger session, when breakpoint reached,
# or after single-step.
function _cmdloop {
    typeset cmd args

    while read -s cmd"?kshdb> " args; do
        case $cmd in
            \*bp ) _setbp $args ;;  # set breakpoint at line num or string.

            \*bc ) _setbc $args ;;  # set break condition.

            \*cb ) _clearbp ;;      # clear all breakpoints.

            \*g  ) return ;;        # start/resume execution

            \*s  ) let _steps=${args:-1} # single-step N times (default 1)
                   return ;;

            \*x  ) _xtrace ;;       # toggle execution trace

            \*\? | \*h ) _menu ;;   # print command menu

            \*q  ) exit ;;          # quit

            \** ) _msg "Invalid command: $cmd" ;;

              * ) eval $cmd $args ;;  # otherwise, run shell command
        esac
    done
}
```

At each iteration, **cmdloop** prints a prompt, reads a command, and processes it. We use **read –s** so that the user can take advantage of command-line editing within *kshdb*. All *kshdb* commands start with ***** to prevent confusion with shell commands. Anything that isn't a *kshdb* command (and doesn't start with *****) is passed off to the shell for execution. Table 9-3 summarizes the debugger commmands.

Table 9-3: kshdb Commands

Command	Action
*bp *N*	Set breakpoint at line *N*
*bp *str*	Set breakpoint at next line containing *str*
*bp	List breakpoints and break condition
*bc *str*	Set break condition to *str*
*bc	Clear break condition
*cb	Clear all breakpoints
*g	Start or resume execution
*s [*N*]	Step through *N* statements (default 1)
*x	Toggle execution tracing
*h, *?	Print a help menu
*q	Quit

Before we look at the individual commands, it is important that you understand how control passes through **_steptrap**, the command loop, and the guinea pig.

_steptrap runs after every statement in the guinea pig as a result of the **trap ... DEBUG** statement in the preamble. If a breakpoint has been reached or the user previously typed in a step command (***s**), **_steptrap** calls the command loop. In doing so, it effectively "interrupts" the shell that is running the guinea pig to hand control over to the user.*

The user can invoke debugger commands as well as shell commands that run in the same shell as the guinea pig. This means that you can use shell commands to check values of variables, signal traps, and any other information local to the script being debugged.

---

*In fact, low-level systems programmers can think of the entire **trap** mechanism as quite similar to an interrupt-handling scheme.

The command loop runs, and the user stays in control, until the user types *g, *s, or *q. Let's look in detail at what happens in each of these cases.

*g has the effect of running the guinea pig uninterrupted until it finishes or hits a breakpoint. But actually, it simply exits the command loop and returns to _steptrap, which exits as well. The shell takes control back; it runs the next statement in the guinea pig script and calls _steptrap again. Assuming there is no breakpoint, this time _steptrap will just exit again, and the process will repeat until there is a breakpoint or the guinea pig is done.

Stepping

When the user types *s, the command loop code sets the variable _steps to the number of steps the user wants to execute, i.e., to the argument given. Assume at first that the user omits the argument, meaning that _steps is set to 1. Then the command loop exits and returns control to _steptrap, which (as above) exits and hands control back to the shell. The shell runs the next statement and returns to _steptrap, which sees that _steps is 1 and decrements it to 0. Then the second **elif** conditional sees that _steps is 0, so it prints a "stopped" message and calls the command loop.

Now assume that the user supplies an argument to *s, say 3. _steps is set to 3. Then the following happens:

1. After the next statement runs, _steptrap is called again. It enters the first **if** clause, since _steps is greater than 0. _steptrap decrements _steps to 2 and exits, returning control to the shell.

2. This process repeats, another step in the guinea pig is run, and _steps becomes 1.

3. A third statement is run and we're back in _steptrap. _steps is decremented to 0, the second **elif** clause is run, and _steptrap breaks out to the command loop again.

The overall effect is that three steps run and then the debugger takes over again.

Finally, the *q command calls the function **_cleanup**, which just erases the temp file and exits the entire program.

All other debugger commands (***bp**, ***bc**, ***cb**, ***x** and shell commands) cause the shell to stay in the command loop, meaning that the user prolongs the "interruption" of the shell.

Breakpoints

Now we'll examine the breakpoint-related commands and the breakpoint mechanism in general. The ***bp** command calls the function **_setbp**, which can set two kinds of breakpoints, depending on the type of argument given. If it is a number, it's treated as a line number; otherwise it's interpreted as a string that the breakpoint line should contain.

For example, the command ***bp 15** sets a breakpoint at line 15, and ***bp grep** sets a breakpoint at the next line that contains the string **grep**—whatever number that turns out to be. Although you can always look at a numbered listing of a file,* string arguments to ***bp** can make that unnecessary.

Here is the code for **_setbp**:

```
# Set breakpoint(s) at given line numbers and/or strings
# by appending lines to breakpoint file
function _setbp {
    if [[ -z $1 ]]; then
        _listbp
    elif [[ $1 = +([0-9]) ]]; then  # number, set bp at that line
        _linebp="${_linebp}$1|"
        _msg "Breakpoint at line " $1
    else                            # string, set bp at next line w/string
        _stringbp="${_stringbp}$@|"
        _msg "Breakpoint at next line containing $@."
    fi
}
```

_setbp sets the breakpoints by storing them in the variables **_linebp** (line number breakpoints) and **_stringbp** (string breakpoints). Both have breakpoints separated by pipe character delimiters, for reasons that will become clear shortly. This implies that breakpoints are cumulative; setting new breakpoints does not erase the old ones.

The only way to remove breakpoints is with the command ***cb**, which (in function **_clearbp**) clears all of them at once by simply resetting the two variables to null. If you don't remember what breakpoints you have set, the command ***bp** without arguments lists them.

---

* **pr -n** *filename* prints a numbered listing to standard output on System V-derived versions of UNIX. Some older BSD-derived systems don't support it. If this doesn't work on your system, try **cat -n** *filename*, or if that doesn't work, create a shell script with this single line:

```
awk '{ print NR, "\t", $0 }' $1
```

The functions **_at_linenumbp** and **_at_stringbp** are called by **_steptrap** after every statement; they check whether the shell has arrived at a line number or string breakpoint, respectively.

Here is **_at_linenumbp**:

```
# See if next line no. is a breakpoint.
function _at_linenumbp {
    [[ $_curline = @(${_linebp%\|}) ]]
}
```

_at_linenumbp takes advantage of the pipe character as the separator between line numbers: it constructs a regular expression of the form @(*N1*|*N2*|...) by taking the list of line numbers **_linebp**, removing the trailing |, and surrounding it with @(and). For example, if **$_linebp** is 3|15|19|, then the resulting expression is @(3|15|19).

If the current line is any of these numbers, then the conditional becomes true, and **_at_linenumbp** also returns a "true" (0) exit status.

The check for a string breakpoint works on the same principle, but it's slightly more complicated; here is **_at_stringbp**:

```
# Search string breakpoints to see if next line in script matches.
function _at_stringbp {
    [[ -n $_stringbp && ${_lines[$_curline]} = *@(${_stringbp%\|})* ]]
}
```

The conditional first checks if **$_stringbp** is non-null (meaning that string breakpoints have been defined). If not, the conditional evaluates to false, but if so, its value depends on the pattern match after the **&&**—which tests the current line to see if it contains any of the breakpoint strings.

The expression on the right side of the equal sign is similar to the one in **_at_linenumbp** above, except that it has * before and after it. This gives expressions of the form *@(*S1*|*S2*|...)*, where the *S*s are the string breakpoints. This expression matches any line that contains any one of the possibilities in the parenthesis.

The left side of the equal sign is the text of the current line in the guinea pig. So, if this text matches the regular expression, then we've reached a string breakpoint; accordingly, the conditional expression and **_at_stringbp** return exit status 0.

_steptrap uses the || ("or") construct in its **if** statement, which evaluates to true if either type of breakpoint occurred. If so, it calls the main command loop.

Break conditions

kshdb has another feature related to breakpoints: the *break condition*. This is a string that the user can specify that is evaluated as a command; if it is true (i.e., returns exit status 0), the debugger enters the command loop.

Since the break condition can be any line of shell code, there's lots of flexibility in what can be tested. For example, you can break when a variable reaches a certain value (e.g., (($x < 0))) or when a particular piece of text has been written to a file (**grep** *string file*). You will probably think of all kinds of uses for this feature.*

To set a break condition, type ***bc** *string*. To remove it, type ***bc** without arguments—this installs the null string, which is ignored.

_steptrap evaluates the break condition $_brcond only if it's non-null. If the break condition evaluates to 0, then the **if** clause is true and, once again, _steptrap calls the command loop.

Execution tracing

The final feature is execution tracing, available through the ***x** command. This feature is meant to overcome the fact that a *kshdb* user can't use **set -o xtrace** while debugging (by entering it as a shell command), because its scope is limited to the **_cmdloop** function.

The function **_xtrace** "toggles" execution tracing by simply assigning to the variable _trace the logical "not" of its current value, so that it alternates between 0 (off) and 1 (on). The preamble initializes it to 0.

Limitations

kshdb was not designed to push the state of the debugger art forward or to have an overabundance of features. It has the most useful basic features, its implementation is compact and (we hope) comprehensible, and it does have some important limitations. The ones we know of are described in the list that follows.

---

*Bear in mind that if your break condition produces any standard output (or standard error), you will see it after every statement. Also, make sure your break condition doesn't take a long time to run; otherwise your script will run very, very slowly.

1. The shell should really have the ability to trap before each statement, not after. This is the way most commercial source-code debuggers work.* At the very least, the shell should provide a variable that contains the number of the line about to run instead of (or in addition to) the number of the line that just ran.

2. String breakpoints cannot begin with digits or contain pipe characters (|) unless they are properly escaped.

3. You can only set breakpoints—whether line number or string—on lines in the guinea pig that contain what the shell's documentation calls *simple commands*, i.e., actual UNIX commands, shell built-ins, function calls, or aliases. If you set a breakpoint on a line that contains only whitespace or a comment, the shell will always skip over that breakpoint. More importantly, control keywords like **while**, **if**, **for**, **do**, **done**, and even conditionals ([[. . .]] and ((. . .))) won't work either, unless a simple command is on the same line.

4. **kshdb** will not "step down" into shell scripts that are called from the guinea pig. To do this, you have to edit your guinea pig and change a call to *scriptname* to **kshdb** *scriptname*.

5. Similarly, nested subshells are treated as one gigantic statement; you cannot step down into them at all.

6. The guinea pig should not trap on the fake signals DEBUG or EXIT; otherwise the debugger won't work.

7. Variables that are **typeset** (see Chapter 4, *Basic Shell Programming*) are not accessible in break conditions. However, you can use the shell command **print** to check their values.

8. Command error handling is weak. For example, a non-numeric argument to ***s** will cause it to bomb.

Many of these are not insurmountable; see the exercises.

Sample kshdb Session

Now we'll show a transcript of an actual session with *kshdb*, in which the guinea pig is the solution to Task 6-2. For convenience, here is a numbered listing of the script, which we'll call *lscol*.

---

*This kind of functionality is expected to be added in the next Korn shell release.

```
1       set -A filenames $(ls $1)
2       typeset -L14 fname
3       let count=0
4       let numcols=5
5
6       while [[ $count -lt ${#filenames[*]} ]]; do
7           fname=${filenames[$count]}
8           print -n "$fname    "
9           let count="count + 1"
10          if [[ $((count % numcols)) = 0 ]]; then
11              print              # NEWLINE
12          fi
13      done
14
15      if [[ $((count % numcols)) != 0 ]]; then
16          print
17      fi
```

Here is the *kshdb* session transcript:

```
$ kshdb lscol /usr/spool
Korn shell Debugger version 1.0

Stopped at line 0
kshdb> *bp 4
Breakpoint at line 4
kshdb> *g
Reached breakpoint at line 4
kshdb> print $count $numcols
0 5
kshdb> *bc [[ $count -eq 10 ]]
Break when true: [[ $count -eq 10 ]]
kshdb> *g
bwnfs           cron            locks           lpd             lpd.lock
mail            mqueue          rwho            secretmail      uucp
Break condition [[ $count -eq 10 ]] true at line 9
kshdb> *bc
Break condition cleared.
kshdb> *bp NEWLINE
Breakpoint at next line containing "NEWLINE".
kshdb> *g

Reached breakpoint at line 11
kshdb> print $count
10
kshdb> let count=9
kshdb> *g
uucp
Reached breakpoint at line 11
kshdb> *bp
Breakpoints at lines:
 4
Breakpoints at strings:
NEWLINE
```

```
No break condition.
kshdb> *g
uucppublic
$
```

First, notice that we gave the guinea pig script the argument /usr/spool, meaning that we want to list the files in that directory. We begin by setting a simple breakpoint at line 4 and starting the script. It stops after executing line 4 (**let numcols=5**). Then we issue a shell **print** command to show that the variables **count** and **numcols** are indeed set correctly.

Next, we set a break condition, telling the debugger to kick in when **$count** is 10, and we resume execution. Sure enough, the guinea pig prints 10 filenames and stops at line 9, on which **$count** is incremented. We clear the break condition by typing ***bc** without an argument, since otherwise the shell would stop after every statement until the condition becomes false.

The next command shows how the string breakpoint mechanism works. We tell the debugger to break when it hits a line that contains the string NEWLINE. This string is in a comment on line 11. Notice that it doesn't matter that the string is in a comment—just that the line it's on contain an actual command. We resume execution, and the debugger hits the breakpoint at line 11.

After that, we show how we can use the debugger to change the guinea pig's state while running. We see that **$count** is still 10; we change it to 9. In the next iteration of the **while** loop, the script accesses the same filename that it just did (*uucp*), increments **count** back to 10, and hits the breakpoint again. Finally, we list breakpoints and let the script execute to its end; it prints out one last filename and exits.

Exercises

We'll conclude this chapter with a few exercises, which are suggested enhancements to *kshdb*.

1. Improve command error handling in these ways:
   a. For numeric arguments to ***bp**, check that they are valid line numbers for the particular guinea pig.
   b. Check that arguments to ***s** are valid numbers.
   c. Any other error handling you can think of.

2. Enhance the ***cb** command so that the user can delete specific breakpoints (by string or line number).

3. Remove the major limitation in the breakpoint mechanism:

   a. Improve it so that if the line number selected does not contain an actual UNIX command, the next closest line above it is used as the breakpoint instead.

   b. Do the same thing for string breakpoints. (Hint: first translate each string breakpoint command into one or more line-number breakpoint commands.)

4. Implement an option that causes a break into the debugger whenever a command exits with non-0 status:

   a. Implement it as the command-line option **-e**.

   b. Implement it as the debugger commands ***be** (to turn the option on) and ***ne** (to turn it off). (Hint: you won't be able to use the ERR trap, but bear in mind that when you enter **_steptrap**, **$?** is still the exit status of the last command that ran.)

5. Add the ability to "step down" into scripts that the guinea pig calls (i.e., non-nested subshells) as the command-line option **-s**. One way of implementing this is to change the *kshdb* script so that it "plants" recursive calls to *kshdb* in the guinea pig. You can do this by filtering the guinea pig through a loop that reads each line and determines, with the **whence -v** and *file(1)* (see the man page) commands, if the line is a call to another shell script.* If it is, prepend *kshdb* **-s** to the line and write it to the new file; if not, just pass it through as is.

6. Add support for multiple break conditions, so that *kshdb* stops execution when any one of them becomes true and prints a message that says which one is true. Do this by storing the break conditions in a colon-separated list or an array. Try to make this as efficient as possible, since the checking will take place after every statement.

7. Add any other features you can think of.

If you add significant functionality to *kshdb*, we invite you to send your version to the author, care of O'Reilly and Associates, at **billr@ora.com** on the Internet or, via US Mail, at:

O'Reilly & Associates, Inc.
103 Morris St., Suite A
Sebastopol, CA 95472

---

*Notice that this method should catch most nested shell scripts but not all of them. For example, it won't catch shell scripts that follow semicolons (e.g., **cmd1**; **cmd2**).

We'll select the best one and publish it in the next revision of our *UNIX Power Tools* CD-ROM. Remember: there is no "official" Korn shell debugger, and as more and more programmers realize how powerful the Korn shell is as a programming environment, a debugger will become more and more necessary. We've made the initial effort, and we leave it up to you to finish the job!

Finally, here is the complete source code for the debugger function file *kshdb.fns*:

```
# Here after each statement in script being debugged.
# Handle single-step and breakpoints.
function _steptrap {
    _curline=$1                      # arg is no. of line that just ran

    (( $_trace )) && _msg "$PS4 line $_curline: ${_lines[$_curline]}"

    if (( $_steps >= 0 )); then      # if in step mode
        let _steps="$_steps - 1"     # decrement counter
    fi

    # first check if line num or string breakpoint reached
    if _at_linenumbp || _at_stringbp; then
        _msg "Reached breakpoint at line $_curline"
        _cmdloop                     # breakpoint, enter debugger

    # if not, check whether break condition exists and is true
    elif [[ -n $_brcond ]] && eval $_brcond; then
        _msg "Break condition $_brcond true at line $_curline"
        _cmdloop

    # next, check if step mode and number of steps is up
    elif (( $_steps == 0 )); then    # if step mode and time to stop
        _msg "Stopped at line $_curline"
        _cmdloop                     # enter debugger
    fi
}


# Debugger command loop.
# Here at start of debugger session, when breakpoint reached,
# or after single-step.
function _cmdloop {
    typeset cmd args

    while read -s cmd"?kshdb> " args; do
        case $cmd in
            \*bp ) _setbp $args ;;   # set breakpoint at line num or string.

            \*bc ) _setbc $args ;;   # set break condition.

            \*cb ) _clearbp ;;       # clear all breakpoints.
```

```
                \*g  ) return ;;              # start/resume execution

                \*s  ) let _steps=${args:-1} # single-step N times (default 1)
                        return ;;

                \*x  ) _xtrace ;;            # toggle execution trace

                \*\? | \*h ) _menu ;;        # print command menu

                \*q  ) exit ;;               # quit

                \**  ) _msg "Invalid command: $cmd" ;;

                *  ) eval $cmd $args ;;      # otherwise, run shell command
        esac
    done
}


# See if next line no. is a breakpoint.
function _at_linenumbp {
    [[ $_curline = @(${_linebp%\|}) ]]
}


# Search string breakpoints to see if next line in script matches.
function _at_stringbp {
    [[ -n $_stringbp && ${_lines[$_curline]} = *@(${_stringbp%\|})* ]]
}


# Print the given message to standard error.
function _msg {
    print "$@" >&2
}


# Set breakpoint(s) at given line numbers and/or strings
# by appending lines to breakpoint file
function _setbp {
    if [[ -z $1 ]]; then
        _listbp
    elif [[ $1 = +([0-9]) ]]; then  # number, set bp at that line
        _linebp="${_linebp}$1|"
        _msg "Breakpoint at line " $1
    else                            # string, set bp at next line w/string
        _stringbp="${_stringbp}$@|"
        _msg "Breakpoint at next line containing $@."
    fi
}


# List breakpoints and break condition.
function _listbp {
```

```
    _msg "Breakpoints at lines:"
    _msg "$(print $_linebp | tr '|' ' ')"
    _msg "Breakpoints at strings:"
    _msg "$(print $_stringbp | tr '|' ' ')"
    _msg "Break on condition:"
    _msg "$_brcond"
}


# Set or clear break condition
function _setbc {
    if [[ -n "$@" ]]; then
        _brcond=$args
        _msg "Break when true: $_brcond"
    else
        _brcond=
        _msg "Break condition cleared."
    fi
}


# Clear all breakpoints.
function _clearbp {
    _linebp=
    _stringbp=
    _msg "All breakpoints cleared."
}


# Toggle execution trace feature on/off
function _xtrace {
    let _trace="! $_trace"
    _msg "Execution trace \c"
    if (( $_trace )); then
        _msg "on."
    else
        _msg "off."
    fi
}

# Print command menu
function _menu {
    _msg 'kshdb commands:
        *bp N               set breakpoint at line N
        *bp str             set breakpoint at next line containing str
        *bp                 list breakpoints and break condition
        *bc str             set break condition to str
        *bc                 clear break condition
        *cb                 clear all breakpoints
        *g                  start/resume execution
        *s [N]              execute N statements (default 1)
        *x                  toggle execution trace on/off
```

```
        *h, *?              print this menu
        *q                  quit'
}


# Erase temp files before exiting.
function _cleanup {
    rm $_dbgfile 2>/dev/null
}
```

In this chapter:
- *Installing the Korn Shell as the Standard Shell*
- *Environment Customization*
- *System Security Features*

10

Korn Shell Administration

System administrators use the shell as part of their job of setting up a system-wide environment for all users. In this chapter, we'll discuss the Korn shell's features that relate to this task from two perspectives: customization that is available to all users and system security. We assume that you already know the basics of UNIX system administration.*

Installing the Korn Shell as the Standard Shell

As a prelude to system-wide customization, we want to emphasize something about the Korn shell that doesn't apply to most other shells: you can install it as if it were the standard Bourne shell, i.e., as */bin/sh*. Just save the real Bourne shell as another filename, such as */bin/bsh*, in case anyone actually needs it for anything (which is doubtful), then rename your Korn shell as */bin/sh*.

Many installations have done this with absolutely no ill effects. Not only does this make the Korn shell your system's standard login shell, but it also makes most existing Bourne shell scripts run faster, and it has security advantages that we'll see later in this chapter.

As we will see in Appendix A, the Korn shell is backward-compatible with the Bourne shell except that it doesn't support ^ as a synonym for the pipe character |. Unless you have an ancient UNIX system, or you have some very, very old shell scripts, you needn't worry about this.

---

*A good source of information on system administration is *Essential System Administration*, a Nutshell Handbook from O'Reilly & Associates, Inc., by AEleen Frisch.

But if you want to be absolutely sure, simply search through all shell scripts in all directories in your **PATH**. An easy way to do this is to use the *file* command, which we saw in Chapter 5, *Flow Control*, and Chapter 9, *Debugging Shell Programs. file* prints "executable shell script" when given the name of one.* Here is a script that looks for ^ in shell scripts in every directory in your **PATH**:

```
IFS=:
for d in $PATH; do
    print checking $d:
    cd $d
    scripts=$(file * | grep 'shell script' | cut -d: -f1)
    for f in $scripts; do
        grep '\^' $f /dev/null
    done
done
```

The first line of this script make it possible to use **$PATH** as an item list in the **for** loop. For each directory, it **cd**s there and finds all shell scripts by piping the *file* command into *grep* and then, to extract the filename only, into *cut*. Then for each shell script, it searches for the ^ character.†

If you run this script, you will probably find several occurrences of ^—but these should be used within regular expressions in *grep*, *sed*, or *awk* commands, not as pipe characters. Assuming this is the case, it is safe for you to install the Korn shell as */bin/sh*.

Environment Customization

Like the Bourne shell, the Korn shell uses the file */etc/profile* for system-wide customization. When a user logs in, the shell reads and runs */etc/profile* before running the user's *.profile*.

We won't cover all the possible commands you might want to put in */etc/profile*. But the Korn shell has a few unique features that are particularly relevant to system-wide customization; we'll discuss them here.

We'll start with two built-in commands that you can use in */etc/profile* to tailor your users' environments and constrain their use of system resources.

---

*The exact message varies from system to system; make sure that yours prints this message when given the name of a shell script. If not, just substitute the message your *file* command prints for "shell script" in the code below.

†The inclusion of */dev/null* in the *grep* command is a kludge that forces *grep* to print the names of files that contain a match, even if there is only one such file in a given directory.

Users can also use these commands in their *.profile*, or at any other time, to override the default settings.

umask

umask, like the same command in most other shells, lets you specify the default permissions that files have when users create them. It takes the same types of arguments that the *chmod* command does, i.e., absolute (octal numbers) or symbolic permission values.

The **umask** contains the permissions that are turned off by default whenever a process creates a file, regardless of what permission the process specifies.*

We'll use octal notation to show how this works. As you should know, the digits in a permission number stand (left to right) for the permissions of the owner, owner's group, and all other users, respectively. Each digit, in turn, consists of three bits, which specify read, write, and execute permissions from left to right. (If a file is a directory, the "execute" permission becomes "search" permission, i.e., permission to **cd** to it, list its files, etc.)

For example, the octal number 640 equals the binary number 110 100 000. If a file has this permission, then its owner can read and write it; users in the owner's group can only read it; everyone else has no permission on it. A file with permission 755 gives its owner the right to read, write, and execute it and everyone else the right to read and execute (but not write).

022 is a common **umask** value. This implies that when a file is created, the "most" permission it could possibly have is 755—which is the usual permission of an executable that a compiler might create. A text editor, on the other hand, might create a file with 666 permission (read and write for everyone), but the **umask** forces it to be 644 instead.

ulimit

The **ulimit** command was originally used to specify the limit on file creation size. But the Korn shell version has options that let you put limits on several different system resources. Table 10-1 lists the options.

---

*If you are comfortable with Boolean logic, think of the **umask** as a number that the operating system logically XORs with the permission given by the creating process.

Table 10-1: ulimit Resource Options

Option	Resource Limited
-a	All (for printing values only)
-c	Core file size (½ kb blocks)
-d	Process data segment (kb)
-f	File size (½ kb blocks)
-n	File descriptors
-s	Process stack segment (kb)
-t	Process CPU time (seconds)
-v	Virtual memory (kb)

Each takes a numerical argument that specifies the limit in units shown in the table. You can also give the argument "unlimited" (which may actually mean some physical limit), or you can omit the argument, in which case it will print the current limit. **ulimit -a** prints limits (or "unlimited") of all types. You can only specify one type of resource at a time. If you don't specify any option, **-f** is assumed.

Some of these options depend on operating system capabilities that don't exist in older UNIX versions. In particular, some older versions have a fixed limit of 20 file descriptors per process (making **-n** irrelevant), and some don't support virtual memory (making **-v** irrelevant).

The **-d** and **-s** options have to do with *dynamic memory allocation*, i.e., memory for which a process asks the operating system at runtime. It's not necessary for casual users to limit these, though software developers may want to do so to prevent buggy programs from trying to allocate endless amounts of memory due to infinite loops.

The **-v** option is similar; it puts a limit on all uses of memory. You don't need this unless your system has severe memory constraints or you want to limit process size to avoid thrashing.

You may want to specify limits on file size (**-f** and **-c**) if you have constraints on disk space. Sometimes users actually mean to create huge files, but more often than not, a huge file is the result of a buggy program that goes into an infinite loop. Software developers who use debuggers like *sdb* and *dbx* should not limit core file size, because core dumps are necessary for debugging.

The −t option is another possible guard against infinite loops. But we would argue that a program that is in an infinite loop but isn't allocating memory or writing files is not particularly dangerous; it's better to leave this unlimited and just let the user kill the offending program.

In addition to the types of resources you can limit, **ulimit** lets you specify hard or soft limits. Hard limits can be lowered by any user but only raised by the superuser (**root**); users can lower soft limits and raise them—but only as high as the hard limit for that resource.

If you give −**H** along with one (or more) of the options above, **ulimit** will set hard limits; −**S** sets soft limits. Without either of these, **ulimit** sets both. For example, the following commands set the soft limit on file descriptors to 64 and the hard limit to unlimited:

```
ulimit -Sn 64
ulimit -Hn unlimited
```

When **ulimit** prints current limits, it prints soft limits unless you specify −**H**.

Types of Global Customization

The best possible approach to globally-available customization would be a system-wide environment file that is separate from each user's environment file—just like */etc/profile* is separate from each user's *.profile*.

Unfortunately, the Korn shell doesn't have this feature. If you assign a filename to the **ENV** environment variable, it could be overridden in a user's *.profile*. This allows you to make a default environment file available for users who don't have their own, but it doesn't let you have a system-wide environment file that runs in addition to the users'.

Nevertheless, the shell gives you a few ways to set up customizations that are available to all users at all times. Environment variables are the most obvious; your */etc/profile* file will undoubtedly contain definitions for several of them, including **PATH** and **TERM**.

The variable **TMOUT** is useful when your system supports dialup lines. Set it to a number *N*, and if a user doesn't enter a command within *N* seconds after the shell last issued a prompt, the shell will terminate. This feature is helpful in preventing people from "hogging" the dialup lines.

You may want to include some more complex customizations involving environment variables, such as the prompt string **PS1** containing the current directory (as seen in Chapter 4, *Basic Shell Programming*).

You can also turn on options, such as emacs- or vi- editing modes, **trackall** to make alias expansion more efficient and system security tighter, and **noclobber** to protect against inadvertent file overwriting. Any shell scripts you have written for general use also contribute to customization.

Unfortunately, it's not possible to create a global alias. You can define aliases in */etc/profile*, but there is no way to make them part of the environment so that their definitions will propagate to subshells. (In contrast, users can define global aliases by putting their definitions in environment files.)

However, you can set up global functions. These are an excellent way to customize your system's environment, because functions are part of the shell, not separate processes. For example, if you define *pushd* and *popd* (see Chapters 4 through 6) as exported functions, the shell will run them almost as if they were built-in commands, as they are in the C shell.

The best way to create global functions is to use the built-in variable **FPATH** and the **autoload** feature that we introduced in Chapter 4, *Basic Shell Programming*. Just define **FPATH** as a function library directory, perhaps */usr/local/functions*, and make it an environment variable by **export**ing it. In other words, put this or similar code in */etc/profile*:

```
FPATH=/usr/local/functions
export FPATH
```

Then put each global function's definition in a file in that directory with the same name as the function, and put **autoload** *fname* for each of these functions in */etc/profile*.

In either case, we suggest using exported functions for global customization instead of shell scripts. Given how cheap memory is nowadays, there is no reason why you shouldn't make generally useful functions part of your users' environment.

System Security Features

UNIX security is a problem of legendary notoriety. Just about every aspect of a UNIX system has some security issue associated with it, and it's usually the system administrator's job to worry about this issue.

The Korn shell has three features that help solve this problem: the *restricted shell*, which is intentionally "brain damaged," the *tracked alias* facility that we saw in Chapter 3, *Customizing Your Environment*, and *privileged mode*, which is used with shell scripts that run as if the user were **root**.

Restricted Shell

The restricted shell is designed to put the user into an environment where his or her ability to move around and write files is severely limited. It's usually used for "guest" accounts. You can make a user's login shell restricted by putting **rksh** or **ksh -r** in the user's */etc/passwd* entry.

The specific constraints imposed by the restricted shell disallow the user from doing the following:

- Changing working directories: **cd** is inoperative. If you try to use it, you will get the error message "ksh: cd: restricted".

- Redirecting output to a file: the redirectors >, >|, <>, and >> are not allowed.

- Assigning a new value to the environment variables **SHELL**, **ENV**, or **PATH**.

- Specifying any pathnames with slashes (/) in them. The shell will treat files outside of the current directory as "not found."

These restrictions go into effect after the user's *.profile* and environment files are run.

This means that the restricted shell user's entire environment is set up in *.profile*. Since the user can't overwrite that file, this lets the system administrator configure the environment as he or she sees fit.

Two common ways of setting up such environments are to set up a directory of "safe" commands and have that directory be the only one in **PATH**, and to set up a command menu from which the user can't escape without exiting the shell.

A System Break-in Scenario

Before we explain the other security features, here is some background information on system security that should help you understand why they are necessary.

Many problems with UNIX security hinge on a UNIX file attribute called the *suid* (set user ID) bit. This is like a permission bit (see **umask** above): when an executable file has it turned on, the file runs with an effective user ID equal to the owner of the file, which is usually **root**. The effective user ID is distinct from the real user ID of the process.

This feature lets administrators write scripts that do certain things that require **root** privilege (e.g., configure printers) in a controlled way. To set a file's *suid* bit, the superuser can type **chmod 4755** *filename*; the 4 is the *suid* bit.

Modern system administration wisdom says that creating *suid* shell scripts is a very, very bad idea.* This has been especially true under the C shell, because its *.cshrc* environment file introduces numerous opportunities for break-ins. The Korn shell's environment file feature creates similar security holes, although the security features we'll see shortly make this problem less severe.

We'll show why it's dangerous to set a script's *suid* bit. Recall that in Chapter 3, *Customizing Your Environment*, we mentioned that it's not a good idea to put your personal *bin* directory at the front of your **PATH**. Here is a scenario that shows how this combines with *suid* shell scripts to form a security hole: a variation of the infamous "Trojan horse" scheme.

For this particular technique to work, the computer cracker has to find a user on the system with an *suid* shell script. In addition, the user must have a **PATH** with his or her personal *bin* directory listed before the public *bin* directories, and the cracker must have write permission on the user's personal *bin* directory.

Once the cracker finds a user with these requirements, he or she does the following:

- Looks at the *suid* script and finds a common utility that it calls. Let's say it's *grep*.

- Creates the Trojan horse: a shell script called *grep* in the user's personal *bin* directory that looks like this:

```
cp /bin/ksh filename
chown root filename
chmod 4755 filename
/bin/grep "$@"
rm ~/bin/grep
```

filename should be some unremarkable filename in a directory with public read and execute permission, such as */bin* or */usr/bin*. The file,

---

*In fact, some versions of UNIX intentionally disable the *suid* feature for shell scripts.

when created, will be that most heinous of security holes: an *suid* interactive shell.

- Sits back and waits for the user to run the *suid* shell script—which calls the Trojan horse, which in turn creates the *suid* shell and then self-destructs.

- Runs the *suid* shell and creates havoc.

Tracked Aliases

The Korn shell protects against this type of scheme in two ways. First, it defines tracked aliases (see Chapter 3, *Customizing Your Environment*) for just about all commonly-used utilities: *ls*, *mv*, *cp*, *who*, *grep*, and many others. Since aliases take priority over executable files, the alias will always run instead of the Trojan horse.

Furthermore, the shell won't let you know about these if you type **alias -t** to see all tracked aliases.* You'll have trouble finding a command to use as your Trojan horse if you want to break in. This is a very clever—and undocumented—security feature.

Privileged Mode

The second type of protection against Trojan horses is *privileged mode*. This is a **set -o** option (**set -o privileged** or **set -p**), but the shell enters it automatically whenever it executes a script whose *suid* bit is set.

In privileged mode, when an *suid* Korn shell script is invoked, the shell does not run the user's environment file—i.e., it doesn't expand the user's **ENV** environment variable. Instead, it runs the file */etc/suid_profile*.

/etc/suid_profile should be written so as to restrict *suid* shell scripts in much the same way as the restricted shell does. At a minimum, it should make **PATH** read-only (**typeset -r PATH** or **readonly PATH**) and set it to one or more "safe" directories. Once again, this prevents any decoys from being invoked.

Since privileged mode is an option, it is possible to turn it off with the command **set +o privileged** (or **set +p**). But this doesn't help the potential system cracker: the shell automatically changes its effective user ID to be the

---

*Unless you type **whence -v** *command* or **type** *command*. If *command* has a tracked alias, this will say so, and it will cause **alias -t** to report it next time.

same as the real user ID—i.e., if you turn off privileged mode, you also turn off *suid.*

Privileged mode is an excellent security feature; it solves a problem that originated when the environment file idea first appeared in the C shell. Tracked aliases make protection against Trojan horses even stronger.

Furthermore, both features are strong arguments for installing the Korn shell as */bin/sh.* Your system will be all the more impervious to break-ins if your standard shell has these security features.

Nevertheless, we still recommend against creating *suid* shell scripts. We have shown how the Korn shell protects against break-ins in one particular situation, but that certainly does not imply that the Korn shell is "safe" in any absolute sense. If you really must have *suid* scripts, you should carefully consider all relevant security issues.

Finally, if you would like to learn more about UNIX security, we recommend the O'Reilly & Associates Nutshell Handbook, *Practical UNIX Security*, by Gene Spafford and Simson Garfinkel.

In this appendix:
- *The Bourne Shell*
- *The IEEE 1003.2 POSIX Shell Standard*
- *wksh*
- *pdksh*
- *bash*
- *Workalikes on PC Platforms*
- *The Future of the Korn Shell*

Related Shells

The fragmentation of the UNIX marketplace has had its advantages and disadvantages. The advantages came mostly in the early days: lack of standardization and proliferation among technically savvy academics and professionals contributed to a healthy "free market" for UNIX software, in which several programs of the same type (e.g., shells, text editors, system administration tools) would often compete for popularity. The best programs would usually become the most widespread, while inferior software tended to fade away.

But often there was no single "best" program in a given category, so several would prevail. This led to the current situation, where multiplicity of similar software has led to confusion, lack of compatibility, and—most unfortunate of all—UNIX' inability to capture as big a share of the market as other operating platforms (MS-DOS, Microsoft Windows, Novell NetWare, etc.).

The "shell" category has probably suffered in this way more than any other type of software. As we said in the Preface and Chapter 1, *Korn Shell Basics*, of this book, several shells are currently available; the differences between them are often not all that great. We believe that the Korn shell is the best of the most widely used shells, but other shells certainly have their staunch adherents, so they aren't likely to fade into obscurity for a while.

Therefore we felt it necessary to include information on shells similar to the 1988 UNIX Korn shell. This Appendix summarizes the differences between the latter and the following:

- The standard Version 7 Bourne shell, as a kind of "baseline"

- The IEEE POSIX 1003.2 shell Standard, to which the Korn shell and other shells will adhere in the future
- The Windowing Korn shell (*wksh*), a Korn shell with enhancements for X Window System programming
- *pdksh*, a widely-used public domain Korn shell
- The *bash* shell, which is another enhanced Bourne shell with some C shell and Korn shell features
- Korn shell workalikes on desktop PC platforms, including the MKS Toolkit shell

We'll conclude this Appendix with a look at the Korn shell's future: the next release's expected features, obsolescent features of the current shell, and other issues.

The Bourne Shell

The Korn shell is almost completely backward-compatible with the Bourne shell. The only significant feature of the latter that the Korn shell doesn't support is ^ (caret) as a synonym for the pipe (|) character.* This is an archaic feature that the Bourne shell includes for its own backward compatibility with earlier shells. No modern UNIX version has any shell code that uses ^ as a pipe.

To describe the differences between the Bourne shell and the Korn shell, we'll go through each chapter of this book and enumerate the features discussed in the chapter that the Bourne shell does *not* support. Although some versions of the Bourne shell exist that include a few Korn shell features,† we refer to the standard, Version 7 Bourne shell that has been around for many years.

Chapter 1, *Korn Shell Basics*
The **cd** *old new* and **cd** - forms of the **cd** command; tilde (~) expansion; the **jobs** command.

Chapter 2, *Command-line Editing*
All. (I.e., the Bourne shell doesn't support any of the history and editing features discussed in Chapter 2, *Command-line Editing.*)

---

*There are also a few differences in how the two shells react to certain extremely pathological input. Usually, the Korn shell processes correctly what causes the Bourne shell to "choke."

†For example, the Bourne shell distributed with System V supports functions and a few other Korn shell features.

Chapter 3, *Customizing Your Environment*

Aliases; **set -o** options. The Bourne shell supports the "abbreviations" listed in the "Options" table in Appendix B—except **-A**, **-h**, **-m**, **-p**, and **-s**. Environment files aren't supported; neither is the **print** command (use *echo* instead).

The following built-in variables aren't supported:

EDITOR	OPTIND
ERRNO	PPID
ENV	PS3
FCEDIT	PS4
FPATH	PWD
HISTFILE	RANDOM
HISTSIZE	REPLY
LINENO	SECONDS
LINES	TMOUT
OLDPWD	VISUAL
OPTARG	

Some of these variables (e.g., **EDITOR** and **VISUAL**) are still used by other programs, like *mail* and news readers.

Chapter 4, *Basic Shell Programming*

Functions; the whence command; pattern-matching variable operators (%, %%, #, ##); advanced (regular expression) wildcards—use the external command *expr* instead. Command substitution syntax is different: use the older `command` instead of $(*command*).

Chapter 5, *Flow Control*

Conditional tests use older syntax: [*condition*] or **test** *condition* instead of [[*condition*]]. These are actually two forms of the same external command (see the *test(1)* manual page). The logical operators **&&** and **||** are **-a** and **-o** instead. Supported test operators differ from system to system.

The **select** construct isn't supported.

Chapter 6, *Command-line Options and Typed Variables*

Use the external command *getopt* instead of **getopts**, but note that it doesn't really do the same thing. Integer arithmetic isn't supported: use the external command *expr* instead of the $((*arithmetic-exp*)) syntax. For integer conditionals, use the old condition test syntax and relational operators **-lt**, **-eq**, etc., instead of ((*arithmetic-expr*)). **let** isn't supported. Array variables and the **typeset** command are not supported.

Chapter 7, *Input/Output and Command-line Processing*
> The following I/O redirectors are not supported:

> >|
> <>
> <&p
> >&p
> |&

> **print** isn't supported (use *echo* instead). None of the options to **read** are supported.

Chapter 8, *Process Handling*
> Job control—specifically, the **jobs**, **fg**, and **bg** commands. Job number notation with %, i.e., the **kill** and **wait** commands only accept process IDs. The - option to **trap** (reset trap to the default for that signal). **trap** only accepts signal numbers, not logical names. Coroutines aren't supported.

Chapter 9, *Debugging Shell Programs*
> The ERR and DEBUG fake signals. The EXIT fake signal *is* supported, as signal 0.

Chapter 10, *Korn Shell Administration*
> The **ulimit** command and privileged mode aren't supported. The Bourne shell's restrictive counterpart, *rsh*, only inhibits assignment to **PATH**.

The IEEE 1003.2 POSIX Shell Standard

There have been many attempts to standardize UNIX. Hardware companies' monolithic attempts at market domination, fragile industry coalitions, marketing failures, and other such efforts are the stuff of history—and the stuff of frustration.

Only one standardization effort has not been tied to commercial interests: the Portable Operating System Interface, known as POSIX. This effort started in 1981 with the */usr/group* (now UniForum) Standards Committee, which produced the */usr/group Standard* three years later. The list of contributors grew to include the Institute of Electrical and Electronic Engineers (IEEE) and the International Organization for Standardization (ISO).

The first POSIX standard was published in 1988. This one, called IEEE P1003.1, covers low-level issues at the system call level. IEEE P1003.2, covering the shell, utility programs, and user interface issues, was ratified in September 1992 after a six-year effort.

The POSIX standards were never meant to be rigid and absolute. The committee members certainly weren't about to put guns to the heads of operating system implementors and force them to adhere. Instead, the standards are designed to be flexible enough to allow for both coexistence of similar available software, so that existing code isn't in danger of obsolescence, and the addition of new features, so that vendors have the incentive to innovate. In other words, they are supposed to be the kind of third-party standards that vendors might actually be interested in following.

As a result, most UNIX vendors currently comply with POSIX 1003.1. Now that POSIX 1003.2 is available, the most important shells will undoubtedly adhere to it in the future. The Korn shell is no exception; it's expected to be 100% POSIX compliant in its next release, which should be within the next two years. Therefore you should pay attention to the differences between the current Korn shell and 1003.2 if you write shell code that you would like to be portable in the not-too-distant future.

POSIX 1003.2 itself consists of two parts. The first, 1003.2, addresses shell script portability; it defines the shell and the standard utilities. The second, 1003.2a, called the User Portability Extensions (UPE), defines standards of interactive shell use and interactive utilities like the *vi* editor. The combined document—on the order of 2000 pages—is available through the IEEE; for information, call (800) 678-IEEE.

The committee members had two motivating factors to weigh when they designed the 1003.2 shell standard. On the one hand, the design had to accomodate, as much as possible, existing shell code written under various Bourne-derived shells (the Version 7, System V, BSD, and Korn shells). These shells are different in several extremely subtle ways, most of which have to do with the ways certain syntactic elements interact with each other.

It must have been quite difficult and tedious to spell out these differences, let alone to reach compromises among them. Throw in biases of some committee members towards particular shells, and you might understand why it took six years to ratify 1003.2.

On the other hand, the shell design had to serve as a standard on which to base future shell implementations. This implied goals of simplicity, clarity, and precision—objectives that seem especially elusive in the context of the above problems.

The designers found one way of ameliorating this dilemma: they decided that the standard should include not only the features included in the shell, but also those explicitly omitted and those included but with unspecified functionality. The latter category allows some of the existing shells' innovations to "sneak through" without becoming part of the standard, while listing omitted features helps programmers determine which features in existing shell scripts won't be portable to future shells.

The POSIX standard is primarily based on the System V Bourne shell, which is a superset of the Version 7 shell discussed earlier in this Appendix. Therefore you should assume that Korn shell features that aren't present in the Bourne shell also aren't included in the POSIX standard.

However, the Korn shell did contribute a few of its features to the POSIX standard, including:

- $((...)) syntax for arithmetic expressions.
- $(...) syntax for command substitution, except that the $(<*filename*) shorthand for $(cat *filename*) isn't supported.
- Tilde expansion (originally derived from the C shell).

The following Korn shell features are left "unspecified" in the standard, meaning that their syntax is acceptable but their functionality is not standardized:

- The ((...)) syntax for arithmetic conditionals. The arithmetic test operators introduced in Chapter 5, *Flow Control*, (e.g., -eq, -lt), however, are included.
- The [[...]] syntax for conditional tests. The external *test* or [...] utility should be used instead.
- The syntax for defining functions that this book uses. The other syntax shown in Chapter 4 (*fname*() instead of function *fname*) is supported; see below.
- The **select** control structure.
- Code blocks ({...}) are supported, but for maximum portability, the curly braces should be quoted (for reasons too complicated to go into here).
- Signal numbers are only allowed if the numbers for certain key signals (INT, TERM, and a few others) are the same as on the most important historical versions of UNIX. In general, shell scripts should use symbolic names for signals.

The POSIX standard supports functions, as shown above, but the semantics are weaker: functions do not have local traps or options, it is not possible to define local variables, and functions can't be exported.

The POSIX standard also has a few new features:

- The command lookup order has been changed to allow certain built-in commands to be overridden by functions—since aliases aren't included in the standard. (Recall that we had to use an alias as "decoy" for a function that superseded the **cd** command in Chapter 5, *Flow Control.*) Built-in commands are divided into two sets by their positions in the command lookup order: some are processed before functions, some after.

  Specifically, the built-in commands **break**, **:** (do nothing), **continue**, **.** (dot), **eval**, **exec**, **exit**, **export**, **readonly**, **return**, **set**, **shift**, **trap**, and **unset** take priority over functions.

- A new built-in command, **command**, allows you to use built-in commands other than the above even if there are functions of the same name.

- A new keyword, !, takes the logical "not" of a command's exit status: if *command* returns exit status 0, ! *command* returns 1; if *command* returns a non-0 value, ! *command* returns 0. ! can be used with **&&**, **||**, and parentheses (for nested subshells) to create logical combinations of exit statuses in conditionals.

- The command **unset -v** is used instead of **unset** (without an option) to remove the definition of a variable. This provides a better syntactic match with **unset -f**, for unsetting functions.

Finally, because the POSIX standard is meant to promote shell script portability, it explicitly avoids mention of features that only apply to interactive shell use—including aliases, editing modes, control keys, and so on. The UPE covers these. It also avoids mentioning certain key implementation issues: in particular, there is no requirement that multitasking be used for background jobs, subshells, etc. This was done to allow portability to non-multitasking systems like MS-DOS, so that, for example, the MKS Toolkit (see below) can be POSIX compliant.

wksh

UNIX System Laboratories released *wksh*, the Windowing Korn shell, in late 1992. It's a full Korn shell, completely compatible with the version this book describes, that has extensions for graphical user interface (GUI) programming in the X Window System environment. It runs on System V Release 4 (SVR4) and SunOS UNIX systems.

wksh supports the OPEN LOOK and OSF/Motif graphical Toolkits by making their routines available as built-in commands. This allows programmers to combine the Korn shell's strength as a UNIX systems programming environment with the power and abstraction of the Toolkits. The result is a unified environment for quick and easy development of graphics-based software.

There are various GUI development tools that allow you to construct user interfaces with a graphics-based editor rather than with programming language code. But such tools are typically huge, expensive, and complex. *wksh*, on the other hand, is inexpensive and unbeatable for the smoothness of its integration with UNIX—it's the only such tool that you can use as your login shell! We recommend it highly to systems programmers who use X-based workstations and need a rapid prototyping tool.

To give you the flavor of *wksh* code, here is a script that implements the canonical "Hello World" program by displaying a small window with that text in it. The code, taken from the *wksh* manual, should hold no surprises for X and Motif programmers:

```
#!/usr/bin/wksh -motif

XtAppInitialize TOPLEVEL hello Hello "$@"
XtCreateManagedWidget L 1 label $TOPLEVEL labelString:"Hello World"
XtRealizeWidget $TOPLEVEL
XtMainLoop
```

For more information on *wksh*, contact:

    UNIX Systems Laboratories, Inc.
    190 River Road
    Summit, NJ 07901
    Phone: (800) 828-UNIX or (908) 522-6000.

pdksh

If your system does not have the November 1988 Korn shell, there is a public domain version known as *pdksh*. *pdksh* is available as source code in various places on the Internet, including the USENET newsgroup comp.sources.unix. It comes with instructions for building and installing it on various BSD-derived UNIX platforms (especially SunOS).

pdksh was written by Eric Gisin, who based it on Charles Forsyth's public domain Version 7 Bourne shell. It has all Bourne shell features plus some of the Korn shell extensions and a few features of its own.

Its emacs editing mode is actually more powerful than that of the 1988 Korn shell. Like the full *emacs* editor, you can customize the keystrokes that invoke editing commands (known as *key bindings* in *emacs* terminology). Editing commands have full names that you can associate with keystrokes by using the **bind** command.

For example, if you want to set up CTRL-U to do the same thing as CTRL-P (i.e., go back to the previous command in the history file), you could put this command in your *.profile*:

```
bind '^U'=up-history
```

You can even set up two-character escape sequences, which (for example) allow you to use ANSI arrow keys as well as control characters, and you can define *macros*, i.e., abbreviations for sequences of editing commands.

The public domain Korn shell's additional features include *alternation* wildcards (borrowed from the C shell) and user-definable tilde notation, in which you can set up ~ as an abbreviation for anything, not just user names. There are also a few subtle differences in integer expression evaluation and aliasing.

Otherwise, *pdksh* lacks a few features of the official version. In particular, it lacks the following:

- The built-in variables **COLUMNS, ERRNO, LINENO, LINES**, and **PS4**.
- Array variables.
- The fake signals ERR and EXIT within functions.
- Advanced (regular expression) wildcards.
- The newer syntax ([[. . .]]) for conditional tests (the older Bourne shell syntax is supported).
- The advanced I/O redirectors >|, <>, <&p, >&p, and |&. Coroutines are not supported.

- The options **errexit, markdirs, noclobber, nolog,** and **privileged**.
- Of the **typeset** options, only **-f** (function) **-i** (integer), **-r** (read-only), and **-x** (export) are supported.

The documentation (manual page) of *pdksh* is incomplete—which is especially a shame because what exists is considerably better organized than the Korn shell's man page! For example, it gives the syntax of command lines and control structures in Extended Backus-Naur Form (BNF), which is not only precise and unambiguous but is the *lingua franca* of computer language experts.

However, *pdksh* is a worthwhile alternative to the C and Bourne shells for those who can't get the official version of the Korn shell.

bash

bash is another popular "third-party" shell that is available on the Internet, via anonymous FTP on prep.ai.mit.edu in the directory */pub/gnu.* You can also order it from its maker:

> The Free Software Foundation (FSF)
> 675 Massachusetts Avenue
> Cambridge MA 02139, phone
> (617) 876-3296.

Bash was written by Brian Fox and Chet Ramey. Its name is in line with the FSF's penchant for bad puns: it stands for Bourne-Again Shell. Although *bash* is easily available and you don't have to pay for it (other than the cost of media, phone calls, etc.), it's not really public domain software. While public domain software doesn't have licensing restrictions, the FSF's software does. But those restrictions are diametrically opposed to those in a commercial license:* instead of agreeing not to distribute the software further, you agree not to prevent it from being distributed further! In other words, you enjoy unrestricted use of the software as long as you agree not to inhibit others from doing the same. Richard Stallman, the founder of the FSF, invented this intriguing and admirable concept.

You may have heard that public domain software tends to be buggy, poorly maintained and documented, etc. Let us emphasize that this is absolutely not the case with software from the FSF. It is among the finest, most full-

---

*Accordingly, the document that spells out these restrictions is called a *copyleft*.

featured, best-maintained, and most technically advanced software in existence.

The FSF has been developing a complete, UNIX-compatible operating system called GNU, which stands for GNU's Not UNIX.* They have already written lots of utilities and software tools for GNU that also run on most varieties of UNIX, the most famous of which is the GNU Emacs editor. The shell for GNU is *bash*.

bash is fully compatible with the Bourne shell. It has several of the most important Korn shell features and the C shell features that the Korn shell has appropriated, including aliases, functions, tilde notation, emacs and vi editing modes, arithmetic expressions, job control, etc.

Yet *bash* is not really a Korn shell workalike. Various aspects of its syntax are different, e.g.:

- Arithmetic expressions have the form $[...].
- Functions conform to the alternate syntax we didn't use in this book (see Chapter 4, *Basic Shell Programming*), although you may use the **function** keyword in addition to the parentheses.
- Condition tests are in the old, Bourne shell style.
- The command **type** does what **whence** does, only better.
- **print** is not supported; you must use **echo**.

Some of these will change as the POSIX 1003.2 standard evolves. *Bash* also doesn't implement various small Korn shell features, including most of those listed above for *pdksh*, and it doesn't support the DEBUG fake signal.

However, *bash* has many features of its own that make it a very powerful and flexible environment. Here are some of the highlights:

- You can put backslash-escapes in the primary prompt string (**PS1**) for which *bash* substitutes things like the date, time, current working directory, machine name, user name, shell, etc.
- The commands **builtin**, **command**, and **enable** give you more control over the steps *bash* goes through to look for commands—i.e., *bash*'s analog to the list of command search steps in Chapter 7, *Input/Output and Command-line Processing*.

---

*This is an example of a *recursive acronym*, in which the first letter stands for the acronym itself. It is the result of a mental disorder caused by a rare brain parasite endemic to the southern part of Cambridge, MA.

- The emacs editing mode is customizable, even more so than its equivalent in *pdksh*. You can use the **bind** command to set up your own keystroke preferences, and there are several more commands available—including the ability to undo your last command.
- You can also rebind keystrokes in vi editing mode.
- *bash* supports ! as a keyword, a la POSIX 1003.2 (see page 297).
- *bash* has online help for built-in commands.
- **pushd** and **popd** are built-in, as they are in the C shell.
- Many new options and variables let you customize your environment with unprecedented flexibility.

We're compelled to say that many users prefer *bash* to the Korn shell. Although the latter is probably used by more people, because of the commercial channels through which it's distributed, *bash* is clearly an excellent choice.

Workalikes on PC Platforms

The proliferation of the Korn shell has not stopped at the boundaries of UNIX-dom. Many programmers who got their initial experience on UNIX systems and subsequently crossed over into the PC world wished for a nice UNIX-like environment (especially when faced with the horrors of the MS-DOS command line!), so it's not surprising that several UNIX shell-style interfaces to small-computer operating systems have appeared, Korn shell emulations among them.

Shells that are called "Korn shell" exist for the Minix and Coherent operating systems, both of which are small, inexpensive UNIX-like systems for IBM PC-type machines. These shells are not very compatible with the 1988 UNIX Korn shell; they only have the most important Korn shell features, such as emacs and vi editing modes and shell functions.

Somewhat better is a version of *pdksh* for OS/2, which you can get in binary form (i.e., the executable, not the source code) from the USENET newsgroup comp.binaries.os2.

But far better than that is the MKS Toolkit, available from Mortice Kern Systems, Inc. The Toolkit is actually a complete UNIX-like environment for MS-DOS (version 2.0 and later) and OS/2 (version 1.2 and later). In addition to its shell, it comes with a *vi* editor and many UNIX-style utilities, including major ones like *awk*, *uucp*, and *make*.

The MKS shell itself is very much compatible with the 1988 UNIX Korn shell, and it has a well-written manual. Its only real syntactic difference is that it doesn't support the Korn shell's condition test syntax; you must use the old Bourne shell syntax instead.

The few other differences are due to limitations in the underlying operating systems rather than the shell itself. Most importantly, MS-DOS does not support multitasking or file permissions, so the MS-DOS version supports none of the relevant Korn shell features. The OS/2 version doesn't support file permissions either.

Specifically, the MKS shell for MS-DOS does not support the following:

- Background jobs: **&** at the end of a command acts like **;** , i.e., as a statement separator.
- Job control: **fg**, **bg**, **jobs**, **kill**, and **wait**; the options **bgnice** and **monitor**; coroutines.

The MKS shells for both MS-DOS and OS/2 do not support the following:

- File permission: **umask**, **newgrp**. The option **privileged** has been renamed to **protected** to reflect the lack of *suid* permission. Some test conditions have different meanings, as shown in Table A-1.

Table A-1: File Permission Test Operators

Operator	UNIX Test	MKS Toolkit Test
-g	*setgid* bit	System attribute
-k	sticky (save text) bit	Archive attribute
-u	*setuid* bit	Hidden attribute

- Filenames: all scripts must have names with the extension *.ksh*. Shell-related files have names that don't conform to MS-DOS file naming rules; Table A-2 shows MKS toolkit equivalents.
- Environment variables that contain directory lists, such as **PATH** and **MAILPATH**, should use semicolons (**;**) instead of colons (**:**) to separate directories, because colons are used in DOS and OS/2 pathnames.

Table A-2: MKS Toolkit Names for Shell Files

UNIX Filename	MKS Toolkit Filename
.profile	*profile.ksh*
.sh_history	*sh_histo*
/etc/profile	*\etc\profile.ksh*
/etc/suid_profile	*\etc\suid_pro.ksh*

- Signals: the only ones supported are INT, ALRM, and STOP. The fake signals ERR and EXIT are supported, but DEBUG is not.
- **PPID** is renamed **PID**.
- Condition tests: **-a** (file existence) is renamed **-e** to avoid clashing with the **-a** operator (for logical "and") in the older *test* or *[. . .]* syntax. The > and < (lexicographic comparisons) aren't supported.

The MKS shell also supports a few features of its own. It uses $[. . .] (a la *bash*) as an alternative syntax for arithmetic expressions, and it includes a few invocation and **set** options that are related to the underlying operating system.

Many UNIX users who have moved to DOS PCs swear by the MKS Toolkit; it's inexpensive ($299 at this writing), and it makes MS-DOS into a reasonable environment for advanced users and software developers. The Toolkit is available through most dealers that sell software tools, or through MKS itself. For more information, contact MKS, 35 King St. North, Waterloo, Ontario, Canada N2J 2W9, or electronically as follows:

Telephone	(800) 265-2797 (US & Canada)
Fax	(519) 884 8861
Internet	toolkit@mks.com
CompuServe	73260,1043
BIX	mks

The Future of the Korn Shell

David Korn continues to enhance the Korn shell at AT&T Bell Labs. At this writing, a new release is in beta test—usually the final step before a piece of software is released. However, negotiations between AT&T and USL (now Novell UNIX Systems Group) over distribution rights could very well postpone the new shell's public release for a couple of years or more.

Nevertheless, the new Korn shell has significant enhancements that make it worth looking forward to. These features are subject to change between the time of this writing and the new shell's public release. Here are some highlights:

- The ability to customize key bindings, as in *bash* and *pdksh* but applicable to vi- as well as emacs-mode. This is implemented as another "fake signal" trap (on keystrokes), so it's extremely flexible.
- Many new customization variables and options.
- A greatly expanded set of string operators, providing substrings, substitutions, and other functionality.
- An enhanced array variable facility that provides for associative arrays, which can be addressed by their contents rather than by indices.
- Better prompt string customization capabilities (with command substitution and arithmetic expression evaluation).
- Floating point (real number) arithmetic.
- An arithmetic **for** loop in the style of the C programming language.
- A new option to **print** that allows C language **printf()**-style output formatting.
- The ability to add new built-in commands, on systems that support dynamic loading (the *dlopen()* system call).
- More user control over command lookup order, as in the POSIX standard and *bash*.
- The ability to set timed "alarms" (with the ALRM signal).
- Expanded debugging support through additional fake signal traps.
- Online help for built-in commands through a standard -? option.

The next release is expected to be incompatible with the 1988 Korn shell in a few ways, some of which are necessary for POSIX compliance (refer to the section on POSIX in this Appendix for more details):

- The **alias** command will never display tracked aliases unless you specify the option -t.
- Functions defined with *fname()* (the syntax not used in this book) will have weaker POSIX-compliant semantics. However, functions defined with **function** *fname* will remain the same.
- Tilde expansion can take place inside ${ . . . }-style variable expressions, whereas in the 1988 Korn shell, tildes in these expressions are treated literally.
- ! will be a keyword, as it is in the POSIX standard.

- Command substitution and arithmetic expression evaluation (in addition to parameter expansion) will be performed on the variables **PS1**, **PS3**, and **ENV** when they are expanded. This will allow for more flexible customization of prompt strings and environment files. It also means that grave accents (`) and $(must be quoted to be taken literally.

- Output of the built-in commands **set**, **typeset**, and **alias** will change so that any words containing special characters are single-quoted—so that these commands' output can be used directly for input.

- A new expansion operator, **$'** ... **'**, is used to delimit strings that conform to the ANSI C language standard for character strings. In the 1988 Korn shell, **$'** causes the dollar sign to be treated literally; in future releases, it must be backslash-escaped.

- **command** will be a built-in command, as in POSIX.

- Command lookup order will change so that built-in commands will be treated as if they were installed in */bin*, i.e., will be found at the same time as */bin* is searched when the shell goes through your **PATH**. The rules will also change to comply with the POSIX standard that allows certain built-in commands to take precedence over functions.

- Signal traps will propagate to subshells (whether nested or shell scripts invoked from shells) until the subshell issues a **trap** command (on any signal). Currently, traps do not propagate to subshells; see Chapter 8, *Process Handling*.

- The built-in variable **ERRNO** will be dropped; exit statuses will reflect system call error numbers.

Finally, the following features are expected eventually to become obsolete:

- The command **fc** will be renamed **hist**; the built-in variable **FCEDIT** will be renamed **HISTEDIT**.

- The **-t** option to **alias**, **set -h**, and **set -o trackall**. Alias tracking will always be on.

- The **-k** or **-o keyword** option. This will always be off (see Chapter 3, *Customizing Your Environment*).

- Grave accents (`) for command substitution. Use $(. . .) instead.

- The **-a** (file existence) condition test will be renamed **-e**, to avoid clashing with the **-a** operator (logical "and") in the old *test* or [. . .] syntax.

- The **=** pattern-matching operator in [[. . .]] condition tests will be replaced by **==** for better syntactic alignment with the C language.

- The arithmetic comparisons **-eq**, **-lt**, etc. Use ((. . .)) instead.

In this appendix:
- *Invocation Options*
- *Built-in Commands and Keywords*
- *Built-in Shell Variables*
- *Test Operators*
- *Options*
- *Typeset Options*
- *Emacs Mode Commands*
- *Vi Control Mode Commands*

B

Reference Lists

Invocation Options

Here is a list of the options you can use when invoking the Korn shell. In addition to these, any **set** option can be used on the command line; see Table B.5 below. Login shells are usually invoked with the options –i (interactive), –s (read from standard input), and –m (enable job control).

Option	Meaning
–c *string*	Execute *string*, then exit.
–s	Read commands from the standard input. If an argument is given, this flag takes precedence (i.e., the argument won't be treated as a script name and standard input will be read).
–i	Interactive shell. Ignore signals TERM, INTR, and QUIT.
–r	Restricted shell. See Chapter 10, *Korn Shell Administration.*

Built-in Commands and Keywords

Here is a summary of all built-in commands and keywords.

Command	Chapter	Summary
:	7	Do nothing (just do expansions of arguments).
.	4	Read file and execute its contents in current shell.
alias	3	Set up shorthand for command or command line.

Command	Chapter	Summary
bg	8	Put job in background.
break	5	Exit from surrounding **for**, **select**, **while**, or **until** loop.
case	5	Multi-way conditional construct.
cd	1	Change working directory.
continue		Skip to next iteration of **for**, **select**, **while**, or **until** loop.
echo	4	Expand and print arguments (obsolete).
exec	9	Replace shell with given program.
exit	5	Exit from shell.
export	3	Create environment variables.
eval	7	Process arguments as a command line.
fc	2	Fix command (edit history file).
fg	8	Put background job in foreground.
for	5	Looping construct.
function	4	Define function.
getopts	6	Process command-line options.
if	5	Conditional construct.
jobs	1	List background jobs.
kill	8	Send signal to process.
let	6	Arithmetic variable assignment.
newgrp		Start new shell with new group ID.
print	1	Expand and print arguments on standard output.
pwd	1	Print working directory.
read	7	Read a line from standard input.
readonly	6	Make variables read-only (unassignable).
return	5	Return from surrounding function or script.
select	5	Menu generation construct.
set	3	Set options.
shift	6	Shift command-line arguments.
time		Run command and print execution times.
trap	8	Set up signal-catching routine.
typeset	6	Set special characteristics of variables.
ulimit	10	Set/show process resource limits.
umask	10	Set/show file permission mask.
unalias	3	Remove alias definitions.
unset	3	Remove definitions of variables or functions.
until	5	Looping construct.
wait	8	Wait for background job(s) to finish.

Command	Chapter	Summary
whence	3	Identify source of command.
while	5	Looping construct.

Built-in Shell Variables

Variable	Chapter	Meaning
#	4	Number of arguments given to current process.
-		Options given to shell on invocation.
?	5	Exit status of previous command.
$	8	Process ID of shell process.
_		Last argument to previous command.
!	8	Process ID of last background command.
CDPATH	3	List of directories for *cd* command to search.
COLUMNS	3	Width of display in columns (for editing modes and **select**).
EDITOR	2	Used to set editing mode; also used by *mail* and other programs.
ERRNO	A	Error number of last system call that failed.
ENV	3	Name of file to run as environment file when shell is invoked.
FCEDIT	2	Default editor for *fc* command.
FPATH	4	Search path for autoloaded functions.
IFS	7	Internal field separator: list of characters that act as word separators. Normally set to SPACE, TAB, and NEWLINE.
HISTFILE	2	Name of command history file.
HISTSIZE	2	Number of lines kept in history file.
HOME	3	Home (login) directory.
LINENO	9	Number of line in script or function that just ran.
LINES	3	Height of display in lines (for **select** command).
MAIL	3	Name of file to check for new mail.
MAILCHECK	3	How often (in seconds) to check for new mail.
MAILPATH	3	List of file names to check for new mail, if MAIL is not set.
OLDPWD	3	Previous working directory.
OPTARG	6	Argument to option being processed by *getopts*.
OPTIND	6	Number of first argument after options.
PATH	3	Search path for commands.

Variable	Chapter	Meaning
PS1	3	Primary command prompt string.
PS2	3	Prompt string for line continuations.
PS3	5	Prompt string for **select** command.
PS4	9	Prompt string for **xtrace** option.
PPID	8	Process ID of parent process.
PWD	3	Current working directory.
RANDOM	9	Random number between 0 and 32767 (2^{15}-1).
REPLY	5,7	User's response to **select** command; result of **read** command if no variable names given.
SECONDS	3	Number of seconds since shell was invoked.
SHELL	3	Full pathname of shell.
TMOUT	10	If set to a positive integer, number of seconds between commands after which shell automatically terminates.
VISUAL	2	Used to set editing mode.

Test Operators

These are the operators that are used with the [[. . .]] construct. They can be logically combined with **&&** ("and") and **||** ("or") and grouped with parenthesis.

Operator	True If . . .
-a *file*	*file* exists.
-b *file*	*file* is a block device file.
-c *file*	*file* is a character device file.
-d *file*	*file* is a directory.
-f *file*	*file* is a regular file.
-g *file*	*file* has its setgid bit set.
-k *file*	*file* has its sticky bit set.
-n *string*	*string* is non-null.
-o *option*	*option* is set.
-p *file*	*file* is a pipe or named pipe (FIFO file).
-r *file*	*file* is readable.
-s *file*	*file* is not empty.
-t *N*	File descriptor *N* points to a terminal.
-u *file*	*file* has its setuid bit set.
-w *file*	*file* is writeable.

Operator	True If . . .
-x *file*	*file* is executable, or *file* is a directory that can be searched.
-z *string*	*string* is null.
-G *file*	*file*'s group ID is the same as that of the shell.
-L *file*	*file* is a symbolic link.
-O *file*	*file* is owned by the shell's user ID.
-S *file*	*file* is a socket.
fileA -nt *fileB*	*fileA* is newer than *fileB*.
fileA -ot *fileB*	*fileA* is older than *fileB*.
fileA -ef *fileB*	*fileA* and *fileB* point to the same file.
string = *pattern*	*string* matches *pattern* (which can contain wildcards).
string != *pattern*	*string* does not match *pattern*.
stringA < *stringB*	*stringA* comes before *stringB* in dictionary order.
stringA > *stringB*	*stringA* comes after *stringB* in dictionary order.
exprA -eq *exprB*	Arithmetic expressions *exprA* and *exprB* are equal.
exprA -ne *exprB*	Arithmetic expressions *exprA* and *exprB* are not equal.
exprA -lt *exprB*	*exprA* is less than *exprB*.
exprA -gt *exprB*	*exprA* is greater than *exprB*.
exprA -le *exprB*	*exprA* is less than or equal to *exprB*.
exprA -ge *exprB*	*exprA* is greater than or equal to *exprB*.

Options

These are options that can be turned on with the **set -o** command. All are initially off except where noted. **Abbrevs**, where listed, are arguments to **set** that can be used instead of the full **set -o** command (e.g., **set -a** is an abbreviation for **set -o allexport**). The abbreviations are actually backward-compatible Bourne shell options.

Option	Abbrev	Meaning
allexport	-a	Export all subsequently defined variables.
errexit	-e	Exit the shell when a command exits with non-0 status.
bgnice		Run all background jobs at decreased priority (on by default).
emacs		Use emacs-style command-line editing.

Option	Abbrev	Meaning
gmacs		Use *emacs*-style command-line editing, but with a slightly different meaning for CTRL-T (See Chapter 2, *Command-line Editing*).
ignoreeof		Disallow CTRL-D to exit the shell.
markdirs		Add / to all directory names generated from wildcard expansion.
monitor	-m	Enable job control (on by default).
noclobber		Don't allow > redirection to existing files.
noexec	-n	Read commands and check for syntax errors, but don't execute them.
noglob	-f	Disable wildcard expansion.
nolog		Disable command history.
nounset	-u	Treat undefined variables as errors, not as null.
privileged	-p	Script is running in *suid* mode.
trackall	-h	Substitute full pathnames for commands in alias expansions.
verbose	-v	Print commands (verbatim) before running them.
vi		Use *vi*-style command-line editing.
viraw		Use *vi* mode and have each keystroke take effect immediately.
xtrace	-x	Print commands (after expansions) before running them.

Typeset Options

These are arguments to the **typeset** command.

Option	Meaning
	With no option, create local variable within function.
-L	Left justify and remove leading blanks.
-R	Right justify and remove trailing blanks.
-f	With no arguments, prints all function definitions.
-f *fname*	Prints the definition of function *fname*.
+f	Prints all function names.
-ft	Turns on trace mode for named function(s).
+ft	Turns off trace mode for named function(s).
-fu	Defines given name(s) as autoloaded function(s).
-i	Declare variable as an integer.

Option	Meaning
-l	Convert all letters to lowercase.
-r	Make variable read-only.
-u	Convert all letters to uppercase.
-x	Export variable, i.e., put in environment so that it is passed to subshells.

Emacs Mode Commands

Here is a complete list of all Emacs editing mode commands.

Command	Meaning
CTRL-A	Move to beginning of line
CTRL-B	Move backward one character (without deleting)
CTRL-C	Capitalize character after point
CTRL-D	Delete one character forward
CTRL-E	Move to end of line
CTRL-F	Move forward one character
CTRL-J	Same as RETURN.
CTRL-K	Delete ("kill") forward to end of line
CTRL-L	Redisplay the line
CTRL-M	Same as RETURN
CTRL-N	Next line
CTRL-O	Same as RETURN, then display next line in history file
CTRL-P	Previous line
CTRL-R	Search backward
CTRL-T	Transpose two characters
CTRL-U	Repeat the following command four times
CTRL-V	Print the version of the Korn shell
CTRL-W	Delete ("wipe") all characters between point and mark (see below)
CTRL-Y	Retrieve ("yank") last item deleted
CTRL-X CTRL-X	Exchange point and mark
CTRL-] x	Search forward for x, where x is any character
DEL	Delete one character backward
CTRL-[	Same as ESC (most keyboards)
ESC b	Move one word backward
ESC c	Change word after point to all capital letters
ESC d	Delete one word forward

Command	Meaning
ESC f	Move one word forward
ESC h	Delete one word backward
ESC l	Change word after point to all lowercase letters
ESC p	Save characters between point and mark as if deleted
ESC CTRL-H	Delete one word backward
ESC CTRL-]x	Search backward for x, where x is any character
ESC SPACE	Set mark at point
ESC #	Insert line in history file for future editing
ESC DEL	Delete one word backward
ESC <	Move to first line of history file
ESC >	Move to last line of history file
ESC .	Insert last word in previous command line after point
ESC _	Same as above
ESC ESC	Do filename completion on current word
ESC *	Do filename expansion on current word
ESC =	Insert line in history file for future editing

Vi Control Mode Commands

Here is a complete list of all vi control mode commands.

Command	Meaning
h	Move left one character
l	Move right one character
w	Move right one word
b	Move left one word
W	Move to beginning of next non-blank word
B	Move to beginning of preceding non-blank word
e	Move to end of current word
E	Move to end of current non-blank word
0	Move to beginning of line
^	Move to first non-blank character in line
$	Move to end of line
i	Insert text before current character
a	Insert text after current character
I	Insert text at beginning of line
A	Insert text at end of line
R	Overwrite existing text
dh	Delete one character backwards

Command	Meaning
dl	Delete one character forwards
db	Delete one word backwards
dw	Delete one word forwards
dB	Delete one non-blank word backwards
dW	Delete one non-blank word forwards
d$	Delete to end of line
d0	Delete to beginning of line
D	Equivalent to **d$** (delete to end of line)
dd	Equivalent to **0d$** (delete entire line)
C	Equivalent to **c$** (delete to end of line, enter input mode)
cc	Equivalent to **0c$** (delete entire line, enter input mode)
x	Equivalent to **dl** (delete character backwards)
X	Equivalent to **dh** (delete character forwards)
k or –	Move backward one line
j or +	Move forward one line
G	Move to line given by repeat count
/*string*	Search forward for *string*
?*string*	Search backward for *string*
n	Repeat search forward
N	Repeat search backward
f*x*	Move right to next occurrence of *x*
F*x*	Move left to previous occurrence of *x*
t*x*	Move right to next occurrence of *x*, then back one space
T*x*	Move left to previous occurrence of *x*, then forward one space
,	Undo motion of last character finding command
;	Redo last character finding command
\	Do filename completion
*	Do wildcard expansion (onto command line)
=	Do wildcard expansion (as printed list)
~	Invert ("twiddle") case of current character(s)
_	Append last word of previous command, enter input mode
v	Run the **fc** command on the current line (actually, run the command **fc -e ${VISUAL:-${EDITOR:-vi}}**). Usually this means run the full *vi* on the current line.
CTRL-L	Start a new line and redraw the current line on it
#	Prepend # (comment character) to the line and send it
@*x*	Insert expansion of alias _*x*

Obtaining Sample Programs

Some of the examples in this book are available electronically in a number of ways: by *ftp*, *ftpmail*, *bitftp*, and *uucp*. The cheapest, fastest, and easiest ways are listed first. If you read from the top down, the first one that works for you is probably the best. Use *ftp* if you are directly on the Internet. Use ftpmail if you are not on the Internet but can send and receive electronic mail to internet sites (this includes CompuServe users). Use BITFTP if you send electronic mail via BITNET. Use UUCP if none of the above works.

FTP

To use FTP, you need a machine with direct access to the Internet. A sample session is shown, with what you should type in boldface.

```
% ftp ftp.uu.net
Connected to ftp.uu.net.
220 FTP server (Version 6.21 Tue Mar 10 22:09:55 EST 1992) ready.
Name (ftp.uu.net:kismet): anonymous
331 Guest login OK, send domain style e-mail address as password.
Password: kismet@ora.com (use your user name and host here)
230 Guest login OK, access restrictions apply.
ftp> cd /published/oreilly/nutshell/ksh
250 CWD command successful.
ftp> binary (Very important! You must specify binary transfer for compressed files.)
200 Type set to I.
ftp> get ksh.tar.Z
200 PORT command successful.
150 Opening BINARY mode data connection for ksh.tar.Z.
226 Transfer complete.
ftp> quit
221 Goodbye.
%
```

If the file is a compressed *tar* archive, extract the files from the archive by typing:

```
% zcat ksh.tar.Z | tar xf -
```

System V systems require the following *tar* command instead:

```
% zcat ksh.tar.Z | tar xof -
```

If *zcat* is not available on your system, use separate *uncompress* and *tar* commands.

FTPMAIL

FTPMAIL is a mail server available to anyone who can send electronic mail to and receive it from Internet sites. This includes any company or service provider that allows email connections to the Internet. Here's how you do it.

You send mail to *ftpmail@online.ora.com*. In the message body, give the FTP commands you want to run. The server will run anonymous FTP for you and mail the files back to you. To get a complete help file, send a message with no subject and the single word "help" in the body. The following is an example mail session that should get you the examples. This command sends you a listing of the files in the selected directory, and the requested example files. The listing is useful if there's a later version of the examples you're interested in.

```
% mail ftpmail@online.ora.com
Subject:
reply alan@ora.com                    (where you want files mailed)
open
chdir /published/oreilly/nutshell/ksh
dir
mode binary
uuencode                              (or btoa if you have it)
get ksh.tar.Z
quit
%
```

A signature at the end of the message is acceptable as long as it appears after "quit."

All retrieved files will be split into 60KB chunks and mailed to you. You then remove the mail headers and concatenate them into one file, and then *uudecode* or *atob* it. Once you've got the desired file, follow the directions under FTP to extract the files from the archive.

VMS, DOS, and Mac versions of *uudecode, atob, uncompress*, and *tar* are available. The VMS versions are on *gatekeeper.dec.com in /archive/pub/VMS.*

BITFTP

BITFTP is a mail server for BITNET users. You send it electronic mail messages requesting files, and it sends you back the files by electronic mail. BITFTP currently serves only users who send it mail from nodes that are directly on BITNET, EARN, or NetNorth. BITFTP is a public service of Princeton University. Here's how it works.

To use BITFTP, send mail containing your *ftp* commands to *BITFTP@PUCC*. For a complete help file, send HELP as the message body.

The following is the message body you should send to BITFTP:

```
FTP  ftp.uu.net  NETDATA
USER  anonymous
PASS your Internet email address (not your bitnet address)
CD  /published/oreilly/nutshell/ksh
DIR
BINARY
GET  ksh.tar.Z
QUIT
```

Once you've got the desired file, follow the directions under FTP to extract the files from the archive. Since you are probably not on a UNIX system, you may need to get versions of *uudecode, uncompress, atob*, and *tar* for your system. VMS, DOS, and Mac versions are available. The VMS versions are on *gatekeeper.dec.com* in */archive/pub/VMS.*

Questions about BITFTP can be directed to Melinda Varian, *MAINT@PUCC* on BITNET.

UUCP

UUCP is standard on virtually all UNIX systems, and is available for IBM-compatible PCs and Apple Macintoshes. The examples are available by UUCP via modem from UUNET; UUNET's connect-time charges apply.

You can get the examples from UUNET whether you have an account or not. If you or your company has an account with UUNET, you will have a system with a direct UUCP connection to UUNET. Find that system, and type:

```
% uucp uunet\!~/published/oreilly/nutshell/ksh/ksh.tar.Z \
    yourhost\!~/yourname/
```

The backslashes can be omitted if you use the Bourne shell (*sh*) instead of *csh*. The file should appear some time later (up to a day or more) in the directory */usr/spool/uucppublic/yourname*. If you don't have an account but would like one so that you can get electronic mail, then contact UUNET at 703-204-8000.

Try to get the file */published/oreilly/nutshell/ksh/ls-lR.Z* as a short test file containing the filenames and sizes of all the files in the directory.

Once you've got the desired file, follow the directions under FTP to extract the files from the archive.

Index

!, built-in variable, 238
  keyword in next release, 305
  negating a condition test, 131, 133
  negation in character sets, 13
  POSIX shell keyword, 297
  regular expression operator, 102, 104
##, pattern-matching operator, 105, 108, 171
#, built-in variable, 92
  comments, 99
  length operator, 108
  pattern-matching operator, 105, 108, 116, 151
  size of an array, 175
$', ANSI C string delimiter in next release, 306
$(( )), (see arithmetic expressions)
$, built-in variable, 31, 237;
    for constructing temp filenames, 238
%%, pattern-matching operator, 105, 107, 117, 151, 153, 171
%, pattern-matching operator, 105, 107-108, 140, 144
  specifying jobs, 223-225, 229, 294
&&, for condition tests, 131, 197, 293
  for exit statuses, 124-125, 153, 297
&, (see background jobs)
(( )), (see condition tests, arithmetic)
\, 68-69
*, accessing entire array, 174
  as default in case statement, 144
  built-in variable, 92;
    as default list in for statement, 136;

    as default list in select statement, 147
  regular expression operator, 102, 104-105
  wildcard, 12, 14, 270
+, regular expression operator, 102, 104-105
.. (directory), 10
., current directory, 11
  to hide files, 11
.kshrc, 82
.mailrc, 186
.profile, 30-31, 60-61, 81, 186, 194
  for setting up restricted shell environment, 287
/bin, 75, 288
/dev/null, 141, 160, 282
/etc/hosts, 197
/etc/passwd, 18, 188, 209, 217, 287
/etc/profile, 145, 147, 183, 194, 282, 285-286
/etc/suid_profile, 289
/etc/termcap, 73
/tmp, 238, 263
/usr/bin, 75, 288
/usr/lib, 263
/usr/tmp, 238
;;, in case statement, 148
<, 17
>, 17
?, built-in variable, 123, 259, 275
  regular expression operator, 102-104
  wildcard, 12, 105
@, built-in variable, 92
  preserving whitespace, 175

@ (cont'd)
    regular expression operator, 102,
        104, 270
[ ] (**wildcard**), 13-14, 105
    (see also condition tests, old syn-
        tax)
[[ ]], (see condition tests)
(**backslash**), 24
    as continuation characters, 26
    for quoting quote marks, 25-26
., to run a script, 85
\:**no-op command**, 234
\, +, 96, 101, 140
    -, 96, 98-100, 116, 271
    =, 96, 100-101
    ?, 96, 99-100, 116
;, statement separator, 62, 127, 275,
    303
^, as pipe character in Bourne shell,
    281-282, 292
    matching beginning of line in regu-
        lar expressions, 37, 282
' (**grave accent**), 306
    archaic command substitution del-
        imiter, 109, 293;
        obsolescence in next release,
        306
|&, background job with two-way
    pipes, 246, 248
|, as case pattern separator, 143
    pipe, 17-18, 281, 292
| |, for condition tests, 131, 293
    for exit statuses, 124-125, 270, 297
~ (**tilde**), 9-10, 204, 208-209, 292, 296
    in public domain Korn shell, 299
    within double quotes, 68
    within variable expressions, 305

                    A

Ada, 88, 97
adb, 253
ADM-3a terminal, 48
AIX, 1, 27
algebraic notation, 246-247, 251
aliases, xvi, 42, 53, 60-65, 186, 293
    defining, 61
    lack of system-wide, 286

on arguments of command line, 64
order of precedence in command
    lookup, 89, 204
output of alias command in next
    release, 306
preventing lookup as, 122
recursive, 63-64, 204
removing (unalias), 65
showing, 65
tracked, 64-65, 77, 286;
    as protection against Trojan
    horses, 289-290;
    defining, 65;
    in next release, 305-306;
    showing, 65, 289
using; as mnemonic, 61-62;
    as shorthand, 62-63;
    for correcting command typos,
    62
ANSI, 299
a.out, 130, 162
Apple Macintosh, xv
    Multifinder, 221
    OS System 7, 221
    OS Version 6, 221
arithmetic expressions, 160, 165, 181,
    296
    bases of numbers, 167
    bash syntax, 301
    condition tests, 169;
        (see also condition tests, arith-
        metic)
    features in next release, 305
    floating point (real number), 305
    MKS Toolkit shell syntax, 304
    operators, 166-167;
        assignment form, 166;
        truth values of relational, 166
    order of evaluation in command-
        line processing, 204
arrays, 173-176, 180, 293, 299
    # (size of), 175
    assigning values to, 174
    assignment with set -A, 174, 180
    associative, 305
    extracting values from, 174
    features in next release, 305
    initializing, 174, 180
    preserving whitespace in, 175

arrays (cont'd)
value of entire, 174
ASCII, 14
assembler, (see assembly language)
assembly language, 128-131
AT&T, 4, 304
autoload, 90, 286
(see also functions, autoloaded.)
A/UX, 1
awk, xvi, 101, 104-105, 105, 209, 282,
302
using instead of cut, 111
using instead of pr -n, 269

B

background jobs, 19-22, 87, 221-222
! variable (process ID of most
recent), 238
creating, 223
lack of in MS-DOS, 303
saving standard output and error
of, 190
with two-way pipes, 246
Backus-Naur Form (BNF), 300
basename, 108
bash, 5, 292, 300-302
obtaining from Internet, 300
bc, 247
bg, 223, 226, 294
biff, 70
/bin, 75, 288
BITFTP, 319
Bourne, Steven, 3
Bourne shell, xv, xvi, 3-5, 29, 66, 88,
91, 101, 109, 127, 147, 159, 166,
185, 189, 245, 253, 281, 291-296,
299-301
break, 148
BSD, 4, 27, 37, 39, 42, 70
built-in commands, ability to add new
in next release, 305
online help for in next release, 305
order of precedence in command
lookup, 89, 206
built-in variables, $, 31
#, 92
*, 92

@, 92
?, 123, 259, 275
* and # in functions, 93
*; as default list in for statement,
136;
as default list in select statement,
147
CDPATH, 77-78
COLUMNS, 69, 199
EDITOR, 69, 81
ERRNO; obsolescence in next
release, 306
FCEDIT, 69
FPATH, 90, 286
LINENO, 256, 260, 265
LINES, 69
list of those not supported in
Bourne shell, 293
list of those not supported in
pdksh, 299
MAILCHECK, 70
MAILPATH, 75
naming convention, 67
OLDPWD, 78, 114, 122, 204
OPTARG, 160
OPTIND, 160
PID, 304
positional parameters; (see posi-
tional parameters)
PS1, 72-73, 110
PS2, 72-73
PS3, 72-73, 148;
command substitution in next
release, 306
PS4, 72-73, 255-256;
in kshdb, 266
RANDOM, 258
REPLY; in read statement, 193;
in select statement, 147, 149, 175
SECONDS, 78
VISUAL, 69
(see also environment variables.)

C

C compilers, 107, 128-131, 143-145,
    161-165
    as pipelines, 214-217
    optimization, 163
    options, 163
C programming language, 4, 14, 85-86,
    88, 103, 121, 124, 129, 136,
    143-144, 148, 150, 152-153, 155,
    159, 166-167, 191, 194, 196, 219,
    253, 305"
C++ programming language, 217, 305
C shell, xv, xvii, 4-6, 37, 61-62, 72, 82,
    88, 91, 109, 114-115, 147, 170,
    189, 286, 288, 290, 299-302"
    history mechanism, xvi, 29, 31, 53
    list of features in Korn shell, xvi
case, 143-146, 158, 175-176, 194, 266
    double-semicolons, 148
    redirecting I/O to, 196
    syntax, 143
cat, 16, 16-17, 17, 186, 237, 263
cd, 10-11, 210, 282, 292
    - (to previous directory), 11, 114
    examples, 10
    inoperative in restricted shell, 287
    substitution form, 11
CDPATH, 77-78
CD-ROM, 130
chapter summary, xviii-xx
chmod, 86, 283
chsh, 6
code blocks, 196-199, 251
    compared to nested subshells,
    249-250
    piping outout to, 198
    POSIX shell syntax, 296
    redirecting standard I/O to, 197
COLUMNS, 69, 199
command substitution, 30, 109-114,
    293, 296
    examples, 109
    I/O redirection within, 109, 296
    order in command-line processing,
    204
    shown in xtrace output, 255
    syntax, 109
command-line options, 155-165

list of, 307-316
command-line processing, 203-217
    effect of eval on, 210
    effect of quoting on, 207
    example, 206
    inside condition tests, 126
    order of steps in, 204
    order of steps in POSIX shell, 297
commands, built-in command in next
    release, 306
    list of, 307
    vi, 314
comments in scripts, 99
compound statements, 196
    redirecting I/O to, 196
compress, 20-21
condition tests, 126-135, 166, 293,
    296, 299, 301
    arithmetic, 167, 169, 296;
        integer values as truth values,
        167, 271
    file attribute operators, 131-134;
        -a, 131, 133, 138, 306;
        -d, 131-133, 138, 151;
        -f, 131, 133, 138;
        -G, 131;
        -nt, 131, 214;
        -O, 131, 133, 138;
        -ot, 131;
        -r, 131, 133, 138;
        -s, 131;
        -w, 131, 133, 138;
        -x, 131-133, 138, 151
    function of, 126
    in while and until statements, 150
    integer comparison operators, 135;
        -eq, 135;
        -ge, 135;
        -gt, 135;
        -le, 135;
        -lt, 135;
        -ne, 135;
        obsolescence in next release,
        306
    old syntax, 126-127, 293, 299, 301,
    303
    processing of text inside, 126

condition tests (cont'd)
  string comparison operators,
    126-131;
    !=, 126;
    <, 126;
    =, 126, 197, 270, 306;
    >, 126;
    −n, 126-127, 147, 151;
    −z, 126-128
  string vs. integer comparisons, 135
  supported in MKS Toolkit shell,
    304
conditionals, (see if)
constants, 182
control keys, 26-28
  clashes with editing modes, 30
  CTRL-\, 28
  CTRL-C, 27
  CTRL-D, 5-6, 28, 148
  CTRL-H, 28
  CTRL-M, 26
  CTRL-Q, 28
  CTRL-S, 28
  CTRL-U, 28
  DEL, 28, 32
conventions, typographical, xx-xxi
core dumps, 227, 235, 250, 284
coroutines, 222, 241-247, 294, 299
  definition, 241
  on multiple-CPU computers,
    243-245
  performance issues, 243-244
  pipelines as example of, 241-242
  two-way pipes; (see two-way
    pipes)
cp, 17, 244
crontab, 31
CTRL-
CTRL-C, 27, 187, 225, 227-228,
    234-235, 238, 250, 259
CTRL-D, 5-6, 28, 148, 186, 237
CTRL-H, 28
CTRL-M, 26
CTRL-Q, 28
CTRL-S, 28
CTRL-U, 28
CTRL-Z, 223, 225-227

cut, 16, 18, 111-112, 112, 142, 188,
    193, 209, 256, 282
  -c (extract columns), 113
  -d (field delimiter), 111, 158
  using awk instead of, 111

D

date, 17, 165
dc, 246-248, 251
debuggers, 162, 253-254
  dbx, 284
  essential features, 261
  sdb, 284
debugging, core dumps, 284
  shell code, xvi, 254-279;
    (see also kshdb), 261;
    basics, 254;
    with print, 254
DEL, 28, 32
/dev/null, 141,160,282
diff, 21, 121
directories, .., 10
  ., 11
  home (login), 9
dirname, 108

E

EBCDIC, 14
echo, xvi, 5, 68, 191, 293-294
  difference in versions of, 191
ed, 81, 105, 187-188, 253
EDITOR, 69, 81
egrep, 101, 103-105, 105
elif, (see if)
emacs, commands, 313
emacs editor, 30, 32, 37, 40-41, 51, 56,
    60, 73, 80-81, 101, 103, 110, 253,
    299
  GNU emacs, 39, 60, 301
  Gosling (Unipress) emacs, 39
  search commands, 37
emacs-mode, xv, xvi, 32-42, 193, 286,
    299
  basic commands, 32-34
  case-changing commands, 41

emacs-mode (cont'd)
  enabling, 30-31
  exchanging point and mark, 41
  filename completion, 37-38
  filename expansion, 38
  history file commands, 36-37
  in workalike shells, 302
  key customization in next release, 305
  keyboard shortcuts with aliases, 42
  line commands, 35
  mark, 41
  point (dot), 33
  repeat counts, 39-40
  searching the history file, 36-37
  terminal requirements, 33
  transpose characters command, 39
  useful command subset, 56
  word commands, 34-35
ENV, 81-82, 285, 294
  command subsitution in next release, 306
  in privileged mode, 289
environment files, 81-82
  compared to .profile, 82
  creating, 81
  customization in next release, 306
  in privileged mode, 289
  in subshells, 249
  lack of system-wide, 285
  security holes in, 288
environment variables, 67
  about, 80
  creating, 80
  ENV, 81-82, 285, 294;
    command substitution in next release, 306;
    in privileged mode, 289
  FCEDIT, 55
  HISTFILE, 31, 69, 80
  HISTSIZE, 32
  HOME, 78, 80, 204
  IFS, 92, 94, 193, 203;
    role in command-line processing, 204
  inheritance by subshells, 249
  LOGNAME, 72, 80
  MAIL, 70-71, 80
  MAILPATH, 70-71, 80, 116, 303

PATH, 75-77, 80, 86, 116, 151-152, 170, 183, 193, 206, 282, 285, 289, 294, 303;
  in restricted shell, 287;
  security problem with, 76, 288
PS1, 208-210, 285, 301;
  command substitution in next release, 306
PWD, 72-73, 78, 80, 122, 204
read-only variables in restricted shell, 287
SHELL, 78, 80-81, 294
  showing, 81
TERM, 73-75, 80, 145-149, 175-176, 194-195, 285
TMOUT, 285
  visibility in subshells, 87
VISUAL, 30
(see also built-in variables.)
environments, 59
ERRNO, obsolescence in next release, 306
/etc/hosts, 197
/etc/passwd, 18, 188, 209, 217, 287
/etc/profile, 145, 147, 183, 194, 282, 285-286
/etc/suid_profile, 289
/etc/termcap, 73
eval, 210-217
  for constructing pipelines, 211-212, 214-217
  role in command-line processing, 210
exec, 263
  with I/O redirectors, 263
executable files, (see files, executable)
exit, 5-6, 123, 238
exit status, 121-125, 128, 271, 275
  conventional values, 121
  in job status messages, 223
  logical combinations, 124-125
  trapping when non-0, 259-260
export, 80-81, 87, 182, 286
expr, xvi, 166, 293

F

fake signals, 257-261
DEBUG, 257, 261, 267, 272, 294,
301, 304
ERR, 257, 259-260, 294, 299, 304
EXIT, 257-259, 264, 272, 294, 299,
304
in next release, 305
trapping in scripts being debugged
with kshdb, 272
fc, 29, 31, 53-56
-e (edit), 54-56
-l (list previous commands), 53-55
obsolescence in next release, 306
FCEDIT, 55, 69
fg, 223-225, 294
to resume suspended jobs, 226
fi, (see if)
file (command), 152-153, 275, 282
file descriptors, 186, 189-191
I/O redirection to/from, 185, 190,
200
of standard I/O, 189
files, environment;(see environment
files)
executable, 75, 128-129, 152;
a.out, 130;
order of precedence in command lookup, 89, 206
modification times, 213
permissions, 86, 283, 303;
octal notation, 283;
suid (see suid shell scripts)
temporary (names for), 238
find, 25
finding commands, order of precedence, 89, 204;
control over in next release, 305;
in next release, 306
PATH, 75-77
tracked aliases, 77
finger, 137-138
flow control, general description, 119
summary of constructs, 119-120
for, 136-143, 180
comparison to for statement in C
and Pascal, 136
in next release, 305

lists of names in, 136
overview, 136
syntax, 136
Forsyth, Charles, 299
FORTRAN, 135, 152
FPATH, 90, 286
Free Software Foundation (FSF),
300-301
from, 82
FTP, 262, 300
full pathnames, 9
functions, xvi, 293, 301
advantages over scripts, 88
autoloaded, 90-91
autoloading, 183, 286
definition, 88
deleting, 88
differences between scripts and, 89
exporting, 183
in next release, 305
in SunOS Bourne shell, 292
in workalike shells, 302
listing, 89, 183
local variables in, 177-178
order of precedence in command
lookup, 89, 206
POSIX shell syntax, 296
preventing lookup as, 123
recursive, 251
running, 88
syntax, 88
system-wide, 286
tracing execution of, 183, 256

G

getopt, xvi, 159, 293
getopts, 159-161, 166, 293
advantages, 161
arguments, 159
error messages, 160
exit status, 159
OPTARG variable, 160
OPTIND variable, 160
summary of functionality, 161
suppressing error messages, 160
Gisin, Eric, 299
GNU, 301

graphical user interface (GUI), 1, 298
grep, xvi, 16, 101, 103, 105, 113, 125,
    141-142, 142, 193, 198, 226, 282,
    288
    -i (case insensitive), 113
    -l, 110
    older BSD version of, 113

H

head, 98, 169, 212
here-documents, 187-189
    deleting leading TABs in, 189
    parameter and command substitu-
    tion in, 188
HISTFILE, 31, 69, 80
history (alias), 54
history file, printing to, 192-193
HISTSIZE, 32
HOME, 78, 80, 204
hostname, 110
HP/UX, 1, 27

I

IEEE, 294
    (see also POSIX)
IEEE POSIX 1003.2, (see POSIX, shell)
if, 120-135, 172-173, 181, 195, 209,
    268, 271
    redirecting I/O to, 196
    syntax, 120
IFS, 92, 94, 193, 203
    role in command-line processing,
    204
incompatibilites in next release,
    305-306
installing the Korn shell as /bin/sh,
    281-282, 290
Institute of Electrical and Electronic
    Engineers, (see IEEE)
INT, 250
Internet, 187, 262, 299-300
interprocess communication (IPC),
    227
I/O, pipelines, 17-18

redirection, 17-19, 185-191, 294,
    299;
    <, 17, 169, 185;
    >, 17, 185, 186;
    <&-, 185;
    <>, 185, 187, 189, 294, 299;
    >&-, 185, 191;
    >>, 185-187;
    >|, 185-187;
    |&, 185;
    |, 185;
    <&-, 191;
    << (see here-documents), ;
    limitations in restricted shell,
    287;
    order in command-line process-
    ing, 206;
    <&p, 185;
    >&p, 185;
    sending standard error to a pipe,
    190;
    to code blocks, 197;
    to functions, 196;
    to multiline flow-control con-
    structs, 196;
    to/from file descriptors, 185, 190,
    200, 202-203;
    with exec, 263
standard I/O, 15-18;
    in kshdb break conditions, 271;
    inheritance by subshells, 249;
    saving standard error in a file,
    190
strings; (see print, read)
ISO, 294

J

job control, xvi, 223-226
    lack of support for in MS-DOS, 303
job numbers, 222-224, 251
    difference between process IDs
    and, 222
    in job status messages, 223

jobs, 190, 251
  background; (see background jobs)
  command, 20, 223-224, 292, 294;
    + and - in output of, 224;
    -l (also list process IDs), 224;
    -n (list suspended or exited
      jobs), 224;
    -p (only list process IDs), 224,
      230;
    similarity to ps, 231
  definition, 222
  resuming, 226;
    in the background, pitfalls of,
      226;
    in the background (see bg)
  status messages, 223
  suspending, 223, 225-226
  ways to refer to; %% (most recent),
    224-225;
    %+ (most recent), 225;
    %- (second most recent),
      224-225;
    by command name, 224-225,
      235;
    by job number, 223, 225, 229;
    by string search, 224-225
jobs (see also processes), 221
Joy, Bill, 4

K

keywords, order of precedence in
    command lookup, 89, 204
kill, 223, 228-230, 235, 294
  arguments to, 228
  default signal sent, 228
  killing runaway processes, 232-233
  -l (list signals), 227
  used with process IDs, 232
Korn, David, 4, 304
kshdb, 253, 262-279
  commands, 267;
    *bc (set break condition), 271;
    *bp (set breakpoint), 269;
    *bp (without arguments), 269;
    *cb (clear breakpoints), 269;
    *g (go), 268;
    *q (quit), 268;

    *s (step), 268;
    *x (execution tracing), 271
  enhancing, 275
  limitations, 271-272
  sample session, 272-274
  source code; debugging functions,
    276-279;
    driver script, 262;
    online availability, 262;
    preamble, 264;
    structure, 262-263

L

let, 168-173, 181, 293
  examples, 168
  syntax, 168
  (see also arithmetic expressions)
LINENO, 256, 260, 265
LINES, 69
linkers, (see linking)
linking, 128-131, 144-145, 162,
    162-163
LISP, 15, 121
LOGNAME, 80
logout command files, 62
lp, 7, 9, 18, 188
ls, 11, 198, 241
  -F (show file type), 63
  -l (long listing), 11, 133-134;
    column formats of, 113

M

mail, 7, 15-16, 60, 70-71, 81, 112, 187,
    202, 237-240, 293
  dead.letter, 238
MAIL, 70, 71, 80
MAILCHECK, 70
MAILPATH, 70-71, 75, 80, 116, 303
make, 213, 302
man, 86, 233
metacharacters, 204
Microsoft Windows, 221, 291
Microsoft Windows NT, 221
mknod, 227
MKS Toolkit, 297, 302

MKS Toolkit (cont'd)
    shell, 292, 302-304;
        names for standard shell files,
        303;
        obtaining, 304
Modula, 88, 97
more, 18, 73, 241
MS-DOS, xv, 12, 56, 139, 141-142, 221,
    291, 297, 302
multitasking, in POSIX shell standard,
    297
mv, 141, 162, 239

N

Network Information Service (NIS),
    217
new features in next release, 305
newgrp, 303
next release, incompatibilities,
    305-306
    new features, 305
    obsolete features in, 306
nice, 22
nohup, 240, 294
Novell, 304
Novell NetWare, 291
null string, 92

O

object-code libraries, 162-163
    C runtime library, 162, 164
    names of, 162
obsolete features in next release, 306
OLDPWD, 78, 114, 122, 204
OPEN LOOK, 298
OPTARG, 160
OPTIND, 160
options, 60, 65-67
    bgnice, 66, 243, 303
    command-line; (see command-line
        options)
    dash; (see command-line options)
    emacs, 31, 66
    ignoreeof, 66
    in next release, 305

    keyword, 80;
        obsolescence in next release,
        306
    list of, 307-316
    list of those not supported in
        pdksh, 300
    list of; set -o, 311;
        typeset, 312
    markdirs, 66
    monitor, 223, 303
    noclobber, 66, 187, 286
    noexec, 254, 257;
        turning on and off, 257
    noglob, 66
    privileged, 289, 303
    trackall, 66, 286;
        obsolescence in next release,
        306
    turning on and off, 66, 257
    verbose, 254-255
    vi, 31, 66
    xtrace, 254-257;
        PS4 prompt in, 255-256;
        tracing function execution, 256
orphans, (see processes, in pathologi-
    cal states)
OS/2, 302-303
    Version 2, 221
OSF/Motif, 298
other shells, (see entries for individual
    shells)

P

parallelizing shell scripts, 243-245
parentheses, for nested subshells, 249
    for grouping condition tests, 132
    for nested subshells, 132
    within arithmetic expressions, 166
Pascal, 85, 88, 91, 97, 121, 124, 136,
    143-144, 150, 153, 155, 219
PATH, 75-77, 80, 86, 116, 151-152, 170,
    183, 193, 206, 282, 285, 289, 294,
    303
    in restricted shell, 287
    security problem with, 76, 288

pathnames, full, 9
   limitations in restricted shell, 287
   relative, 9
pattern-matching operators, ##, 105,
   108, 171
   #, 105, 108, 116, 151
   %%, 105, 107, 117, 151, 153, 171
   %, 105, 107, 108, 140, 144
   examples, 106
   syntax, 105-106
PCs, 74, 292, 302
pdksh, (see public domain Korn shell)
PID, 304
pipelines, 204, 241-242
   system calls used in, 241-242
pipes, 222
   compared to two-way pipes, 248
   to code blocks, 198
   two-way; (see two-way pipes)
popd, 114-117, 126-127, 170-173, 286,
   302
   additional arguments, 170
   functionality, 115
positional parameters, 92-95, 155-156,
   256, 264
   in functions, 93-94
   number of (#), 92
   syntax for higher than nine, 95
POSIX, 1003.1, 294
   1003.2a (UPE), 295, 297
   1003.2; (see POSIX, shell)
   history, 294-295
   shell, 292, 294-297;
      Korn shell features in, 296
pr, 269
   using awk instead of pr -n, 269
print, 23-24, 67-68, 191-193, 200, 203,
   272, 293-294
   as debugging aid, 254
   escape sequences, 191-192
   features in next release, 305
   for emulating eval, 211
   options, 192-193;
     -n, 101, 192;
     -n (suppress LINEFEED), 133, 181;
     -p, 192, 246, 248;
     -r, 192;
     -s, 192-193;
     -u, 192

priorities, 22
privileged mode, 289-290, 294
   /etc/suid_profile as environment
     file, 289
   turning off, 289
process IDs, 222, 231, 251, 294
   $ variable (ID of current shell), 31,
     237;
      for constructing temp filenames,
      238
   ! variable (process ID of most
     recent background job), 238
   difference between job numbers
     and, 222
processes, daemons, 233
   group leaders, 231, 233
   in pathological states, 233, 242
   performance characteristics of, 243
   (see also jobs), 221
prompting, in read statement, 200
prompts, 72-73
   customizing; features in next
     release, 305-306;
     with command number, 72;
     with current directory, 72-73,
     208-210;
     with machine name, 110;
     with user name, 72
   primary, 72
   processing of PS1, 209
ps, 230-233, 251
   -a; BSD version, 233;
     System V version, 231-232
   -ax (BSD), 233
   -e (System V), 233
   listing all processes on the system,
     233
   output of BSD version, 231
   output of System V version, 230
PS1, 72-73, 110, 208-210, 285, 301
   command subsitution in next
     release, 306
PS2, 72-73
PS3, 72-73, 148
   command subsitution in next
     release, 306
PS4, 72-73, 255-256
   in kshdb, 266

PS4 (cont'd)

public domain Korn shell, xv, 292,
  299-300
  documentation, 300
  for OS/2, 302
pushd, 114-117, 121-122, 132,
  170-173, 286, 302
  additional arguments, 170
  functionality, 115
PWD, 72-73, 78, 80, 122, 204

Q

quoting, 23-26
  and variables, 68-69
  arithmetic expressions in double
    quotes, 165
  command substitution with double
    quotes, 110
  difference between single and
    double quotes, 207
  double quotes with $@ and $*,
    94-95
  examples, 207
  in command-line processing, 207
  rules for quoting character strings,
    165

R

r (alias), 55
RANDOM, 258
read, 193-203
  exit status of, 195
  from files, 195-197
  from user input, 199-201;
    continuing on next line, 201;
    prompting, 200
  options, 201;
    -p, 201, 246, 248;
    -r, 201-202;
    -s, 201-202, 267;
    -u, 201-202, 202-203
  syntax, 193
readonly, 182, 289

regular expressions, xvi, 101-105, 293,
  299
  ! operator, 102, 104
  * operator, 102, 104, 105
  + operator, 102, 104, 105
  ? operator, 102-104
  @ operator, 102, 104
  compared to awk and egrep,
    104-105
  operator examples, 102
  order of evaluation in command-
    line processing, 205
  relationship to wildcards, 105
  syntax, 102
relative pathnames, 9
REPLY, in read statement, 193
  in select statement, 147, 149, 175
restricted shell, 287
  installing as a user's login shell, 287
  restrictions, 287
  role of .profile in, 287
return, 123-124
Reverse Polish Notation (RPN),
  246-247, 251
rksh, (see security, restricted shell)
rm, 238
root, 8

S

SCO, 27
scripts, built-in commands imple-
    mented as, 86
  comments in, 99
  order of precedence in command
    lookup, 89, 206
  running, 85-88
SECONDS, 78
security, xvii, 65, 286-290
  Korn shell features pertaining to,
    286
  problem with PATH, 76, 288
  restricted shell; (see restricted
    shell)
  suid interactive shells, 288
  Trojan horse schemes, 288-289
sed, 16, 101, 105, 282

select, xvi, 147-149, 175-176, 199-200, 293, 296
  description, 147
  lists of names in, 147
  PS3 prompt in, 148
  redirecting I/O to, 196
  syntax, 147
set, -A (array assignment), 174, 180
  +o (turn off option), 66, 257
  -o (turn on option), 66, 257, 293
  output of in next release, 306
  (see options)
SHELL, 78, 80-81, 294
shell compilers, 253
shell variables, list of, 309
shift, 156-160
signals, 223, 227-232
  ALRM, 304-305
  DEBUG; (see fake signals)
  description, 227
  effect of on processes, 229
  ERR; (see fake signals)
  EXIT; (see fake signals)
  fake; (see fake signals)
  hangup; (see HUP)
  HUP, 239-240
  ignoring, 239
  in POSIX shell, 296
  INT, 227-229, 235-236, 238, 258, 296, 304
  KILL, 228-230, 232
  lack of propagation to subshells, 249, 306
  listing, 227
  other types of, 228
  propagation to subshells in next release, 306
  QUIT, 227-230, 232
  sending with control keys, 227-228
  shown in background job status messages, 229
  specifying in trap command, 234
  STOP, 304
  TERM, 228-230, 235, 238, 258, 296
  trapping; (see traps)
  TSTP, 223, 227-228
sleep, 234
SNOBOL, 91
sort, 16-18, 20-21, 98, 142, 193, 226

special characters, 95
spell, 86
stacks, 114
Stallman, Richard, 300
standard I/O, (see I/O)
string I/O, (see print, read)
string operators, 96-101
  ; +, 96;
    -, 96, 98-100, 116, 271;
    =, 96, 100-101;
    ?, 96, 99-100, 116;
    +, 101, 140;
  # (length), 108
  in next release, 305
  summary of functionality, 96
  syntax, 96-97
stty, 27
  to customize control-key signals, 228
subprocesses, 79-80
subshells, 86-88, 221, 248-250
  information passed from parent processes, 79
  inheritance of properties from parent shells, 249
  nested, 249-251, 272, 297;
    compared to code blocks, 249-250
suid, 303
suid shell scripts, 287-289, 289-290
  creating, 288
  dangers of, 288-289
SunOS, 1, 4, 27, 113
system calls, exec, 241
  fork, 241
  pipe, 241
  wait, 241
System III, 27
System V, 27, 73
System V Release 4, 4-5

T

tail, 142
TCP/IP, 197
tee, 190
temporary files, 238

TERM, 73-75, 80, 145-149, 175-176, 194-195, 285
termcap, 73
terminfo, 73-75, 148
test, xvi, 126
  (see also condition tests, old syntax.)
test operators, list of, 310
testopt, 67
thrashing, (see processes, performance characteristics of)
tilde (˜) notation, 9-10, 204, 208-209, 292, 296
  ˜+ (current directory), 204
  ˜- (previous directory), 204
  within double quotes, 68
  within variable expressions, 305
TMOUT, 285
/tmp, 238, 263
TOPS-20, 37, 51
tr, 16, 139-140, 181
trap, (see traps, trap command)
traps, 234-241, 294
  after every statement, 261
  for ignoring signals, 239
  lack of propagation to subshells, 249, 306
  listing, 234
  propagation to subshells in next release, 306
  resetting defaults, 240
  setting global traps within functions, 236-237
  trap command, 234;
    - (to reset default), 240;
    null string argument (for ignoring signals), 239;
    syntax, 234
  trapping fake signals, 257-261, 264, 267
  within functions, 235-237
troff, 7, 152, 226
true, 234
tty, 146
two-way pipes, xvi, 245-248
  compared to standard pipes, 248
  creating, 246
  flow of I/O, 246

for building interfaces to existing programs, 248
  relationship to standard I/O, 246
typeset, 176-183, 293
  function options; +f, 183;
    -f, 183;
    +ft, 183;
    -ft, 183, 256;
    -fu, 183;
  making variables local to functions, 94, 177-178
  options supported in pdksh, 300
  output of in next release, 306
  string formatting options, 178-182;
    combined effect, 179;
    examples, 179;
    -L, 180, 203;
    -l, 181;
  syntax, 176
  turning off options, 179
  type and attribute options, 182-183;
    -f, 182-183;
    -i, 182;
    -r, 182, 182-183, 289;
    -x, 182
  variables in kshdb break conditions, 272
  with no arguments (to list variables), 183
typographical conventions, xx-xxi

U

ulimit, 283-285, 294
  hard vs. soft limits, 285
  options; -a (print all limits), 283-284;
    -c (core file size), 283-284;
    -d (process data segment), 283-284;
    -f (file size), 283-284;
    -n (file descriptors), 283;
    -s (process stack segment), 283-284;
    -t (process CPU time), 283, 285;
    -v (virtual memory), 283-284

ulimit (cont'd)
    privileged (superuser) options to, 285
    removing limits, 284
Ultrix, 1, 4, 27
umask, 283, 303
    as logical NAND with file permission, 283
unalias, 65
uncompress, 20
UNIX, Command Syntax Standard Rules, 159, 161
    documentation conventions, 99
    filenames in BSD, 198
    filenames in System V, 180, 198
    interprocess communication in, 227
    Programmer's Manual, 222, 233
    security; (see security)
    shell history, 3-4
    terminal interface, 30, 37, 39, 42
    utilities, 16
    versions; AIX, 1, 27, 230;
        A/UX, 1;
        BSD, 4, 27, 37, 39, 42, 68, 70, 111, 113, 198, 227, 230, 233, 269, 295, 299;
        HP/UX, 1, 27, 230;
        SCO, 27;
        SunOS, 1, 4, 27, 113, 230, 292, 298-299;
        System III, 27, 223;
        System V, 27, 68, 73, 180, 198, 223, 227, 230-231, 269, 295-296;
        System V Release 4, xv, 4-5, 162, 298;
        that don't support job control, 223;
        Ultrix, 1, 4, 27, 230;
        UTS, 1;
        Version 6, 101;
        Version 7, 3-4, 292, 295-296, 299;
        Xenix, 1, 27, 223;
    workalikes; Coherent, 302;
        Minix, 302
UNIX commands, uucp, 319
UNIX System Laboratories (USL), 4, 298, 304
    address and phone number, 298
unset, in POSIX shell, 297

until, 148, 150, 153
    differences with while, 150
    redirecting I/O to, 196
    syntax, 150
USENET, comp.binaries.os2 newsgroup, 302
    comp.sources.unix newsgroup, 299
user-controlled multitasking, 221
/usr/bin, 75, 288
/usr/lib, 263
/usr/tmp, 238
UTS, 1
uucp, 188, 302
uucp command, 319

V

variables, 60, 67-68
    and quoting rules, 68-69
    arrays; (see arrays)
    assignment to, 67
    built-in; (see built-in variables)
    compared to conventional programming languages, 91
    defining, 67
    deleting, 67
    environment; (see environment variables)
    global, 93
    in next release, 305
    integer, 165, 168-173, 182, 293
    integer (see also let), 168
    integer; (see also arithmetic expressions; let; typeset -i).)
    listing, 183
    local (in functions), 93, 177-178
    order of substitution in command-line processing, 204
    pattern-matching operators; (see pattern-matching operators)
    positional parameters; (see positional parameters)
    string operators; (see string operators)
    value of; full syntax, 95;
        short form, 67

variables, value of (cont'd)
VAX/VMS, 12, 19, 103, 113, 142-143, 221
Version 7, 3-4
version of Korn shell, determining, xv
vi editor, 30, 42, 56, 60, 73, 80, 101, 105, 226, 253, 302
vi-mode, xvi, 42-53, 193, 286
  basic control mode commands, 43-45
  case-changing command, 52
  character-finding commands, 50-51
  control mode, 42
  delete buffer, 47
  deletion commands, 46-47
  enabling, 30-31
  entering and changing text, 45-46
  entering input mode, 45-46
  filename completion, 51
  filename expansion, 51
  in workalike shells, 302
  input mode, 42-43
  key customization in next release, 305
  keyboard shortcuts with aliases, 53
  moving around in the history file, 48-49
  repeat counts, 43
  retrieving words from previous commands, 53
  searching the history file, 49
  undelete commands, 47
  word definitions, 43
VISUAL, 30, 69
VM/CMS, xv, 19, 221
VT100 terminal, 74

W

wait, 242, 294
  arguments to, 242
wc, 169-170
whence, 30, 89, 151, 293, 301
  -p, 109
  -v, 89, 275;
    to show tracked aliases, 289

while, 136, 148, 150-153, 171, 180-181, 195, 198, 201, 203, 209
  differences with until, 150
  redirecting I/O to, 196
  syntax, 150
who, 112
  who am i, 187
wildcards, *, 12, 14
  ?, 12, 105
  [ ], 13-14, 105
  basic, 12
  character ranges, 13
  examples, 13
  in alias expansions, 63
  order of expansion in command-line processing, 205
Windowing Korn shell (wksh), 292, 298
wksh, 292
words, 2
  order of separation in command-line processing, 204

X

X Window System, 31, 60, 74-75, 187, 232, 247, 292, 298
xcalc, 247
Xenix, 1, 27
xterm, 31, 74-75, 187, 232
xtrace mode, (see options, xtrace)

Y

y.tab.c, 107

Z

zombies, (see processes, in pathological states)

About the Author

Bill Rosenblatt is co-author, with Deb Cameron, of the O'Reilly Nutshell Handbook *Learning GNU Emacs*. He is a software development manager at Moody's Investors Service in New York City, and he moonlights as a writer for *SunWorld* and other magazines.

Bill received a B.S.E. from Princeton University, and an M.S. and A.B.D. from the University of Massachusetts at Amherst, each in some variant of Computer Science. His interests in the computing field include software engineering, object-oriented systems, databases, and pro- ↵ gramming language theory. Outside of the computing field, he's interested in jazz, classical music, antique maps, and Sherlock Holmes pastiche novels.

Bill lives on the Upper West Side of Manhattan. He wishes his landlord allowed pets so that he could truthfully claim to have a dog and cat with suitably droll names like "Coltrane" and "Ravel".

Colophon

Our look is the result of reader comments, our own experimentation, and distribution channels.

Distinctive covers complement our distinctive approach to technical topics, breathing personality and life into potentially dry subjects. UNIX and its attendant programs can be unruly beasts. Nutshell Handbooks help you tame them.

The animal featured on the cover of *Learning the Korn Shell* is the hawksbill turtle. The name "hawksbill" refers to its prominent hooked beak. This marine reptile is one of the smaller sea turtles, having a carapace (upper shell) length of about two feet and weighing about one hundred pounds. Among pelagic turtles, the hawksbill alone has the tendency to feed and breed in the same area, preferring the tropical shoals and reefs of the world's oceans.

Primarily carnivorous, the hawksbill feeds on crabs, fish, sponges, and jellyfish. The turtle's flesh can be poisonous; in some places fishermen test for poison by throwing the turtle's liver to the crows. If the birds reject the liver, the hawksbill is toxic.

The hawksbill turtle is the sole source of authentic "tortoiseshell" which comes from the scutes, or outer layer of the carapace. Tortoiseshell has been harvested through the years—from ancient Egypt to the present—and is highly valued for its beauty and plasticity. As a result, the hawksbill is endangered. Illegal trade continues to threaten this species' existence.

Edie Freedman designed this cover and the entire UNIX bestiary that appears on other Nutshell Handbooks. The beasts themselves are adapted from 19th-century engravings from the Dover Pictorial Archive. The cover layout was produced with Quark XPress 3.1 using the ITC Garamond font.

The inside layout was formatted in sqtroff by Lenny Muellner using ITC Garamond Light and ITC Garamond Book fonts, and was designed by Edie Freedman. The figures were created in Aldus Freehand 3.1 by Chris Reilley.

More Titles from O'Reilly

Unix Basics

Unix Basics

sed & awk, 2nd Edition

By Dale Dougherty & Arnold Robbins
2nd Edition March 1997
432 pages, ISBN 1-56592-225-5

sed & awk describes two text manipulation programs that are mainstays of the UNIX programmer's toolbox. This new edition covers the sed and awk programs as they are now mandated by the POSIX standard and includes discussion of the GNU versions of these programs.

SCO UNIX in a Nutshell

By Ellie Cutler &
the staff of O'Reilly & Associates
1st Edition February 1994
590 pages, ISBN 1-56592-037-6

The desktop reference to SCO UNIX and Open Desktop®, this version of UNIX in a Nutshell shows you what's under the hood of your SCO system. It isn't a scaled-down quick reference of common commands, but a complete reference containing all user, programming, administration, and networking commands.

UNIX in a Nutshell: System V Edition

By Daniel Gilly &
the staff of O'Reilly & Associates
2nd Edition June 1992
444 pages, ISBN 1-56592-001-5

You may have seen UNIX quick-reference guides, but you've never seen anything like UNIX in a Nutshell. Not a scaled-down quick reference of common commands, UNIX in a Nutshell is a complete reference containing all commands and options, along with generous descriptions and examples that put the commands in context. For all but the thorniest UNIX problems, this one reference should be all the documentation you need. Covers System V, Releases 3 and 4, and Solaris 2.0.

Volume 3M: X Window System User's Guide, Motif Edition, 2nd Edition

By Valerie Quercia & Tim O'Reilly
2nd Edition January 1993
956 pages, ISBN 1-56592-015-5

The X Window System User's Guide, Motif Edition orients the new user to window system concepts and provides detailed tutorials for many client programs, including the xtermterminal emulator and the twm, uwm, and mwmwindow managers. Later chapters explain how to customize the X environment. Revised for Motif 1.2 and X11 Release 5.

UNIX Tools

Exploring Expect

By Don Libes
1st Edition December 1994
602 pages, ISBN 1-56592-090-2

Written by the author of Expect, this is the first book to explain how this part of the UNIX toolbox can be used to automate Telnet, FTP, passwd, rlogin, and hundreds of other interactive applications. Based on Tcl (Tool Command Language), Expect lets you automate interactive applications that have previously been extremely difficult to handle with any scripting language.

Writing GNU Emacs Extensions

By Bob Glickstein
1st Edition April 1997
236 pages, ISBN 1-56592-261-1

This book introduces Emacs Lisp and tells you how to make the editor do whatever you want, whether it's altering the way text scrolls or inventing a whole new "major mode." Topics progress from simple to complex, from lists, symbols, and keyboard commands to syntax tables, macro templates, and error recovery.

UNIX Tools

Programming with GNU Software

By Mike Loukides & Andy Oram
1st Edition December 1996
260 pages, ISBN 1-56592-112-7

This book and CD combination is a complete package for programmers who are new to UNIX or who would like to make better use of the system. The tools come from Cygnus Support, Inc., and Cyclic Software, companies that provide support for free software. Contents include GNU Emacs, *gcc*, C and C++ libraries, *gdb*, RCS, and *make*. The book provides an introduction to all these tools for a C programmer.

Applying RCS and SCCS

By Don Bolinger & Tan Bronson
1st Edition September 1995
528 pages, ISBN 1-56592-117-8

Applying RCS and SCCS is a thorough introduction to these two systems, viewed as tools for project management. This book takes the reader from basic source control of a single file, through working with multiple releases of a software project, to coordinating multiple developers. It also presents TCCS, a representative "front-end" that addresses problems RCS and SCCS can't handle alone, such as managing groups of files, developing for multiple platforms, and linking public and private development areas.

lex & yacc, 2nd Edition

By John Levine, Tony Mason & Doug Brown
2nd Edition October 1992
366 pages, ISBN 1-56592-000-7

This book shows programmers how to use two UNIX utilities, lex and yacc, in program development. The second edition contains completely revised tutorial sections for novice users and reference sections for advanced users. This edition is twice the size of the first, has an expanded index, and covers Bison and Flex.

Managing Projects with make, 2nd Edition

By Andrew Oram & Steve Talbott
2nd Edition October 1991
152 pages, ISBN 0-937175-90-0

make is one of UNIX's greatest contributions to software development, and this book is the clearest description of *make* ever written. It describes all the basic features of *make* and provides guidelines on meeting the needs of large, modern projects. Also contains a description of free products that contain major enhancements to *make*.

Software Portability with imake, 2nd Edition

By Paul DuBois
2nd Edition September 1996
410 pages, ISBN 1-56592-226-3

This Nutshell Handbook®—the only book available on *imake*—is ideal for X and UNIX programmers who want their software to be portable. The second edition covers the current version of the X Window System (X11R6.1), using *imake* for non-UNIX systems such as Windows NT, and some of the quirks about using *imake* under OpenWindows/ Solaris.

Porting UNIX Software

By Greg Lehey
1st Edition November 1995
538 pages, ISBN 1-56592-126-7

This book deals with the whole life cycle of porting, from setting up a source tree on your system to correcting platform differences and even testing the executable after it's built. It exhaustively discusses the differences between versions of UNIX and the areas where porters tend to have problems.

UNIX Tools

UNIX Power Tools, 2nd Edition

By Jerry Peek, Tim O'Reilly &
Mike Loukides
2nd Edition August 1997
1120 pages, Includes CD-ROM
ISBN 1-56592-260-3

Loaded with even more practical advice about almost every aspect of UNIX, this new second edition of *UNIX Power Tools* addresses the technology that UNIX users face today. You'll find increased coverage of POSIX utilities, including GNU versions, greater *bash* and *tcsh* shell coverage, more emphasis on Perl, and a CD-ROM that contains the best freeware available.

Tcl/Tk Tools

By Mark Harrison
1st Edition September 1997
678 pages, Includes CD-ROM
ISBN 1-56592-218-2

One of the greatest strengths of Tcl/Tk is the range of extensions written for it. This book clearly documents the most popular and robust extensions—by the people who created them—and contains information on configuration, debugging, and other important tasks. The CD-ROM includes Tcl/Tk, the extensions, and other tools documented in the text both in source form and as binaries for Solaris and Linux.

Unix Programming

UNIX Systems Programming for SVR4

By David A. Curry
1st Edition July 1996
620 pages, ISBN 1-56592-163-1

Presents a comprehensive look at the nitty gritty details on how UNIX interacts with applications. If you're writing an application from scratch, or if you're porting an application to any System V.4 platform, you need this book. It thoroughly explains all UNIX system calls and library routines related to systems programming, working with I/O, files and directories, processing multiple input streams, file and record locking, and memory-mapped files.

Programming with curses

By John Strang
1st Edition 1986
78 pages, ISBN 0-937175-02-1

curses is a UNIX library of functions for controlling a terminal's display screen from a C program. This handbook helps you make use of the *curses* library. Describes the original Berkeley version of *curses*.

Pthreads Programming

By Bradford Nichols, Dick Buttlar &
Jacqueline Proulx Farrell
1st Edition September 1996
284 pages, ISBN 1-56592-115-1

POSIX threads, or pthreads, allow multiple tasks to run concurrently within the same program. This book discusses when to use threads and how to make them efficient. It features realistic examples, a look behind the scenes at the implementation and performance issues, and special topics such as DCE and real-time extensions.

Unix Programming

Programming Python

By Mark Lutz
1st Edition October 1996
906 pages, ISBN 1-56592-197-6

Programming Python describes how
to use Python, an increasingly popular
object-oriented scripting language.
This book, full of running examples, is
the most comprehensive user material
available on Python. It's endorsed by
Python creator Guido van Rossum and complements reference
materials that accompany the software. Includes CD-ROM with
Python software for all major UNIX platforms, as well as
Windows, NT, and the Mac.

POSIX Programmer's Guide

By Donald Lewine
1st Edition April 1991
640 pages, ISBN 0-937175-73-0

Most UNIX systems today are
POSIX compliant because the
federal government requires it for its
purchases. Given the manufacturer's
documentation, however, it can be
difficult to distinguish system-specific
features from those features defined
by POSIX. The *POSIX Programmer's Guide*, intended as an
explanation of the POSIX standard and as a reference for the
POSIX.1 programming library, helps you write more portable
programs.

Power Programming with RPC

By John Bloomer
1st Edition February 1992
522 pages, ISBN 0-937175-77-3

RPC (Remote Procedure Calling) is
the ability to distribute the execution of
functions on remote computers. Written
from a programmer's perspective, this
book shows what you can do with RPCs,
like Sun RPC, the de facto standard on
UNIX systems. It covers related program-
ming topics for Sun and other UNIX systems and teaches through
examples.

POSIX.4

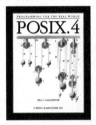

By Bill O. Gallmeister
1st Edition January 1995
568 pages, ISBN 1-56592-074-0

A general introduction to real-time
programming and real-time issues,
this book covers the POSIX.4
standard and how to use it to solve
"real-world" problems. If you're at
all interested in real-time applications—which include just about
everything from telemetry to transaction processing—this
book is for you. An essential reference.

How to stay in touch with O'Reilly

1. Visit Our Award-Winning Site

http://www.oreilly.com/

★ "Top 100 Sites on the Web" —*PC Magazine*
★ "Top 5% Web sites" —*Point Communications*
★ "3-Star site" —*The McKinley Group*

Our web site contains a library of comprehensive product information (including book excerpts and tables of contents), downloadable software, background articles, interviews with technology leaders, links to relevant sites, book cover art, and more. File us in your Bookmarks or Hotlist!

2. Join Our Email Mailing Lists

New Product Releases

To receive automatic email with brief descriptions of all new O'Reilly products as they are released, send email to:
listproc@online.oreilly.com
Put the following information in the first line of your message (*not* in the Subject field):
subscribe oreilly-news

O'Reilly Events

If you'd also like us to send information about trade show events, special promotions, and other O'Reilly events, send email to:
listproc@online.oreilly.com
Put the following information in the first line of your message (*not* in the Subject field):
subscribe oreilly-events

3. Get Examples from Our Books via FTP

There are two ways to access an archive of example files from our books:

Regular FTP

• ftp to:
  ftp.oreilly.com
  (login: anonymous
  password: your email address)
• Point your web browser to:
  ftp://ftp.oreilly.com/

FTPMAIL

• Send an email message to:
  ftpmail@online.oreilly.com
  (Write "help" in the message body)

4. Contact Us via Email

order@oreilly.com
To place a book or software order online. Good for North American and international customers.

subscriptions@oreilly.com
To place an order for any of our newsletters or periodicals.

books@oreilly.com
General questions about any of our books.

software@oreilly.com
For general questions and product information about our software. Check out O'Reilly Software Online at **http://software.oreilly.com/** for software and technical support information. Registered O'Reilly software users send your questions to:
website-support@oreilly.com

cs@oreilly.com
For answers to problems regarding your order or our products.

booktech@oreilly.com
For book content technical questions or corrections.

proposals@oreilly.com
To submit new book or software proposals to our editors and product managers.

international@oreilly.com
For information about our international distributors or translation queries. For a list of our distributors outside of North America check out:
http://www.oreilly.com/www/order/country.html

O'Reilly & Associates, Inc.

101 Morris Street, Sebastopol, CA 95472 USA
TEL   707-829-0515 or 800-998-9938
        (6am to 5pm PST)
FAX   707-829-0104

O'REILLY™

Titles from O'Reilly

International Distributors

UK, EUROPE, MIDDLE EAST AND NORTHERN AFRICA (except France, Germany, Switzerland, & Austria)

INQUIRIES
International Thomson Publishing Europe
Berkshire House
168-173 High Holborn
London WC1V 7AA, UK
Telephone: 44-171-497-1422
Fax: 44-171-497-1426
Email: itpint@itps.co.uk

ORDERS
International Thomson Publishing Services, Ltd.
Cheriton House, North Way
Andover, Hampshire SP10 5BE,
United Kingdom
Telephone: 44-264-342-832 (UK)
Telephone: 44-264-342-806 (outside UK)
Fax: 44-264-364418 (UK)
Fax: 44-264-342761 (outside UK)
UK & Eire orders: itpuk@itps.co.uk
International orders: itpint@itps.co.uk

FRANCE

Editions Eyrolles
61 bd Saint-Germain
75240 Paris Cedex 05
France
Fax: 33-01-44-41-11-44

FRENCH LANGUAGE BOOKS
All countries except Canada
Telephone: 33-01-44-41-46-16
Email: geodif@eyrolles.com

ENGLISH LANGUAGE BOOKS
Telephone: 33-01-44-41-11-87
Email: distribution@eyrolles.com

GERMANY, SWITZERLAND, AND AUSTRIA

INQUIRIES
O'Reilly Verlag
Balthasarstr. 81
D-50670 Köln
Germany
Telephone: 49-221-97-31-60-0
Fax: 49-221-97-31-60-8
Email: anfragen@oreilly.de

ORDERS
International Thomson Publishing
Königswinterer Straße 418
53227 Bonn, Germany
Telephone: 49-228-97024 0
Fax: 49-228-441342
Email: order@oreilly.de

JAPAN

O'Reilly Japan, Inc.
Kiyoshige Building 2F
12-Banchi, Sanei-cho
Shinjuku-ku
Tokyo 160 Japan
Tel: 81-3-3356-5227
Fax: 81-3-3356-5261
Email: kenji@oreilly.com

INDIA

Computer Bookshop (India) PVT. Ltd.
190 Dr. D.N. Road, Fort
Bombay 400 001 India
Tel: 91-22-207-0989
Fax: 91-22-262-3551
Email: cbsbom@giasbm01.vsnl.net.in

HONG KONG

City Discount Subscription Service Ltd.
Unit D, 3rd Floor, Yan's Tower
27 Wong Chuk Hang Road
Aberdeen, Hong Kong
Telephone: 852-2580-3539
Fax: 852-2580-6463
Email: citydis@ppn.com.hk

KOREA

Hanbit Publishing, Inc.
Sonyoung Bldg. 202
Yeksam-dong 736-36
Kangnam-ku
Seoul, Korea
Telephone: 822-554-9610
Fax: 822-556-0363
Email: hant93@chollian.dacom.co.kr

TAIWAN

ImageArt Publishing, Inc.
4/fl. No. 65 Shinyi Road Sec. 4
Taipei, Taiwan, R.O.C.
Telephone: 886-2708-5770
Fax: 886-2705-6690
Email: marie@ms1.hinet.net

SINGAPORE, MALAYSIA, AND THAILAND

Longman Singapore
25 First Lok Yan Road
Singapore 2262
Telephone: 65-268-2666
Fax: 65-268-7023
Email: daniel@longman.com.sg

PHILIPPINES

Mutual Books, Inc.
429-D Shaw Boulevard
Mandaluyong City, Metro
Manila, Philippines
Telephone: 632-725-7538
Fax: 632-721-3056
Email: mbikikog@mnl.sequel.net

CHINA

Ron's DataCom Co., Ltd.
79 Dongwu Avenue
Dongxihu District
Wuhan 430040
China
Telephone: 86-27-83892568
Fax: 86-27-83222108
Email: hongfeng@public.wh.hb.cn

AUSTRALIA

WoodsLane Pty. Ltd.
7/5 Vuko Place, Warriewood NSW 2102
P.O. Box 935,
Mona Vale NSW 2103
Australia
Telephone: 61-2-9970-5111
Fax: 61-2-9970-5002
Email: info@woodslane.com.au

ALL OTHER ASIA COUNTRIES

O'Reilly & Associates, Inc.
101 Morris Street
Sebastopol, CA 95472 USA
Telephone: 707-829-0515
Fax: 707-829-0104
Email: order@oreilly.com

THE AMERICAS

McGraw-Hill Interamericana Editores,
S.A. de C.V.
Cedro No. 512
Col. Atlampa 06450
Mexico, D.F.
Telephone: 52-5-541-3155
Fax: 52-5-541-4913
Email: mcgraw-hill@infosel.net.mx

SOUTHERN AFRICA

International Thomson Publishing Southern Africa
Building 18, Constantia Park
138 Sixteenth Road
P.O. Box 2459
Halfway House, 1685 South Africa
Tel: 27-11-805-4819
Fax: 27-11-805-3648

O'REILLY™

TO ORDER: **800-998-9938** • **order@oreilly.com** • **http://www.oreilly.com/**
OUR PRODUCTS ARE AVAILABLE AT A BOOKSTORE OR SOFTWARE STORE NEAR YOU.
FOR INFORMATION: **800-998-9938** • **707-829-0515** • **info@oreilly.com**

O'REILLY™

O'Reilly & Associates, Inc.
101 Morris Street
Sebastopol, CA 95472-9902
1-800-998-9938

Visit us online at:
http://www.ora.com/
orders@ora.com

O'REILLY WOULD LIKE TO HEAR FROM YOU

Which book did this card come from?

_____

Where did you buy this book?
- ❏ Bookstore   ❏ Computer Store
- ❏ Direct from O'Reilly   ❏ Class/seminar
- ❏ Bundled with hardware/software
- ❏ Other _____

What operating system do you use?
- ❏ UNIX   ❏ Macintosh
- ❏ Windows NT   ❏ PC(Windows/DOS)
- ❏ Other _____

What is your job description?
- ❏ System Administrator   ❏ Programmer
- ❏ Network Administrator   ❏ Educator/Teacher
- ❏ Web Developer
- ❏ Other _____

❏ Please send me O'Reilly's catalog, containing
a complete listing of O'Reilly books and
software.

Name _____   Company/Organization _____

Address _____

City _____ State _____ Zip/Postal Code _____ Country _____

Telephone _____   Internet or other email address (specify network) _____

Nineteenth century wood engraving
of a bear from the O'Reilly &
Associates Nutshell Handbook®
Using & Managing UUCP.

BUSINESS REPLY MAIL
FIRST CLASS MAIL   PERMIT NO. 80   SEBASTOPOL, CA

Postage will be paid by addressee

O'Reilly & Associates, Inc.
101 Morris Street
Sebastopol, CA 95472-9902